Expatriate Manager's Adaption and Knowledge Acquisition

Yan Li

Expatriate Manager's Adaption and Knowledge Acquisition

Personal Development in Multi-National Companies in China

Springer

Yan Li
School of Management
Xiamen University
Xiamen, Fujian
China

ISBN 978-981-10-0052-2 ISBN 978-981-10-0053-9 (eBook)
DOI 10.1007/978-981-10-0053-9

Library of Congress Control Number: 2015953782

Springer Singapore Heidelberg New York Dordrecht London

Printed on acid-free paper

Springer Science+Business Media Singapore Pte Ltd. is part of Springer Science+Business Media
(www.springer.com)

Contents

Chapter 1
Introduction

1.1 Research Background

Growing influx of foreign investment in emerging markets (e.g. Brazil, Russia, India, China) drives an increasing demand for global managers with the specific capabilities required to manage in these culturally, economically and institutionally distant markets (Harvey et al. 1999; Li and Scullion 2010). Multinational companies (MNCs) have known for some time that it is imperative to attract, select, develop, and retain managers who can live and work effectively outside of their own national borders for periods that can often span several years (Caligiuri 2000). These employees are commonly referred to as expatriate workers (Edstrom and Galbraith 1977). Clear benefits can be realised for international organisations that utilise managers already socialised into the organisation, known to them, and trusted by them compared with local managers from the host country who are largely an unknown quantity.

Organizational interventions for enhancing global management effectiveness range from didactic training programs to intensive cultural experiences gained from international assignments. International assignments are aimed at cultivating individuals to think more globally by exposing them to the challenges of living and working in a foreign environment and the topic has an established pedigree in the international human resource management research literature (Stahl and Bjorkman 2006). Both short-term and long-term international assignments are increasingly being adopted by organizations to nurture their global managers (Hall et al. 2001). Despite some concerns over expatriate performance and sometimes failure (Dowling and Welch 2004), the utility of expatriate managers in emerging markets is inevitable because of the strategic roles these managers play and the severe shortage of talent within these economies, particularly qualified local senior executives (Lenartowicz and Johnson 2007). International assignments are regularly positioned as beneficial to organisational success and individual career progression,

Y. Li, *Expatriate Manager's Adaption and Knowledge Acquisition*,
DOI 10.1007/978-981-10-0053-9_1

implying mutual benefit for the individual and the organisation (Dickmann and Doherty 2008). Research clearly demonstrates that firms led by CEOs with international experience perform better financially (Carpenter et al. 2001; Daily et al. 2000) and that these managers attest living and working abroad to be the most powerful experience in developing their career capital (Dickmann and Doherty 2008).

However, managing international assignments has been both challenging and complex for organisations and unsuccessful attempts can be detrimental to a MNCs global business. As Zeira and Banai (1989) aptly remind us, the real cost of an unsuccessful international management assignment extends beyond the monetary expenses of compensation because inevitably there are also negative impacts on future interactions between the MNCs and the host countries. Given the strategic importance MNCs place on global assignments (e.g. high level negotiations, foreign subsidiary management, new market development), the harm caused by an unsuccessful expatriate in the host country can be significant. A high risk of repatriate turnover has also been demonstrated by several studies (e.g. Furuya et al. 2009) which suggests that MNCs may not always be able to capitalise on benefits of international assignments once the assignee returns to his or her home country (repatriates). Despite the high risk of turnover, the factors that determine whether employees with international assignment experience choose to remain with their organisations are largely unclear and this is becoming a priority for MNCs. This is because a key motive for international assignments is not only to accomplish a specific task during the assignment, but also to contribute to the long-term development of both individual talent and the larger organisation.

For these reasons, international HR practitioners and management researchers alike are interested in evaluating international assignments and understanding how to best predict individuals who can live and work successfully in cross national settings (Caligiuri 2000) and subsequently be retained by the organisation. Previous research indicates considerable variation in the types of criteria used in evaluating how successful expatriate assignments have been. Three common criteria for evaluating expatriate success are: cross cultural adjustment; performance on the global assignment; and completion of the assignment. Cross cultural adjustment has been argued to be the antecedent of both performance and completion of the global assignment. Given that these are both important for MNCs, a better understanding of the factors which impact cross cultural adjustment is necessary.

Local knowledge in emerging markets (e.g. China) has been argued to have a special nature in that it is highly tacit and fast-changing and its acquisition will depend on intensive socialized activities and experiences in these markets (Li and Scullion 2010). Successful adaptation of expatriates will hinge on how well they learn from experiences in these foreign operations (Ng et al. 2009). Learning and knowledge acquisition by expatriates is deemed to be an underestimated strategic outcome in the study of expatriate adaptation and according to a recent theoretical study (Yamazaki and Kayes 2007) different learning strategies may be required for effective adaptation in various host countries. However, previous studies have mainly focused on managers' performance and adaptation (Bhaskar-Shrinivas et al. 2005) in assessing the effectiveness of international assignments and few have considered the importance of these in the context of expatriate management learning. According to Senge (1990) learning describes how people recreate themselves in response to external changes to gain a new appreciation of the world and this involves a holistic process of adaptation, including the functions of thinking, feeling, perceiving and behaving (Yamazaki and Kayes 2007). A country's culture is believed to shape peoples' preferred modes of learning and has been argued to be one of the most powerful socialisation agents that impact on individuals styles of learning. Despite this, there is a dearth of studies that have researched learning in the context of cross-cultural adaptation or knowledge acquisition (Armstrong and Mahmud 2008) during the course of expatriate managers' international work assignments. This study seeks to fill this gap by examining how expatriate managers learn, adjust, and acquire new knowledge in a host culture through the lens of Experiential Learning Theory.

1.2 Research Purposes and Questions

This research examines how Western expatriate managers adapt, learn, and develop during their international assignments in China using an experiential learning approach. This study also investigates how Western expatriate managers differ from host Chinese counterpart managers to gain a comprehensive understanding of expatriate learning and development. Concerning the purpose of this study, this research highlights four specific research questions as follows:

1. How do Western expatriate managers adapt when working in China?
2. What do Western expatriate managers learn from their international assignments in China?
3. How do Western expatriate managers learn from their international assignments in China?
4. To what extent do Western expatriate managers differ from host Chinese managers?

This study applies experiential learning theory (ELT) (Kolb 1984) to expatriate learning to understand how expatriate managers learn from their international assignment experiences to become qualified global managers. Questions of this study draw on three disciplinary areas: Experiential learning; knowledge acquisition and knowledge management; and international assignment and cross-cultural adjustment research. In this respect, the present study seeks to contribute to these three bodies of literature.

(a) Significance for experiential learning theory (ELT)

First, in line with an inquiry about the relationship between learning styles and cultures, this study will help to understand how are environmental changes and cultural transitions relate to the change of learning styles. It will also help us understand the relationship between learning styles transition and adaptive flexibility. Second, this research will contribute to our understanding of how environmental change relates to the development of adaptive flexibility. Third, this study will contribute to further understanding of the relationship between adaptive flexibility and self-development.

(b) Significance for expatriate and international assignment research

First, in line with an inquiry about the relationship between expatriate learning and expatriate adaptation, this study will help further our understanding of how expatriate learning leads to successful expatriate adaptation and what kinds of learning strategies expatriates tend to adopt for expatriate adaptation in intercultural business contexts. Second, this study will contribute to our understanding of expatriates' learning outcomes from international assignments. Moreover, based on the expatriate learning outcomes, it will further add useful suggestions for expatriate training prior to international assignments. Third, by comparing Western expatriates with different lengths of assignment tenure, this study will help us to understand how expatriates learn and develop over time during their international assignments. It will also help us to understand temporal aspects associated with how long expatriates take to achieve successful adaptation and performance during their international assignments.

(c) Significance for cross-cultural research

By comparing Western expatriates with host Chinese managers, this study will help us understand what the differences are between Western and Chinese managers in terms of learning styles.

This research consists of seven chapters. Chapter 1 is the introduction. It consists of research background, research purposes and questions, and research significance and structure of the thesis. Chapter 2 develops the research conceptual framework. It consists of literature review and the development as well as integration of a research framework and a series of hypotheses and exploratory questions. The literature review and the development consist of five parts: international assignments, experiential learning, expatriate adjustment, managerial tacit knowledge, and expatriate learning. Chapter 3 presents research design and methodology. It consists of research design, population and sampling, and research instruments. Chapter 4 presents data analysis using a Structure Equation Modelling (SEM) method. It consists of an introduction to SEM, data analysis regarding the measurement models, and data analysis regarding the structure model. Chapter 5 presents the research results of western expatriate managers. It consists of: descriptive statistics; expatriate adjustment and expatriate time; learning style and expatriate time; managerial tacit knowledge and expatriate time; adaptive flexibility and expatriate time; learning style and managerial tacit knowledge; learning style and adaptive flexibility; learning style and expatriate adjustment; adaptive flexibility and expatriate adjustment; managerial tacit knowledge and expatriate adjustment; and finally conclusions. Chapter 6 presents the research results for Chinese managers. It consists of: descriptive statistics; learning style; and managerial tacit knowledge. Chapter 7 presents the discussion and conclusions. It consists of a summary of the results of the research questions, conclusions, implications, and limitations.

References

Armstrong, S. J., & Mahmud, A. (2008). Experiential learning and the acquisition of managerial tacit knowledge. *Academy of Management Learning and Education, 7*(2), 189–208.

Bhaskar-Shrinivas, P., Harrison, D. A., Shaffer, M. A., & Luk, D. M. (2005). Input-based and time-based models of international adjustment: Meta-analytic evidence and theoretical extensions. *Academy of Management Journal, 482*, 25–281.

Caligiuri, P. M. (2000). Selecting expatriates for personality characteristics: A mediating effect of personality on the relationship between host national contact and cross-cultural adjustment. *Management International Review, 40*, 61–80.

Carpenter, M. A., Sanders, W. G., & Gregersen, H. B. (2001). Bundling human capital with organizational context: The impact of international assignment experience on multinational firm performance and CEO pay. *Academy of Management Journal, 44*, 493–511.

Daily, C. M., Certo, S. T., & Dalton, D. R. (2000). International experience in the executive suite: The path to prosperity? *Strategic Management Journal, 21*, 515–523.

Dickmann, M., & Doherty, N. (2008). Exploring the career capital impact of international assignments within distinct organizational contexts. *British Journal of Management, 19*, 145–161.

Dowling, P., & Welch, D. (2004). *International human resource management: Managing people in a global context* (4th ed.). London: Thomson Learning.

Edstrom, A., & Galbraith, J. R. (1977). Alternative policies for international transfers of managers. *Management International Review, 17*(2), 11–22.

Furuya, N., Stevens, M. J., Bird, A., Oddou, G., & Mendenhall, M. E. (2009). Managing the learning and transfer of global management competence: Antecedents and outcomes of Japanese repatriation effectiveness. *Journal of International Business Studies, 40*(2), 200–215.

Harvey, M. G., Speier, C., & Novicevic, M. M. (1999). The impact of emerging markets on staffing the global organization: A knowledge-based view. *Journal of International Management, 5*, 167–186.

Hall, D. T., Zhu, G., & Yan, A. (2001). Developing global leaders: To hold on to them, let them go! *Advances in Global Leadership, 2*: 327–349.

Hocking, J. B., Brown, M., & Harzing, A.-W. (2007). Balancing global and local strategic contexts: expatriate knowledge transfer, applications, and learning with a transnational organization. *Human Resource Management, 46*(4), 513–533.

Kolb, D. A. (1984). *Experiential learning: Experience as the source of learning and development*. Englewood Cliffs, NJ: Prentice-Hall.

Lenartowicz, T., & Johnson, J. P. (2007). Staffing managerial positions in emerging markets: A cultural perspective. *International Journal of Emerging Markets, 2*(3), 207–214.

Li, S., & Scullion, H. (2010). Developing the local competence of expatriate managers for emerging markets: A knowledge-based approach. *Journal of World Business, 45*, 190–196.

Maertz, C. P, Jr, Hassan, A., & Magnusson, P. (2009). When learning is not enough: A process model of expatriate adjustment as cultural cognitive dissonance reduction. *Organizational Behaviour and Human Decision Processes, 108*, 66–78.
Ng, K. Y., Dyne, L. V., & Ang, S. (2009). From experience to experiential learning: Cultural Intelligence as a learning capability for global leader development. *Academy of Management Learning and Education, 8*(4), 511–526.
Senge, P. M. (1990). *The fifth discipline: The art and practice of the learning organization*. New York: Currency Doubleday.
Stahl, G. K., & Bjorkman, I. (Eds.) (2006). *Handbook of research in international human resource management*. Cheltenham, UK: Edward Elgar.
Yamazaki, Y., & Kayes, D. C. (2007). Expatriate learning: exploring how Japanese managers adapt in the United States. *International Journal of Human Resource Management, 18*(8), 1373–1395.
Zeira, S., & Banai, R. (1989). A practical but theory-based framework for selecting cross-cultural training methods. *Human Resource Management*, *28*(4), 511–539.

Chapter 2
Expatriate Adjustment and Expatriate Learning

2.1 International Assignments

2.1.1 Definition and Classification of International Assignments

International work experience is one of the major requirements for promotion to higher-level managerial positions. International assignments are a powerful mechanism through which managers acquire new business skill sets, international perspectives, and basic cross-cultural assumptions (Furuya et al. 2009). The topic of international assignments (IAs) has an established pedigree in the international management literature and has in particular dominated the research agenda of international human resource management (IHRM) for over three decades (Collings et al. 2007; Stahl and Bjorkman 2006). It has been argued that entrepreneurs have recognised the importance of physically relocating managers to foreign locations where business operations are based since approximately 1900 B.C. (Collings et al. 2007). Owners of international organisations realised the benefits of utilising people known to them and socialised into the organisation in minimising the agency problems associated with managing spatially diverse organisations from an early stage. This is because these individuals had built a level of trust with their superiors and thus were considered to be more likely to act in the best interests of the organisation, relative to local managers from the host country who were largely an unknown quantity. Thus, international assignments were used as a means of addressing agency issues as a result of the separation of ownership and management and their amplification through distance.

The most widely recognized and long-standing typology of international assignments is that of Edstrom and Galbraith (1977). Edstrom and Galbraith (1977) proposed a distinctive three-fold subdivision of international assignments based on assignment purposes: fill positions, develop organization, and develop managers.

Y. Li, *Expatriate Manager's Adaption and Knowledge Acquisition*,
DOI 10.1007/978-981-10-0053-9_2

Firstly, fill positions refers to when suitably qualified host country nationals were not available. Secondly, as a means of organisational development, aim at increasing knowledge transfer within the MNC and modifying and sustaining organizational structure and decision processes. Thirdly, as a means of management development, aim at developing the competence of the individual manager. Although it is important to note that assignments generally have more than one rationale (Sparrow et al. 2004), Edstrom and Galbraith's (1977) typology provides a useful point of departure for the consideration of why MNCs use international assignments and expatriates. Hocking et al. (2004) argue that Edstrom and Galbraith (1977)' classification of international assignments lack a strong conceptual framework to explain the underlying strategic significance of the categories and their relationships. They reclassify the principal strategic purpose of international assignments and present the underlying relationships. According to Hocking et al. (2004, 2007), international assignments' principal purposes comprise three categories: business applications, organization applications, and expatriate learning. In particular, expatriate learning refers to either business- or organization-related knowledge acquisition by the expatriate, which equivalent to the two knowledge application categories: business applications and organization applications.

Alongside the conventional international assignment (usually more than one year and involving the relocation of the expatriate), there is the emergence of a portfolio of alternatives to the traditional international assignment, referred to as a non-standard international assignment including: short-term assignments (SIAs); commuter assignments; international business travel; and virtual assignments (Brookfield Global Relocation Trends 2005; Collings et al. 2007). Research suggests there is little evidence of a significant decline in the use of long-term (traditional) international assignments but does identify the growing use of alternative forms of international assignments (Collings et al. 2007). A recent survey by Brookfield Global Relocation Trends (2005) reported that 62 % of respondents suggested that their organizations were seeking alternatives to long-term assignments. This suggests that what is happening is the emergence of a portfolio of international assignments within the MNC (Roberts et al. 1998).

The most popular form of non-standard assignments appears to be the short-term international assignment (SIA). Compared to traditional assignments, SIA has three key advantages: flexibility; simplicity; and cost effectiveness. Long-term IAs had uncertain benefits and potential drawbacks. Many expatriates felt that they had to work harder to preserve the home network and their social capital suffered through the traditional IAs. Short-term international assignment seems to be a better choice (Tharenou and Harvey 2008). Managers can be assigned to some challenging tasks in a foreign country. They are not away from the headquarters for a long period of time and can be assigned to several different countries before they are appointed to some important managerial position. Such an approach optimizes the economic efficiency of human resources—providing required skills and developing international capabilities simultaneously (Tharenou and Harvey 2008). However, Yamazaki and Kayes (2007) claim that if MNCs expect their expatriates to perform successfully within their assignment periods, they may need to provide the expatriates with at least a three-year tenure. Therefore, this study adopts a pseudo longitudinal research method that examines expatriates with different lengths of assignment tenure to investigate whether short-term international assignments are as effective for expatriate adjustment and learning as traditional long-term international assignments.

2.1.2 Expatriates and International Assignments

An expatriate is the person that MNCs assign to an international assignment. Expatriates usually are home country nationals or third country nationals. Edstrom and Galbraith (1977) define expatriates as individuals who, irrespective of their national origin, are transferred outside their native country to another country specifically for employment purposes. Expatriates are usually classified into three broad categories based on their national origin relative to that of the parent company (Shaffer et al. 1999). *Parent country nationals* (PCNs) are expatriates who are from the home country of the MNC; *third country nationals* are non-PCN immigrants in the host country (e.g., those transferred between foreign subsidiaries); *inpatriates* are employees from foreign subsidiaries who are assigned to work in the parent country. There are several reasons why MNCs select various types of expatriates. For example, parent country nationals facilitate communication between corporate and foreign offices, while third country nationals tend to be more sensitive to cultural and political issues.

Harzing (2001) identified three specific control roles of expatriates, namely: the bear, the bumble-bee, and the spider. Bears act as a means of replacing the centralisation of decision-making in MNC and provide a direct means of surveillance over subsidiary operations. The title highlights the degree of dominance these assignees have over subsidiary operations. Bumble bees fly 'from plant to plant' and create cross-pollination between the various 'offshoots' (Harzing 2001:369). These expatriates can be used to control subsidiaries through socialisation of host employees and the development of informal communication networks. Finally spiders, as the name suggests control through the weaving of informal communication networks within the MNC. Significantly, Harzing (2001) argues that although expatriates generally appear to perform their role as bears regardless of the situation, the study suggests that their roles as spiders and bumble bees tend to be more contexts specific. Specifically, the bumble bee and spider roles appeared to be more significant in longer established subsidiaries (longer than 50 years) while the bumble bee role appeared to be important in newly established subsidiaries also. Besides, the level of localization of subsidiary operations and further lower levels of international integration (the subsidiary was not greatly reliant on the headquarters for sales and purchases) were positively related to the likelihood of expatriates performing the bumble bee and spider roles.

2.1.3 *Cultural Differences Between Nations*

2.1.3.1 High-Context Versus Low-Context Cultures

Hall (1977) claims a cultural classification of high-context culture and low-context culture based on how, in each individual, identity rests on total communication frameworks. In high-context cultures, surrounding situations, external physical environments, and non-verbal behaviours are all important for its members to determine the meanings of messages conveyed in communication. Covert clues in these contexts make differences to the members and are used to search for a real meaning beyond verbal messages. In a high-context culture, its members tend to be related to each other in relatively long lasting relationships. For their effective communications, high-context culture requires its members to become sensitive to immediate environments through feelings. Yamazaki (2005) contends that the communication patterns in high-context cultures are conceptually associated with the Concrete Experience learning mode. Chinese, French, Japanese, and Arabic countries are classified as high-context cultures (Hall 1977).

In a low-context culture, on the other hand, surrounding situations, external physical environments, and non-verbal behaviours are relatively less important in generating and interpreting meanings, whereas explicit verbal messages are crucial in communication (Hall 1977). Most information is conveyed in explicit codes and therefore, explicit communicative styles in logical forms are placed with high importance. In low-context culture, interpersonal relationships last for a relatively shorter period. The communication patterns of low-context cultures focus less on interpersonal relationships while more on rationally detached analyses. Yamazaki (2005) contends that the communicative traits of low-context culture are consonant with the characteristics of the Abstract Conceptualization learning mode and thereby, individuals in low-context culture are likely to learn by logical thinking and analytical cognition. The United States, the United Kingdom, Canada, Australia, Germany, and Switzerland are classified as low-context cultures (Hall 1977). In the present research, the sample of western expatriates constitutes: 35.5 % of the sample comes from the United Kingdom, 29.8 % from the United States, 21.5 % from Canada, 9.1 % from Australia, and 4.1 % from other countries. Basically, western expatriate managers participated in this research are assigned from countries with low-context cultures to a country with high-context culture, China.

2.1.3.2 Collectivism Versus Individualism Cultures

Hofstede (1997) proposes five dimensions of cultural differences: individualism versus collectivism, masculinity versus feminity, long-term orientation versus short-term orientation, power distance, and uncertainty avoidance (see Fig. 2.1). This section begins with a discussion of the dimension collectivism versus individualism.

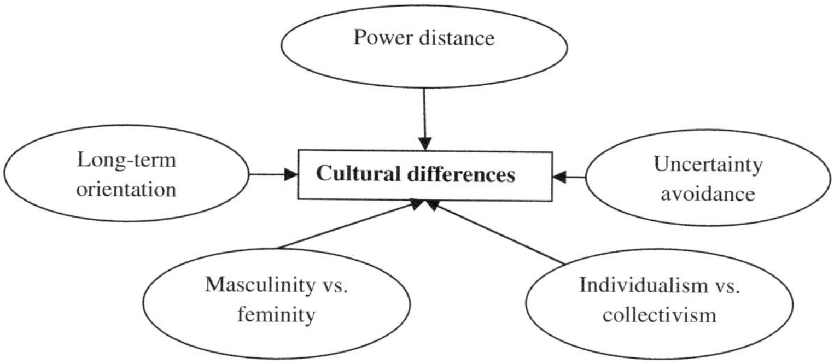

Fig. 2.1 Hofstede's 5 cultural dimension model

Hofstede (1997) defines the collectivism and individualism cultural dimension as 'the degree to which a society reinforces individual or collective achievement and interpersonal relationships'. The fundamental issue addressed by this dimension is the degree of interdependence a society maintains among its members. It has to do with whether people's self-image is defined in terms of 'I' or 'we'. A high score on individualism indicates that individuality and individual rights are paramount within the society. In individualistic cultures, individuals tend to form a large number of looser relationships and they are supposed to look after themselves and their direct family only (Hofstede 2010). On the other hand, a low score on individualism, or a high score on collectivism, indicates that the society has a more collectivist nature with close ties between individuals. In collectivist cultures, the society reinforces extended families and collectives and everyone takes responsibility for fellow members of their group. Markus and Kitayama (1991) examined the culturally different self-construal and proposed two classifications: interdependent-self and independent-self, each of whose attributes differs among cultures. Interdependent-self is represented as the self-construal of people in Asian, African, Latin American, and many southern European cultures, while independent-self is exemplified as the self-construal of those in American culture as well as many western European cultures (Markus and Kitayama 1991). Triandis (1995) and Hofstede (1997) categorized this cultural dimension of interdependent-self versus independent-self as analogous to that of collectivism versus Individualism. Anderson (1988) supports this cultural dimension from a cognitive perspective. He illustrates that Eastern cultures are holistic, relational, and field-dependent, while Western cultures are analytical and field-independent.

People with collectivism cultures have the strong sense of belongingness to social contexts and relationships (Hofstede 1997). Markus and Kitayama (1991) claim that individuals with interdependent-self tend to base the relationship with others as a crucial and functional unit of conscious reflection and, they have a strong tendency to seek information about others' perception about self in the relationship. In contrast, independent-self, the American and western European notion of self, is seen as separate from context (Markus and Kitayama 1991). There is a widespread belief that people are inherently detached and distinct in individualistic cultures where the cultural norm is to become independent from others and to express one's uniqueness. Collectivistic cultures, such as the cultures of most Asian countries, emphasize a communication style in which 'most of the information is either in the physical context or internalized in the person' (Hall 1976: 79), whereas individualistic cultures, such as those of the United States, Germany, and the United Kingdom, use a 'low-context' communication style (Hall 1976). Chinese and Japanese are classified with high collectivist culture, while the North American and most western European countries are classified with individualistic cultures (Hofstede 2010). According to the national culture comparisons of Hofstede (2010), China is a highly collectivist culture where people act in the interest of the group and not necessarily of themselves. In-group considerations affect hiring and promotions with closer in-groups (such as family) are getting preferential treatment. Whereas relationships with colleagues are cooperative for in-groups, they are cold or even hostile to out-groups. In China, personal relationships prevail over task and organization (Hofstede 2010).

In the present research, western expatriate managers are assigned from countries with individualistic cultures to a country with a high collectivist culture, China. As we can see, the collectivists' cultural characteristics of China may present a major obstacle for western expatriates. The researcher suggests that an awareness of the history, culture, and behaviour of Chinese people would reduce expatriates level of frustration, anxiety, and concern.

2.1.3.3 Power Distance

Hofstede (1997) defines power distance as 'the degree of equality, or inequality, between people in the country's society'. Power distance refers to 'the extent to which the less powerful members of institutions and organisations within a country expect and accept that power is distributed unequally' (Hofstede 1997). High scores on a Power distance index indicate that inequalities of power and wealth have been allowed to grow within the society. These societies are more likely to follow a caste system that does not allow significant upward mobility of its citizens. Low scores on a Power distance index, on the other hand, indicate that the society deemphasizes the differences between citizen's power and wealth. In these societies, equality and opportunity for everyone is stressed.

According to the national culture comparisons in Hofstede centre (Hofstede 2010), China sits in the higher rankings of his Power Distance Index, i.e. a society that believes that inequalities amongst people are acceptable. The subordinate-superior relationship tends to be polarized and there is no defense against power abuse by superiors. Individuals are influenced by formal authority and sanctions and are in general optimistic about people's capacity for leadership and initiative. People should not have aspirations beyond their rank. On the other hand, the United State, the United Kingdom, and most western European countries are classified with low power distance cultures (Hofstede 2010). Within organizations in low power distance societies, hierarchy is established for convenience, superiors are always accessible and managers rely on individual employees and teams for their expertise. Both managers and employees expect to be consulted and information is shared frequently. At the same time, the communication is informal, direct, and participative. In the present research, western expatriate managers are assigned from countries with lower power distance cultures to a country with a high power distance culture, China.

2.1.3.4 Strong Uncertainty Avoidance Versus Weak Uncertainty Avoidance Cultures

Hofstede (1997) defines uncertainty avoidance as 'the extent to which the members of a culture feel threatened by uncertain or unknown situations'. Furthermore, uncertainty avoidance index refers to the level of tolerance for uncertainty and ambiguity. High scores on uncertainty avoidance index indicates that the country has a low tolerance for uncertainty and ambiguity and is a rule-oriented society that institutes laws, rules, regulations, and controls in order to reduce the amount of uncertainty. On the other hand, a low score on the uncertainty avoidance index indicates that the country has less concern about ambiguity and uncertainty and has more tolerance for a variety of opinions. A society with weak uncertainty avoidance culture is less rule-oriented and more readily accepts change. The characteristics of strong uncertainty avoidance are reflected in Chinese culture (Hoppe 1990). The main concern of the society is to control everything in order to eliminate or avoid the unexpected. As a result, the society does not readily accept change and is risk adverse.

Organizational members in strong uncertainty avoidance countries have a feeling of anxiety or fear when encountering unfamiliar risks, deviant ideas, or conflicts in their work place. Those members need to take time for action until they acquire enough knowledge and information to reduce or resolve unclear and unstructured situations. In contrast, organizational members in weak uncertainty avoidance countries tend to feel less uncomfortable in unclear and unstructured circumstances and are more likely to take risks in unfamiliar situations when encountering deviant or innovative ideas and behaviours (Hofstede 1997). Self-actualization in a weak uncertainty-avoidance work place functions as a great motivational factor, while no failure is the main concern in a strong uncertainty-avoidance work place. Hoppe (1990) tested the relationship between the strong/weak uncertainty avoidance cultural dimension and Kolb's (1986) learning styles. He examined a sample of 1544 adults from 19 countries: 17 European countries (Great Britain, Germany, France, Italy, and so on), the US, and Turkey. His results showed that people from strong uncertainty avoidance cultures tend to learn through the reflective observation learning mode, while those from weak uncertainty-avoidance cultures tend to learn through the active experimentation learning mode.

Japanese, South Korea, and Germany are classified with strong uncertainty avoidance cultures; Chinese is classified with medium to strong uncertainty avoidance culture; the United State, the United Kingdom, Australia, and Denmark are classified with weak uncertainty avoidance cultures (Hofstede 2010). In the present research, western expatriate managers are assigned from countries with weak uncertainty avoidance cultures to a country with a medium to strong uncertainty avoidance culture, China.

2.1.3.5 Long-Term Orientation

Hofstede (1997) defines Long-term orientation as 'the degree to which a society embraces, or does not embrace, long-term devotion to traditional, forward thinking values'. High scores on a Long-term orientation index indicate that the country prescribes to the values of long-term commitments and respect for tradition. This is thought to support a strong work ethic where long-term rewards are expected as a result of today's hard work. In a society with a long-term orientation, businesses may take longer to develop, particularly for an 'outsider'. Low scores on a Long-term orientation index, on the other hand, indicate that the country does not reinforce the concept of long-term, traditional orientation. In a society with this culture, change can occur more rapidly as long-term traditions and commitments do not become impediments to change.

According to the national culture comparisons in Hofstede centre (Hofstede 2010), China is a highly long-term oriented society in which persistence and perseverance are normal. Resources and investment tend to be in long-term projects, such as real estate. The United States, on the other hand, is classified as a short-term culture. American businesses tend to measure their performance on a short-term basis, with profit and loss statements being issued on a quarterly basis. This also drives its people to strive for quick results within the work place. In the present research, western expatriate managers are assigned from countries with relatively short-term orientation cultures to a country with a highly long-term oriented culture, China.

2.1.3.6 Masculinity Versus Feminity

Hofstede (1997) defines the Masculinity/Feminity cultural dimension as 'the degree to which a society reinforces, or does not reinforce, the traditional masculine work role model of male achievement, control, and power'. High scores on the Masculinity index indicate that the country experiences a high degree of gender differentiation. Males dominate a significant portion of the society and power structure, with females being controlled by male domination. On the other hand, low scores on the Masculinity index indicate that the country has a low level of differentiation and discrimination between genders. Females are treated equally to males in all aspects of the society. In the present research, western expatriate managers are assigned to a country with a slight Masculinity oriented culture, China.

In summary, Chinese culture is highly contrasted with western (American and Western Europe) cultures. China is distinct different from most other countries. From a western perspective, China 'is seen as the most foreign of all foreign places. Its culture, institutions, and people appear completely baffling—a matter of absolute difference' (Chen 2001: 17). Also, companies in different cultures have different ways of conducting business. There is a wealth of evidence that cultural differences can act as important barriers for business expatriates. According to Torbiorn (1988), the more dissimilar, foreign, or strange a situation appears, the more negative the expatriates' attitudes towards those situations. Psychological cultural barriers are typically associated with negative reactions towards another culture, norms of the other culture appear as less familiar, less normal, less good, and so forth than those to which the individual is acculturated (Selmer 2004). A psychological cultural barrier is said to be more obvious when two cultures are different in terms of language and other cultural norms (Selmer 2004).

2.2 Expatriate Adjustment

International assignments involve significant changes in the job the individual performs and the corporate culture in which responsibilities are executed. It also involves dealing with unfamiliar norms related to the general culture, living conditions, weather, food, health care, daily customs, and political systems. It is estimated that 20–40 % of all expatriates sent on foreign assignments return home prematurely. McGinley (2008) suggests that expatriate failure rates vary from country to country. National Foreign Trade Council (2006) demonstrates that the rate of early return from expatriate assignment was approximately 21 %. However, failure rates are said to increase further when repatriation failure (expatriates who return from overseas assignments but then leave their firms within one year) rates are considered (McGinley 2008). Expatriate failure is a significant issue for MNCs due to the high costs of expatriate failure which are both direct (e.g. salary, training costs, travel and relocation expenses) and indirect (damaged relations with host country organizations and loss of market share). Research suggests that the latter should be considered as the most significant costs by MNCs, as damage to reputation in key strategic foreign markets could be highly detrimental to the prospects of successfully developing international business in particular regions. Expatriate failure also bears considerable costs for managers themselves, including loss of self-esteem, self-confidence, and reputation. In summary, the literature indicates that the failure rate of expatriates has been reported to range from 10 to 80 %, costing MNCs from $40,000 to $1million for each failed assignment. The inability of expatriates to successfully adjust to foreign environments has been cited as one of the most frequent reasons for unsuccessful international assignments (Black et al. 1991; Shaffer et al. 1999; Takeuchi et al. 2005; Okpara and Kabongo 2010).

Liu and Lee (2008) contend that management researchers have largely failed to study systematically the psychological, social and behavioural concerns of managing overseas operations. In order to advance the research on expatriate failure and increase our understanding on expatriate adjustment, additional research is needed, particularly from a non-western context like China, because the majority of the researches conducted on these issues have been done in the west (Black et al. 1991; Grainger and Nankervis 2001; Selmer 2004).

Expatriate adjustment is generally described as a process where a manager leaves a familiar cultural environment and enters an unfamiliar one. It is the perceived degree of psychological comfort and familiarity an expatriate has working with the new culture (Black et al. 1991). Scholars have only focused their research efforts on the problem of expatriate adjustment and effectiveness since the late 1970s (Black et al. 1991). Previous to that time, some research had been conducted on Peace Corps volunteers and foreign exchange students, but little work was done on expatriate managers (Church 1982, cited in Black et al. 1991). Selmer (2004) contends that psychological adjustment is a main component of expatriate adjustment. Psychological adjustment connotes subjective well-being or mood states (e.g. depression, anxiety, tension, and fatigue), emphasizing attitudinal factors of the process of adjustment. The theoretical concept of subjective well-being is associated with the psychological aspects of international adjustment (Selmer 2004).

The concept of socio-cultural adjustment has been proposed and defined in the literature on international adjustment (Searle and Ward 1990; Ward and Searle 1991). Research on international assignments highlights psychological or socio-cultural adjustment as the vital construct underlying the rewards and costs of expatriate experiences to individuals, their families, and their firms (Bhaskar-Shrinivas et al. 2005). Socio-cultural adjustment relates to the ability to 'fit in' or effectively interact with members of the host culture (Ward and Kennedy 1992). Socio-cultural adjustment has been associated with variables that promote and facilitate culture learning and acquisition of social skills in the host culture (Selmer 2006). The socio-cultural notion of adjustment is based on cultural learning theory and highlights social behaviours and practical social skills underlying attitudinal factors (Black and Mendenhall 1991). Selmer (2006) claims that Black et al.'s (1991) theoretical framework of international adjustment covers socio-cultural aspects of international adjustment. A significant amount of existent empirical research supports a positive correlation between expatriates' international adjustment and their work performance (Caligiuri 1997; Selmer 2006).

2.2.1 Expatriate Adjustment Dimensions and Process

Black (1988) contends that expatriate adjustment to the cross-cultural environment can be viewed as having three primary dimensions: *degree*, *mode*, and *facet*. *Degree* of adjustment can be viewed as both a subjective and objective concept. Subjectively, it is the degree of comfort the expatriate feels in the new role and the degree to which he/she feels adjusted to the role requirements. Objectively, on the other hand, it is the degree to which the expatriate has mastered the role requirements and is able to demonstrate that adjustment via his/her performance (Black 1988). *Mode* of adjustment refers to the manner in which the expatriate adjust to the new role, i.e. expatriates can adjust by altering the new role to match better themselves or by altering their own attitudes and behaviours to match better the role expectations or altering both to compromise. Black (1988) proposes that there are at least two *facets* of expatriate adjustment: work adjustment and general adjustment. Black and Stephens (1989) further extended this framework and suggest that there are three specific facets of expatriate adjustment: adjustment to work, which encompasses supervision, responsibilities, and performances; adjustment to interacting with host nationals; adjustment to the general environment, which encompasses life conditions in the foreign country. Several researchers have confirmed this typology (Black and Gregersen 1991; Shaffer et al. 1999; Okpara and Kabongo 2010).

Expatriate adjustment is the process of adaptation to living and working in a foreign culture. Torbion (1988) proposed that cross-cultural adjustment occurred in four phases which is often referred to the U-curve. It depicts a progression of adjustment through four sequential stages: honeymoon, culture shock, adjustment, and mastery. The trajectory of adjustment over time resembles a U-curve: initially rising during the honeymoon, falling when culture shock occurs, recovering as adjustment take place, and stabilizing during mastery.

Black and Mendenhall (1991) explained the U-curve in terms of social learning theory. The first phase occurs during the first few weeks after arrival. At this time, the new arrival is fascinated with the new and different aspects of the foreign culture and country (Torbion 1988). During the initial stage, the person has not had sufficient time and experience in the new country to discover that many of his/her past habits and behaviours are inappropriate in the new culture. This lack of negative feedback and the newness of the foreign culture combine to produce the 'honeymoon' effect. Once the newcomer begins to cope seriously with the real conditions of everyday life, the second phase of cross-cultural adjustment begins. This stage is characterized by frustrations and hostility toward the host country and its people (Torbion 1988). This is because the person discovers that his/her past behaviours are inappropriate in the new culture but as yet has not learned what to substitute. Torbion (1988) argues that culture shock generally occurs at the transition between phase two and phase three when the person has received the maximum amount of negative feedback but as yet has very little idea about what the appropriate behaviours are. The third stage begins as the person acquires some language skills and adaptive ability to move around on his/her own. In the third phase, the person begins to learn not only how to get around but also some new appropriate behaviours. By the third phase, the person also has developed some proficiency in performing the new set of behaviours (Black 1988). In the fourth phase, the person's adjustment is generally complete and the incremental degree of adjustment is minimal. In this stage, the person now knows and can properly perform the necessary behaviours to function effectively and without anxiety to cultural differences

(Black 1988). Bhaskar-Shrinivas et al.'s (2005) Meta-analyses, using data from 8474 expatriates in 66 studies, provided support for the U-curve, or sideways S-shape, to expatriate adjustment's trajectory.

Integrating the international and domestic adjustment literatures, Black et al. (1991) propose two major components (including seven dimensions) of the expatriate adjustment process. Figure 2.2 presents Black et al.'s (1991) International adjustment model. The first component, anticipatory adjustment, describes issues that exist before expatriates leave their home countries; the second component, in-country adjustment, deals with issues that become relevant after the expatriates arrive at their foreign assignments. Anticipatory adjustment includes three dimensions: pre-departure training, previous overseas experience, and organizational selection mechanisms. In-country adjustment, on the other hand, includes four dimensions: individual skills, job-related factors, organizational factors, and non-work factors. Shaffer and Harrison (2001) propose that an expatriate's language skills should also be considered in anticipatory adjustment. Black (1988) explains that in both domestic and international adjustment literatures, an individual leaves a familiar setting and enters an unfamiliar one. However, because international adjustment usually entails greater disruptions of old routines than domestic adjustment, the magnitude of uncertainty is usually higher in international versus domestic adjustment. In general, the domestic adjustment literature has focused on pre- and post-entry adjustment variables, especially those related to the job and the organization, whereas the international adjustment literature has focused on individual and

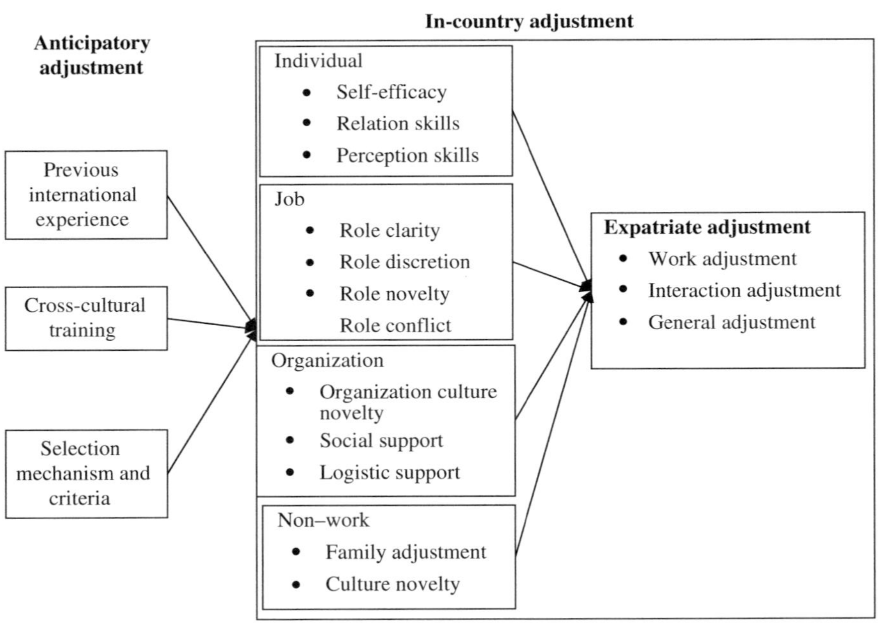

Fig. 2.2 Black et al.'s (1991) International adjustment model

non-job variables and on degree of adjustment (Black et al. 1991). Black et al. (1991) further suggest that general adjustment and interaction adjustment may be much stronger predictors of organizational commitment, intent to leave, or turnover in the case of international adjustment versus domestic adjustment. Hechanova et al. (2003) argue that the adjustment model proposed by Black et al.'s (1991) has instigated and galvanized a large body of evidence. While Tan et al. (2005) argue that Black et al.'s (1991) cross-cultural adjustment model is mainly descriptive and needs to be more prescriptive, Bhaskar-Shrinivas et al. (2005) produced evidence that strongly supported the model, through meta-analyses using data from 8474 expatriates in 66 studies. They contend that Black et al.'s (1991) model is the most influential and often-cited theoretical treatment of expatriate experiences.

2.2.2 *Factors Influencing Expatriate Adjustment*

The present research will discuss the factors that influence expatriate adjustment from four aspects: individual factors, job-related factors, organizational factors, and non-work factors based on Black et al.'s (1991) International adjustment model (see Fig. 2.2). It should also be noted that different adjustment influencing factors may have different impacts on each facet of expatriate adjustment (general adjustment, work adjustment, and interaction adjustment).

2.2.2.1 Individual Factors

The present research will discuss the individual factors that influence expatriate adjustment from two aspects: individual characteristics (including self-efficacy and interpersonal skills) and previous international experience.

1. Individual characteristics

Black (1988) reviewed the individual factors that were hypothesized to facilitate expatriate adjustment and reported a summary of these which includes: (1) the individual's desire to adjust; (2) technical or managerial competence (Hays 1971, cited in Black 1988); (3) a person's social relation skills orientation (Ratiu 1983); (4) an individual's tolerance for ambiguity or open mindedness (Ratiu 1983); (5) an individual's self-confidence. Mendenhall and Oddou (1985) reviewed the individual skills necessary for a manager to be effective in a cross-cultural setting. They categorized all these skills into three dimensions: the self-dimension, which encompasses skills that enable the expatriate to maintain mental health, psychological well-being, self-efficacy, and effective stress management; the relationship dimension, which constitutes the array of skills necessary for the fostering of relationships with host nationals; and the perception dimension, which entails the cognitive abilities that allow the expatriate to correctly perceive and evaluate the host environment and its actors (Mendenhall and Oddou 1985). Ones and

Viswesvaran (1997) confirmed the appropriateness of using individual traits and temperaments for understanding differences in how managers respond to expatriate and repatriate experiences. More recently, Mol et al. (2005) conducted a quantitative review of the Big Five personality factors and found that they were as predictive of expatriate performance. However, Tan et al. (2005) contend that expatriates' emotions should also be considered as an important individual factor in the international adjustment model. They claim that expatriates' emotions play a major role in cross-cultural success, especially for individualists working in collectivistic culture for long periods of time. They further suggest that emotional demands caused by cultural differences in expatriate encounters impact negatively on their experience. Klein and Lee (2006) found that certain personality traits, such as openness, increased expatriate adjustment and their learning. Despite criticisms such as these, Okpara and Kabongo (2010) contend that Black et al.'s (1991) international adjustment model is a well-established theoretical model and allows for further inclusion of related factors on each level.

'Self-efficacy' was initially conceptualized as a belief in a person's ability to succeed in the enactment of a specific task (Bandura 1977). Sherer et al. (1982, cited in Shaffer et al. 1999) explored the concept of general 'self-efficacy' and defined it as 'an individual's past experiences with success and failure in a variety of situations which should result in a general set of expectations that the individual carries into new situations'. In case of expatriate adjustment, 'self-efficacy' refers to the ability to believe in one self and one's ability to deal effectively with the foreign surroundings, even in the face of great uncertainty (Mendenhall and Oddou 1985). Bandura (1977) first explored the impact of the concept 'self-efficacy' in social learning. Bandura (1977) suggests that individuals with higher levels of self-efficacy tend to persist in exhibiting new behaviours that are being learned longer than do individuals with less self-efficacy. Based on this, Black et al. (1991) propose that high level of self-efficacy would drive the expatriate to persist in exhibiting new behaviours which, in turn, would facilitate his/her degree of adjustment. They contend that expatriates with high overall self-efficacy persist in exhibiting newly learned behaviours despite negative feedback; they use the resulting learning to improve their adjustment.

Relational skills, or interpersonal skills, refer to a repertoire of tools and techniques that facilitate the formation of one's interpersonal ties. Through those ties, expatriates obtain necessary information and behaviour-relevant feedback in host cultures (Black et al. 1991). Interaction with host nationals is another important adjustment facilitating factor. Because interaction with host nationals can provide cues concerning appropriate behaviour in the new culture, greater interaction with host nationals would reduce novelty and positively affect adjustment.

Black et al. (1991) propose that the accuracy of the expectations held by expatriates is a key to effective international adjustment. The more accurate expectations expatriates can form, the more uncertainty they will reduce and the better their adaptation will be. Relational skills, or interpersonal skills, provide an important means of increasing the cues expatriates receive about what is expected and how they are doing regarding the expectations. In summary, interpersonal skills have two main beneficial impacts on expatriate adjustment. First, the greater expatriates' interpersonal skills, the easier it is for them to interact with host nationals (Mendenhall and Oddou 1985). Second, the more expatriates interact with host nationals, the more information they can receive about what is and what isn't appropriate in the host culture and how they are doing. Black (1988) found a significant positive relationship between percentage of time spent with host nationals and general international adjustment. Bhaskar-Shrinivas et al. (2005) claim that relational skills allow the expatriates to gain familiarity with what is acceptable and/or unacceptable in the host cultures.

2. Prior international experience

Prior international experience refers to individuals' prior experience in living and/or working abroad. Prior international (working and/or non-work) experience that expatriates possess is likely to influence their adjustment to a host country (Okpara and Kabongo 2010). Previous international non-work experiences, such as travelling and studying, are likely to be associated with the extent to which expatriates adjust to foreign cultures (Okpara and Kabongo 2010). When people travel to foreign countries, they learn the behaviors, customs, and norms of those cultures through direct experience or through observation of the host nationals' behaviours (Bandura 1977). Past international experience provides expatriates with direct opportunities to learn a variety of skills. Intercultural communication, relocation, and adaptive skills will be gained, all of which should have a positive influence on the expatriates' cross-cultural adjustment (Black et al. 1991; Selmer 2002, 2004; Shaffer et al. 1999). Black (1988) suggests that the experience of a prior expatriation lowers the difficulties related to work adjustment. Black et al. (1991) suggest that previous international experience is an important source of information from which accurate expectations can be formed and the accuracy of the expectations held by expatriates is a key to effective international adjustment. Yamazaki (2005) argue that previous experience may change how expatriates adjust by allowing them to ignore what had not worked for them in the past and to concentrate on what did work. Research examining the extent of prior international working experience (Black 1988; Okpara and Kabongo 2010) has generally indicated a slightly positive association with adjustment, especially with work adjustment. However, Torbiorn (1988) found that specific length of previous overseas experience was not related to higher levels of adjustment. Therefore, quantity of prior international experience does not seem to necessarily relate to current international adjustment. These inconsistent findings indicate that exactly how previous international experience influences expatriate adjustment and what factors inhibit or magnify the impact of previous experience needs to be comprehensively investigated.

Selmer (2002) explored the possibility that prior international experience moderated the relationship between current assignment tenure and adjustment, studying western expatriates in Hong Kong. His results showed that the impact of prior Asian experience on the novice group (less than one year on an international assignment) was significant, but prior international experience outside Asia was not significant for either group. In the light of Selmer's (2002) research results,

Takeuchi et al. (2005) organized previous international experience along two dimensions (domain (work/non-work) and cultural specificity) and examined the effects of expatriates' current past international experience on their cross-cultural adjustment. They targeted 243 Japanese expatriates working in the United States and their results indicate that past international experience moderates the relationship between current assignment tenure and both general and work adjustment. Takeuchi et al. (2005) made explanations to previous inconsistent research findings regarding the impact of prior international experience: the interaction effects of previous international experience differed depending on the measurement mode being used. The interaction figures for the length-based measures of prior international experience illustrated both direct and indirect effects, while the number-based measure of prior international experience only exhibited the mediating effects. Takeuchi et al. (2005) further conclude that previous international experience acts as a moderator rather than as an antecedent to expatriates' cross-cultural adjustment. Bhaskar-Shrinivas et al. (2005) also examined the mediating influences of prior overseas assignments. They suggest that time spent on current assignment may enhance the effect of previous international experience on work adjustment and expatriates may leverage past experiences better as they stay on assignments longer. As their assignments progress, expatriates may be better able to pick out the experiences that best enable them to adjust to their work surroundings.

2.2.2.2 Job-Related Factors

Black (1988) reviewed the job-related factors that were hypothesized to influence (facilitate or inhibit) expatriate adjustment based on both international adjustment and domestic adjustment literature and proposes four job-related factors that can increase the uncertainty, uncontrollability, unfamiliarity, or unpredictability of the new work role and consequently inhibit the adjustment. These four adjustment inhibiting job-related factors are: role novelty (role novelty involves the difference between the past role and the new role), role ambiguity, role conflict, and role overload. Moreover, he proposed three job-related factors that have the potential for reducing the uncertainty and facilitating expatriate adjustment: role discretion, previous transfer or previous overseas work experience, and pre-departure knowledge.

International assignments are often associated with policy and procedural conflicts with parent companies (Gregersen and Black 1992). Bhaskar-Shrinivas et al. (2005) further explain that role clarity refers to exact understanding of position requirements; role discretion refers to decision-making autonomy; role novelty refers to differences between host and native country work roles; and role conflict refers to incompatible cues regarding job expectations. These four job-related factors are likely to influence expatriates' ability to adjust to the new environment. For example, role clarity may reduce the ambiguity associated with foreign work surroundings, whereas role discretion may enable expatriates to use previously employed behavioural mechanisms to minimize that ambiguity. Bhaskar-Shrinivas et al.'s (2005) meta-analyses using data from 8474 expatriates in 66 studies provided support for a significant correlation between job role clarity and work adjustment. Obviously, the uncertainty regarding objectives and role requirements are the strongest stressors in expatriates' overseas work environments.

(a) Current assignment tenure

Black (1988) also found a significantly positive relationship between the length of current assignment tenure and work adjustment. It is reasonable to argue for a positive relationship between the length of time in a current work assignment (current international assignment tenure) and expatriate adjustment. When expatriates initially arrive in the host country, they face considerable uncertainty about many different aspects of both life and work. However, over time, they are likely to acquire information that enables them to function more effectively in the new environment. With prolonged exposure to the differences of the host culture, expatriates are likely to become more familiar with the general surroundings and find more suitable standards and become better adjusted (Takeuchi et al. 2005).

Takeuchi et al. (2005) examined the effects of current assignment tenure on expatriate adjustment, studying 243 Japanese expatriates working in the United States. Their results showed that current assignment tenure had significant relationships with expatriates' general and work adjustment. Takeuchi et al. (2005) propose that the time spent in an international assignment is very important for expatriates' work adjustment and suggest researchers adopt a time perspective for understanding expatriate adjustment. Longer tenure increases opportunities for expatriates to learn appropriate work behaviours through direct as well as vicarious modelling (Bandura 1977). In addition, an extended period of time is also required before expatriates are fully accepted by their peers and develop work relationship with their peers. Accordingly, the length of current assignment tenure is related to an enhanced understanding of the culture of a host country and an increased ability to adapt to the host country (Takeuchi et al. 2005). Black and Mendenhall (1991) define 'time to proficiency' as the period it takes an employee in a new job to reach an acceptable performance level. The time expatriates take to become proficient after transfers may have several important implications both for themselves and their organizations. Typically, the total costs for an organization of an international assignment will exceed the total contribution an expatriate makes for some time during a post-entry period of settling-in. Hence, the longer the time to proficiency, the greater the balance of costs will be to the organization. It would be in the interest of both the expatriate and the assigning organization to keep the time to proficiency as short as possible.

2.2.2.3 Organizational Factors

Organizations' selection criteria and mechanisms are also important expatriate adjustment influencing factors. Black et al. (1991) claim that the closer the selected expatriate matches the needs of the organization, the easier the expatriate's adjustment after entering the international assignment. Also, the greater the difference between the organizational culture of the subsidiary organization in the foreign country compared to the organization in the home country (i.e. high organizational culture novelty) the more difficult the expatriate adjustment would be (Black et al. 1991).

Moreover, logistical support from the organization, parent firm assistance with day-to-day living, such as help with housing, schools, grocery stores, and so on, could potentially reduce uncertainty associated with international assignments and therefore facilitate expatriate adjustment (Black et al. 1991). Social support from co-workers and logistical support from the parent company can play important roles in easing adjustment. By providing expatriates with information about culturally suitable norms and behaviours in their work context, social support from co-workers reduces uncertainty emanating from an expatriate's new circumstances. Logistical support, on the other hand, could assist adjustment by making critical resources available to the expatriate at times of necessity and thus, meeting the demands of the new environment. In a study by Guzzo et al. (1994), expatriates' judgments of sufficiency of employer benefits and their perceptions of support were significant predictors of organizational commitment and intention to leave. Organization's social support, defined in terms of the sources and quality of helping relationships, acts as a stress buffer and has an indirect effect on strains such as job dissatisfaction.

2.2.2.4 Non-work Factors

The present research will also discuss the non-work factors that influence expatriate adjustment from two aspects: expatriate's family's adjustment and host culture novelty.

(a) Expatriate's family's adjustment

Poor cross-cultural adjustment of a spouse is likely to inhibit an expatriate's adjustment. In Tung's (1982) survey of American MNC executives, she found that these executives believed that a spouse's inability to adjust to the foreign host culture was the number one reason for expatriate failures. Tung (1982) further claims that an expatriate's family's inability to adjust is the biggest reason for the expatriate's inability to make the transition. Black (1988) contends that the expatriate's family's ability to adjust to the new culture/country has a significant impact on the expatriate's transition at work and adjustment. Black and Stephens (1989) investigated a large sample of American expatriates on assignment in several different countries and their spouses. They found positive and significant relationships between expatriates and spouse cross-cultural adjustment. In a recent study by Black and Stephens (1989), family situation was rated by expatriates as the most important contributor to successful international assignments. Bhaskar-Shrinivas et al.'s (2005) meta-analyses using data from 8474 expatriates in 66 studies provided support for the idea that there is a strong correlation between spouse and expatriate adjustment.

(b) Culture novelty

There is a wealth of evidence that cultural differences can act as important barriers for business expatriates. As we discussed in Sect. 2.1.3 ('cultural differences between nations'), Chinese culture is highly contrasted with western (American and Western Europe) cultures. Western expatriate managers experience high culture novelty when they work in China. Mendenhall and Oddou (1985) refer to culture novelty as culture toughness and suggest that some countries, like China, seem to be more difficult to adapt to than others. They claim that the greater the difference between the cultures of the host country compared to the home country, i.e. high culture novelty, the more difficult would be the expatriate adjustment. Torbiorn (1988) noted that culture novelty has its largest impact on expatriates during the first two years of their assignments. After that, the impact of culture novelty diminishes somewhat. Some authors such as Pires and Stanton (2005) question the efficacy of culture immersion strategies. They contend that cultural values and norms in the individual typically are not changed by simply living in, or learning the language of another culture.

According to Selmer's (2002) study of 36 UK-based companies, he found that respondents from similar cultures (e.g., USA) were as likely to report adjustment problems as expatriates assigned to more dissimilar cultures like China. He concluded that the degree of cultural novelty of the country does not seem to have any correlation with the outcome of the international assignment. Based on in-depth interviews of ethnic Hong Kong Chinese business managers assigned to China, Selmer and Shiu (1999) found that the perceived cultural closeness seemed to build up expectations of easy and quick adjustment, which could, if it was not accomplished, result in frustration and withdrawal. Furthermore, comparing the adjustment of western and overseas Chinese business expatriates in China, Selmer (2002) found that although the westerners perceived a higher degree of culture novelty than the overseas Chinese, they were better adjusted in work environment. More recently, Selmer (2006) examined 165 western business expatriates assigned by western firms to China to find out whether the culture novelty is a relevant factor in assessing the adjustment of business expatriates. Their results showed that there was no significant relationship between culture novelty and expatriate adjustment.

A possible explanation for this is that an expatriate from a very different culture, may be tolerated and given the benefit of the doubt going through the process of trying to adjust to a new culture. An expatriate from a similar or presumed identical culture, on the other hand, could be treated with less patience and given less latitude for culturally deviant behaviours (Selmer 2006). Expatriates, overlooking any possible cultural differences that may exist in foreign locations with a similar culture, exhibiting even minor inappropriate behaviours, will most probably be unfavourably assessed. Hung (1994) argues that in China, Hong Kong Chinese may be judged by different standards and more harshly than a westerner for any mistake made because he/she is presumably knowledgeable about Chinese etiquette and manners and would be expected to fully understand the appropriate social protocol and behave accordingly.

2.2.3 Adjustment of Expatriates in China

Since the introduction of the 'Open Door' policy in the late 1970s, China has undergone enormous social and economic transformations. In 1979, when China opened up for foreign investment, foreign businesses started to move into claim a share of the country's vast markets. China continues to attract more foreign direct investment than any other developing country. However, many parts of the Chinese mainland still have the character of a developing country. China has enjoyed an average annual growth rate of 9 per cent since 1980, partly because of a huge inflow of foreign direct investment (FDI). The country's entry into the World Trade Organization has accentuated its importance as a current and potential market for Western and other international business firms. China has emerged as the world's most desirable market (Selmer 2006).

Selmer (2006) indicate that wholly owned subsidiaries in mainland China perform better if the companies have subsidiaries elsewhere in Greater China. The area 'Greater China' encompasses mainland China, Hong Kong, Singapore, and Taiwan (Selmer 2006). In doing so, business firms may accumulate substantial benefits in terms of enhanced experience of their expatriate staff that may facilitate their eventual entry into mainland China. Selmer (2006) examined the comparative adjustment of expatriates in Greater China and their empirical findings suggest that adjustment of business expatriates is better elsewhere in Greater China than in mainland China. He further proposed an expansion strategy for the internationalization of an organization that using other Greater China locations, like Singapore or Hong Kong, as a stepping-stone and source of experience in the ultimate quest to enter mainland China.

Obviously, interpersonal interactions are relatively difficult in China in the absence of a common language. The official language of China is Mandarin, but, beside that, local dialects are spoken in different regions. Business expatriates in China tend to see language differences as a fundamental obstacle to interaction adjustment. The language barrier is substantial, despite the fact that the level of English proficiency is generally rising in China. Accordingly, there is reason to believe that western expatriate managers in China have a lower degree of interaction adjustment than their general adjustment. Many western business expatriates found their assignment in China frustrating (Selmer 2006). General adjustment for western expatriates in Beijing and Shanghai, China should be relatively easy. Both Beijing and Shanghai are highly dynamic cities with a good provision of modern conveniences. Living conditions in general are good, with ample supply of Western and Asian food, excellent shopping, good housing conditions, good health care facilities as well as modern entertainment facilities and opportunities. With regard to anticipatory adjustment, it has been argued that previous international experience may be an important source from which accurate expectations can be formed (Church 1982) and that 'several previous international adjustment experiences would provide more information from which uncertainties could be reduced and accurate expectation formed' (Black et al. 1991, p. 306). Empirical evidence has also shown that prior international experience facilitates an individual's ability to function and work effectively (Takeuchi et al. 2005; Selmer 2002) and the more contact assignees have had with the host culture, the greater their cross-cultural adjustment. This leads to the present research's first hypothesis:

Hypothesis 1 Duration of managers' international experiences in the host culture will positively influence their adjustment to the current international assignment.

2.3 Experiential Learning Theory

Experiential learning theory (ELT) is a learning theory that is characterized by six basic propositions (Kolb 1984).

1. Learning is best conceived as a process, not in terms of outcomes (p. 26).
2. Learning is a continuous process grounded in experience (p. 27).
3. The process of learning requires the resolution of conflicts between dialectically opposed modes of adaptation to the world (p. 29).
4. Learning is a holistic process of adaptation to the world (p. 31).
5. Learning involves transactions between the person and the environment (p. 34).
6. Learning is the process of creating knowledge (p. 36).

Despite the wide acceptance of Kolb's experiential learning theory, there are salient issues concerning the structure and validity of its use. Kolb's theory has been criticized for logical inconsistencies in theory construction and for the psychometric properties of the learning style inventory. In the 1970s, critical analysis began to emerge regarding the theoretical limitations of Kolb's theory. Critics mainly questioned the psychometric properties of its measure. In response to these criticisms, Kolb redesigned the inventory in 1986 (Mainemelis et al. 2002). Research results indicated that the updated versions largely addressed earlier concerns related to measurement validity (Mainemelis et al. 2002). However, researchers still pointed out several issues concerning data validity and ipsative measurement of the revised model of the learning style inventory. Reynolds (1997) claim that Kolb's experiential learning theory is in decontextualizing learning the concept of style which may provide a discriminatory basis for dealing with difference in gender or race. DeCiantis and Kirton (1996) argue that Kolb's theory conflated three unrelated elements (cognitive style, cognitive level and cognitive process) and attempted to measure all three using a single instrument. They further contend that the experiential learning model is unrelated to style but rather is a 'map' of the learning process (DeCiantis and Kirton 1996). De vita (2001) claims that the cognitive nature of Kolb's theory over-emphasizes the role of the individual and dedecontextualizes the learning process. Kolb (1999) responded to this critique by saying that this critique has been more focused on the theory than the instrument examining the underlying assumptions of the experiential learning theory; however, if the role of the learner is disproportionate to the process, results from the measure instrument would not have consistency and validity. Kolb's experiential learning theory emphasizes the central role of the experiences and the individual. Since the experiential learning theory (ELT)'s first statement in 1971 (Kolb 1971, cited in Kolb 1986), there have been many studies using ELT to advance the theory and practice of experiential learning. The July 2005 update of the Experiential Learning Theory Bibliography (Kolb and Kolb 2005) includes 1876 studies. Because Experiential Learning Theory is a holistic theory of learning that identifies learning style differences among different academic specialties, it is not surprising to see that ELT research is highly interdisciplinary, addressing learning and educational issues in many areas. An analysis of the 1004 entries in the 1999 ELT bibliography (Kolb et al. 2001) shows that 207 studies in management, 430 in education, 104 in information science, 101 in psychology, 72 in medicine, 63 in nursing, 22 in accounting, and 5 in law. About 55 % of this research has appeared in refereed journal articles, 20 % in doctoral dissertations, and 10 % in books and book chapters.

2.3.1 Experiential Learning Process and Cycle

Kolb (1984) defines learning as 'the process whereby knowledge is created through the transformation of experiences'. According to ELT, learning requires people to resolve a dialectic confrontation both when they grasp experience and when they transform experience. The learning processes lie in the bases of four adaptive learning modes that create the experiential learning cycle (Mainemelis et al. 2002). These four adaptive learning modes are concrete experience, reflective observation, abstract conceptualization, and active experimentation respectively. Zull (2002) supported ELT's learning cycle from a biological perspective of human brain mechanisms, based on the examination of left-brain functions that correspond to the four adaptive learning modes.

2.3.2 Learning Style

According to ELT, an effective learner is required to use each of the four fundamental learning abilities at the base of these four adaptive modes (Kolb 1984). Kolb's learning style that he proposed in his Experiential Learning Theory (1984) is influential in explaining aspects of individual differences in modes of adaptation and adjustment in learning. Yamazaki (2005) illustrates that learning styles refer to cognitive, affective, and physiological behaviours that perform as relatively stable indicators of how people perceive, interplay with, and respond to their outside environment in learning situations. In Kolb's learning model, concrete experience (CE) abilities call for being involved in experiences and dealing with immediate human situations in a subjective manner; in contrast, abstract conceptualization (AC) abilities require using logic, ideas, and concepts. Reflective observation (RO) abilities require understanding the meaning of thoughts and situations by carefully watching and listening; in contrast, active experimentation (AE) abilities demand actively influencing people and changing situations.

A combination of two learning abilities constitutes an associated learning style (Kolb 1984; Kolb and Fry 1975). Learning style denotes an individual's general preference for using two sets of learning abilities over other two. The diverging learning style specializes in the two modes CE (feeling) and RO (reflecting), while the converging learning style specializes in AC (thinking) and AE (acting). The assimilating learning style specializes in AC and RO, whereas the accommodating learning style specializes in CE and AE. It should be noted that the names quoted to these learning styles were originally diverger, converger, assimilator, and accommodator. To emphasize the dynamic nature of learning style, the latest version of the learning style inventory has changed the style names from diverger to diverging, from converger to converging, from assimilator to assimilating, and from accommodator to accommodating accordingly (Kolb and Kolb 2005).

Individuals with diverging learning styles are best at viewing concrete situations from many different points of view (Kolb 1984). The style is labelled 'diverging' because a person with it performs better in situations that call for generation of ideas, such as a 'brainstorming' session. People with diverging learning styles have broad cultural interests and like to gather information. They are interested in people and tend to be imaginative and emotional. On the other hand, an individual with a converging learning style is best at finding practical uses for ideas and theories (Kolb 1984). They have the ability to solve problems and make decisions based on finding solutions to questions or problems. People with converging learning styles prefer to deal with technical tasks and problems rather than with social and interpersonal issues.

Individuals with assimilating learning styles are best at understanding a wide range of information and putting it into concise, logical form (Kolb 1984). People with assimilating learning styles are less focused on people and more interested in ideas and abstract concepts. An individual with an accommodating learning style is best at doing things, carrying out plans and tasks, and getting involved in new experiences. They prefer to solve problems in a trial-and-error manner, relying on their own intuition or other people for information, rather than their own analytic ability. People with accommodating learning styles are inclined to learn from primarily "hands-on" experience. Accommodating learning style is important for effectiveness in action-oriented careers where one must adapt oneself to changing circumstances (Armstrong and Mahmud 2008). People with accommodating learning styles tend to pursue careers in organizations and businesses where they can bring to bear their competencies in acting skills: Leadership, Initiative, and

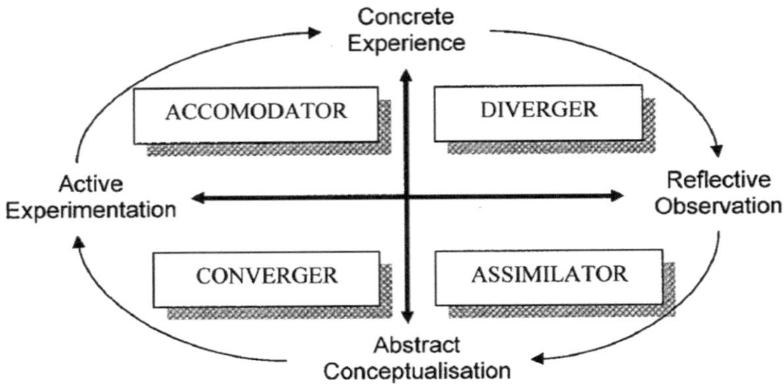

Fig. 2.3 Kolb's learning styles

Action (Kolb et al. 2001). Diverging, assimilating, converging, and accommodating learning styles are the four fundamental learning styles in experiential learning theory. Figure 2.3 describes Kolb's experiential learning style model.

Recent theoretical and empirical work shows that the original four learning styles can be expanded to nine distinct styles (Kolb and Kolb 2005). Learning styles appear as an individual's preference for a particular region of the learning space that enables us to discriminate the individual preference in more detail. Kolb (1984) identified four additional learning styles, which they identified as Northerner, Easterner, Southerner, and Westerner. Kolb and Kolb (2005) describe and develop these styles in more detail based on Hunt's analysis, which emphasizes the impact of the style's weakest learning mode on the learner's learning process.

The Northerner specializes in CE while balancing AE and RO, in which feeling serves as an integrative link between acting and reflecting dialectic modes. People with northern learning styles learn by involving themselves in new and challenging situations while being comfortable in the outer world of action and the inner world of reflection. The Easterner specializes in RO while balancing CE and AC, in which reflection and observation serve as an integrative link between feeling and thinking dialectic modes. People with eastern learning styles learn by deep reflection as well as the ability to be both feeling oriented and conceptual. The Southerner specializes in AC while balancing AE and RO, in which thinking serves as an integrative link between acting and reflecting dialectic modes. People with southern learning styles excel in inductively developing a particular concept or idea and deductively evaluating the validity and practicality of that concept or idea by testing them in the real world. The Westerner specializes in AE while balancing CE and AC, in which acting serves as an integrative link between feeling and thinking dialectic modes. People with western learning styles combine the ability of finding solutions to questions or problems based on their technical analysis as well as by relying on people and immediate concrete situations as sources of information. The balancing learning style (Mainemelis et al. 2002) refers to individuals who position

CONCRETE EXPERIENCE

ACTIVE EXPERIMENTATION

REFLECTIVE OBSERVATION

NW Feeling-Acting Accommodating	N Feeling Acting-Reflecting Northerner	NE Feeling-Reflecting Diverging
W Acting Feeling-Thinking Westerner	C Feeling Acting + Reflecting Thinking Balancing	E Reflecting Feeling-Thinking Easterner
SW Thinking-Acting Converging	S Thinking Acting-Reflecting Southerner	SE Thinking-Reflecting Assimilating

ABSTRACT CONCEPTUALIZATION

Fig. 2.4 Kolb's nine-region learning style type grid

themselves in the central region. People with balancing learning style integrate CE and AC and RO and AE. They are equally comfortable in moving across two dialectic modes in a balanced manner. Overall, Fig. 2.4 describes Kolb's Nine-Region Learning Style Type Grid.

2.3.2.1 Influence of Culture on Learning Style

Among learning theories, Kolb's experiential learning model has received special attention to the examination of cross-cultural activities (Hoppe 1990). In examining cross-cultural differences in learning styles and other learning programs, Kolb's learning model has been extensively applied in the field of cross-cultural and international studies (e.g., Katz 1988; Hoppe 1990; Yuen and Lee 1994; Jackson 1995; Auyeung and Sands 1996; Fridland 2002; Barmeyer 2004; Yamazaki and Kayes 2007, etc.). Learning styles are determined by the interplay between people and their environment (Kolb 1984). Kolb (2001) further explains that such interplay shapes learning styles at five levels (Kolb et al. 2001): psychological type, educational specialization, professional career, current job, and adaptive competencies. In addition to these five levels, Yamazaki and Kayes (2004) indicate that the culture of the country around people is the sixth level of interplay that shapes learning styles. The continuity and development of a certain learning situation fitted to each country relates to the way in which learning styles vary among cultures. Culture as an environmental characteristic has a great influence on learning styles. Certain learning styles within one country tend to developed in learning environments that are influenced by its particular culture. Many researchers have examined the interplay between the person and the environment at the cultural level. Hayes and Allinson (1988) suggest that the culture of a country may be one of the powerful socialization agents that have a great impact upon the development of individuals' learning styles. Hofstede (1997) contends that a country's culture shapes its peoples' preferred modes of learning through their socialization experiences. Pratt (1991) also argues that learning styles may be distinguishable across cultures according to his comparative study of self-conceptions between China and the United States. Furthermore, Yamazaki (2005) conducted a comprehensive analysis on which culture is related to which learning style or learning ability. He concentrated on a theoretical and empirical comparative analysis between Kolb's learning styles and six cultural typologies (high context vs. low context cultures, shame vs. guilt cultures, strong uncertainty avoidance vs. weak uncertainty avoidance cultures, M-type organizations vs. O-type organizations, interdependent-self vs. independent-self, and field-dependent vs. field-independent cultures) in three research areas: Anthropology, Cross-cultural management, and Cross-cultural psychology. Yamazaki (2005) proposes a close examination between the cultural component and the other five levels of factors (i.e. psychological type, educational specialization, professional career, current job, and adaptive competencies) to further explore how individual learning styles are shaped and developed in a particular culture.

Kaze (1988, cited in Yamazaki 2005) examined the learning styles of 821 Israeli undergraduates with different majors by using Kolb's original 9-item learning style inventory. She suggests that the interplay between the typical Israeli culture and learning style is evident in the orientation toward the AE mode. She also made the cross-cultural comparison of learning styles between Israel and the US revealed that the Israeli are far more orientated toward the active mode than the American. Smith and Kolb (1985) examined 1446 American samples and suggest that the overall American subjects are shifted more toward the AC and AE mode. Therefore, they concluded that the converging learning style may be a typical learning style of the American samples as a whole. Yuen and Lee (1994) investigated 1032 Singapore undergraduates with eight different majors and compared the learning styles of Singapore students with those of the American undergraduate students in Ruble's research (Yuen and Lee 1994). Their study reveals that the Singapore students are more abstract and reflective than the American students are. McMurray (1998) investigated the learning styles of 160 Japanese undergraduates with economics and science majors. He found that the learning preferences of Japanese subjects were stable during two consecutive semesters and were orientated toward the CE and RO modes, which is different from the American subjects that are orientated toward AC and AE modes (Kolb 1984; Smith and Kolb 1985). Barmeyer (2004) examined learning styles of 132 French students, 98 German students, and 123 Quebecois students in business administration and found that French and Quebecois students are significantly more concrete than German students; German students are significantly more abstract and active than French and Quebecois students. French students are significantly skewed toward the reflective observation learning mode. Focusing on the learning style distribution of these students, the dominant learning styles of French students and Quebecois students are both Assimilating and Diverging, while that of German students are Assimilating and Converging.

More recently, Yamazaki (2005) summarized five research studies about learning styles on American subjects: Smith and Kolb (1985), Kolb and Fry (1975), Geiger and Pinto (1991), and Boyatzis and Mainemelis (2000) and concluded that American subjects possess more abstract and active learning modes and tend to prefer the converging learning style. Pratt (1991) conducted a comparative study of self-conceptions between Chinese and Western societies and claimed that learning styles are distinguishable across these two cultures. Therefore, there is a variation of learning styles among different countries and societies. The relationship between the learning style and countries and societies suggest that a dominant learning style in one country will be indicative of learning characteristics in that country at a macro environmental level. Existing research has demonstrated cultural distinctions between Western countries and China on several important dimensions. As we have discussed in the section 'cultural differences western expatriates experienced in China', Chinese culture tends to be a high-context culture whereas Western countries tend to toward a low-context culture (Hall 1976). Chinese culture is more collective and the Western culture is more individualistic (Hofstede 1997).

2.3.2.2 Chinese Learning Style Versus Western Learning Style

Auyeung and Sands (1996) examined the relationship between the Individualistic-Collective cultural dimension and Kolb's (1984) learning style. They analyzed learning styles from a total of 303 Australian accounting students, whose country is representative of Individualism culture, and 172 accounting students from Hong Kong and 157 accounting students from Taiwan, whose country is representative of Collective culture. Their results illustrated that Individualistic culture is more linked with the Active learning mode, while Collective culture is more associated with the reflective learning mode. Students from Chinese cultures are significantly more reflective and abstract and less active and concrete than are the Australian students. Fridland (2002) examined learning style difference between Chinese teachers (N = 100) of English as a foreign language and American teachers (N = 105) of English as a second language and reported that Chinese learning styles were distributed more at the diverging learning style (42 % of the Chinese teachers is the diverging learning style, 28 % is the assimilating style, 18 % is the converging style, and 12 % is the accommodating style), while American learning styles stayed more at the accommodating learning style. With regard to the differences in learning abilities, Fridland (2002) contends that Chinese are oriented more toward the reflective observation and less toward the active experimentation, while Americans' learning orientations are quite opposite to Chinese ones.

Japanese culture derives from Chinese culture and Confucian ethics is rooted into both of them. It is reasonable to agree that Chinese and Japanese have similar learning preferences. Considering Japanese learning style also supports the present research's main hypothesis that Chinese learning preferences are oriented toward the concrete experience and the reflective observation learning modes. McMurray

(1998 cited by Yamazaki 2005) investigated the learning styles of 160 Japanese undergraduate students with economic and science majors and found that the learning preferences of Japanese participants were highly skewed toward the concrete experience and the reflective observation learning modes.

In light of American learning style, several studies in the field of management learning are harmonized with their results, which indicate that American managers are inclined toward the abstract conceptualization and the active experimentation learning modes (Boyatzis and Mainemelis 2000). Boyatzis and Mainemelis (2000) claim that American managers' learning styles are mostly associated with the Converging and the Assimilating learning styles. Yamazaki and Kayes (2007) examined cultural differences in learning styles between Japanese managers (N = 267) and American mangers (N = 126) within the same Japanese MNCs operated in the US. They concluded that Japanese managers are more concrete and reflective, whereas American managers are more abstract and active. They proposed that the dominant learning style of Japanese managers is the diverging learning style and that of American managers is the converging learning style.

Learning styles are affected by the interplay between people and their environment (Kolb 1984) and according to Kolb et al. (2001) such interplay shapes learning styles at five levels: psychological type, educational specialization, professional career, current job, and adaptive competencies (Kolb 1984; Kolb et al. 2001). Yamazaki and Kayes (2004) later extended Kolb's model to account for cultural influences on the process of learning and learning styles. Previous researchers have also argued that cultures have an influence on how people learn (e.g. Hayes and Allinson 1988). With regard to cultural differences in learning styles, Smith and Kolb (1985), Kolb and Fry (1975), Geiger and Pinto (1991), and Yamazaki and Kayes (2007) all concluded that American subjects possess more abstract and active learning modes and therefore tend to adopt a converging learning style. Research has also demonstrated cultural distinctions between Western countries and China with regard to preferred ways of grasping experience. For example, Hall (1976) claimed that Chinese culture tends to be a high-context culture whereas Western countries such as the USA tend to toward a low-context culture. The former requires its members to be sensitive to immediate environments through feelings, and long lasting interpersonal relationships are crucial for determining the meanings of messages conveyed in communication. Yamazaki (2005) reasoned that these high context cultures (e.g. China) are associated with the CE learning mode where members tend to grasp experience through feeling in proximate contexts. Conversely, in low context cultures, the immediate environment and non-verbal behaviours are less crucial in generating and interpreting meanings, whereas explicit verbal messages are more important in communications (Hall 1976). Yamazaki (2005) reasoned that these low context cultures (e.g. USA) are conceptually associated with the AC mode where abstract and symbolic presentation in a logical manner forms the central method of communicating with others.

Other comparative studies of Chinese and American societies also demonstrated that learning styles are distinguishable across these two cultures (Pratt 1991). In particular, Yamazaki (2005) re-analysed the data from a number of previous studies of learning styles across cultures to determine which country or culture is related to which learning style. With regard to transforming experience during the learning process (AC-RO), he concluded that Chinese culture is highly contrasted with American culture reporting that 'Chinese are oriented more toward reflective observation and less toward active experimentation, while Americans' learning orientations are quite the opposite to Chinese ones' (pp. 538).

Summarising the literature reviewed above, it can be concluded that Chinese are generally oriented more toward RO than AE and more toward CE than AC. Conversely, Westerners' learning orientations are generally more toward AE than RO and more toward AC than CE. This leads to one exploratory question regarding the influence of culture on learning styles.

Exploratory Question 1: To what extent do Western expatriate managers differ from host Chinese managers with regard to learning styles?

2.3.2.3 Influence of Environmental Change on Learning Style

The change of environmental demands also accrues the shift of learning style. The longer the exposure of the environmental demands, the greater the tendency for a person to specialize more in the learning style that is matched with such demands. This is similar as a socialization process in which individual learning style as a personal attribute grow to more closely match the environmental demands (Kolb 1984). Zhang (2001) contends that styles can change with situations, time, and demands and therefore, it is possible to provide avenues for change to match needs or effectiveness.

Gyen (1980, cited in Kolb, 1984) examined learning style transitions/adaptations in two professional careers: engineers and social workers. His study illustrated that a change of job demands directs the orientation of learning styles over their career paths. The engineers' dominant learning style was the converging orientation, but they developed concrete experience and reflective observation learning modes after they participated in managerial jobs. On the other hand, the diverging learning style was the typical learning style of social workers, but they developed abstract conceptualization and active experimentation learning modes after they held responsibilities for management and administration. The study of Gyen (1980) illustrated the influence of changing environmental demands upon learning styles: learning styles will change according to changes in the environment.

It could be inferred that expatriates' learning styles may change according to the learning orientation that is demanded by the host country. Environmental change may also cause expatriates' learning styles to be shifted towards the ones matched with the demands produced by new environments in the host country. The transition of learning styles is likely to occur in accordance with the amount of continuous time the expatriates have spent in the host country. Expatriates' learning styles may evolve from one place to another in keeping with the consistency of their environmental change direction (Yamazaki and Kayes 2004). In this study, the researcher will examine western expatriate managers' learning style transitions over time when they working in China.

2.3.3 *Learning Skills*

While learning styles involve four learning abilities and refer to generic adaptive competencies to the environment, learning skills reflect more situational, specific competencies required for effective performance on a variety of tasks (Kolb 1984). Because of the more explicit form of adaptive competencies in response to job demands in more confined environmental boundaries, learning skills may be easily discernible and detectable. The concrete experience (CE) mode encompasses three interpersonal skills: relationship building, leadership, and helping and understanding people. The reflective observation (RO) mode involves three perceptual skills: sense making, information gathering, and information analysis. The abstract conceptualization (AC) mode involves three analytical skills: theory integration, quantitative, and technology skills. Finally, the active experimentation (AE) mode includes three behavioural skills: goal setting, action, and initiative taking. Figure 2.5 presents the relationship between the four experiential learning modes and learning skills.

Yamazaki (2005) outlines a taxonomy of skills necessary for cross-cultural learning based on Kolb's experiential learning theory (1984). He identifies 73 learning skills that cluster into 10 thematic cross-cultural learning competencies. He also suggested that the difference between expatriates' cultural backgrounds may be reflected in the variation of expatriate adaptation strategies: which specific intercultural skills based on the ELT need to be developed for their intercultural adaptation.

2.3.3.1 The Relationship Between Learning Skills and Learning Styles

In terms of understanding the relationship between learning styles and learning skills, Curry's (1983) three layer onion model which is built upon her study of 21 cognitive and learning style instruments provides us with a useful heuristic (see Fig. 2.6). Curry (1983) proposes a heuristic model to organize the theory, resembling layers of an onion in which she places individual difference constructs. In the outer layer, Curry (1983) places what has been labelled as 'Instructional Preference' which refers to the individual's choice of environment in which to learn. She explains that the outer layer of the onion model is the most observable and interacts most directly with outward learning environments. This layer seems to be most related to the concept of the learning skills of experiential learning theory because

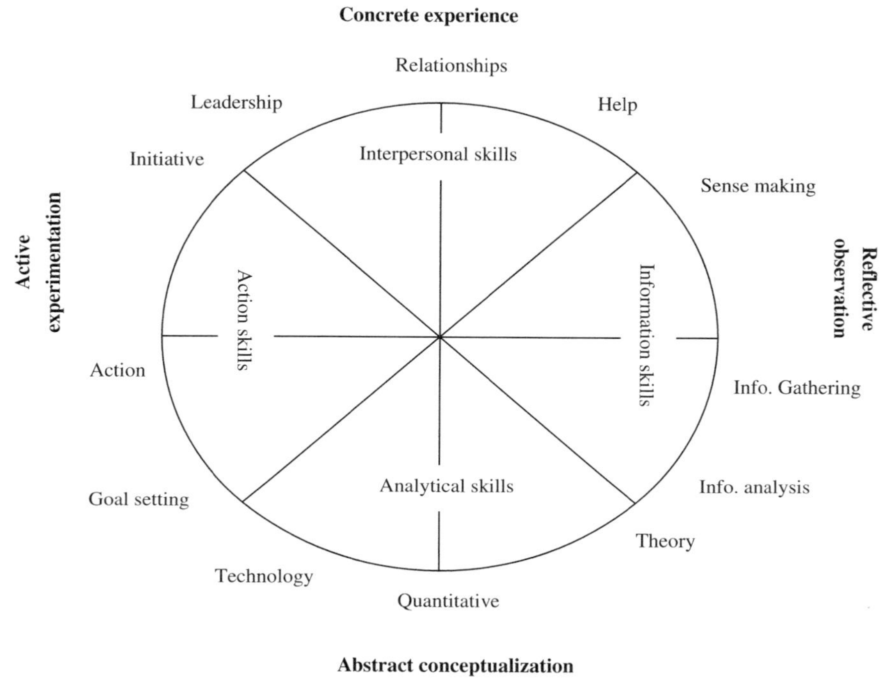

Fig. 2.5 Experiential learning modes and learning skills

interplay between individuals and their situational environments makes a direct difference to the outer layer. Such interplay produces specific skills that can be greatly observed on the external surface where people perform in order to meet particular demands derived from their environments.

The middle layer of the onion model, labelled as 'Information Processing Style', is regarded as an individual's approach to assimilating information. Due to its relative de-coupling from the environment, it is believed to be more stable than the outer layer, though it can still be modified to a degree by learning strategies. The second layer represents information processing dimensions as a set of processes that function at the intersection between fundamental personality levels/individual differences and environmentally provided learning format choices. Experiential learning styles would be managed within this middle layer (Curry 1983, p. 11). The innermost layer of the model is labelled as 'Cognitive Personality Style', defined as an individual's approach to adapting and assimilating information, which does not interact directly with the environment and is believed to be a relatively permanent personality dimension. The innermost layer of the onion model concerns cognitive personality dimensions (such as cognitive style) that are characterized as reflective of the underlying and relatively permanent personality (Curry 1983, p. 14).

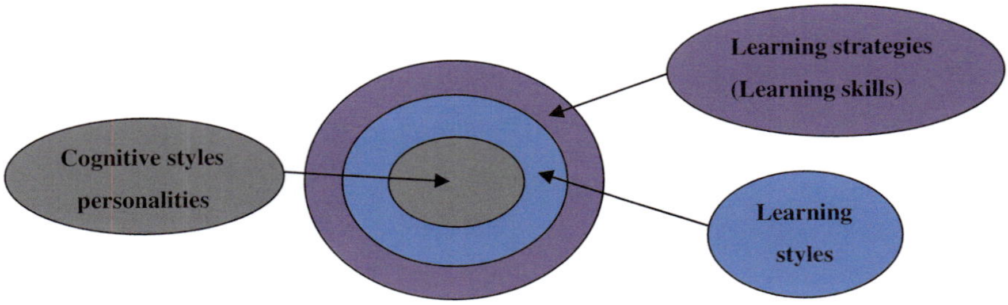

Fig. 2.6 Curry's three layer onion model

2.3.4 Adaptive Flexibility

Based on the work of Piaget et al. (1984) in experiential learning theory suggests that adaptive flexibility is related to the degree that one integrates the dual dialectics of the learning process—conceptualizing/experiencing and acting/reflecting. Unlike learning style, which refers to more generic adaptive competencies to the world, and learning skill, which refers to more specific and situational competencies, adaptive flexibility describes the relatively stable changes that occur as individuals learn to adapt to changing circumstances over time. Adaptive flexibility describes how an individual learns to manage competing demands and deal with environmental complexity.

Kolb (1984), Boyatzis and Kolb (1993) suggest several strategies to increase adaptive flexibility. First, increase our ability to 'read' the situations and to use various learning styles in response. This can be accomplished through practice. When confronted with a situation, try to envision different approaches, i.e. learning styles, and the possible advantages of each. Second, strengthen our association with others who have a facility with the styles we are 'weakest' in. Including these people in our development process and utilizing their skills in dealing with unclear situations. Moreover, use our strengths to develop our weak areas. For example, a person can use his/her Active Experimentation style to set a priority to develop Reflective Observation skills; use his/her Concrete Experience style to solicit input from people high in Abstract Conceptualization.

2.3.4.1 The Relationship Between Adaptive Flexibility and Self-development

Individual self-development is the dialectic process that is reaching toward a higher-level synthesis between social specialization and individual integrative fulfilment. It is attained through a dialectic process of adaptation to the world. Adaptive flexibility and the mobility it provides are the primary vehicles of individual self-development (Kolb 1984).

There have been many empirical studies about the relationship between adaptive flexibility and self-development. Kolb (1984) investigated the relationship between adaptive flexibility as measured by the Adaptive Style Inventory (ASI) and the level of ego development as measured by Loevinger's sentence completion instrument. In his study, there was a significant positive relationship between total adaptive flexibility and ego development level. Moreover, most of this co-variation in adaptive flexibility occurred in reflective observation and abstract conceptualization. Kolb (1984) also examined the relationship between adaptive flexibility as measured by the ASI and the level of self-direction as measured in a self-assessment workshop. The relationship between total adaptive flexibility and the person's degree of self-directedness was significantly positive in this study. In this research, the co-variation in adaptive flexibility was determined primarily in active experimentation. This suggests that those at higher levels of adaptive flexibility are more self-directed and display that directedness through wide variation of their active behaviour in different situations.

The development in experiential learning theory describes affective development in concrete experience as a process of increasing complexity in one's conception of personal relationships, resulting from integration of the four learning modes. As a result, experiential learning theory (1984) predicts that increasing adaptive flexibility, particularly in the realm of concrete experience, would be associated with increased richness in construing one's interpersonal world. A major component of internal structural complexity is the constructions which can be called upon to describe and manipulate one's thoughts and interactions with the interpersonal environment (Kolb 1984, p. 220). Kolb (1984) examined the relationship between adaptive flexibility as measured by the ASI and the level of cognitive complexity in relationships as measured by the total number of constructs a person used to describe his or her interpersonal world, which is also known as a cognitive mapping method. The result showed that total adaptive flexibility is positively correlated with individual cognitive complexity in relationships, especially in the area of concrete experience adaptive flexibility. Taken together, Kolb's results (1984, 1975) above suggest that overall adaptive flexibility and adaptive flexibility in the four adaptive modes are meaningful indicators of self-development. Total adaptive flexibility is significantly related to the level of ego development, to self-direction, and to the level of cognitive complexity in relationships.

Mainemelis et al. (2002) adds further construct validity for the hypothesis that individual adaptive flexibility is predictive of highly integrated and complex levels of adult development in their study through testing the relationship between balanced/specialized learning styles and adaptive flexibility. Their study also suggests that learning style that balances experiencing and conceptualizing shows greater adaptive flexibility in responding to experiencing and conceptualizing learning contexts. In this study, the researcher will examine the influence of international assignment experiences on the development of western expatriate managers' adaptive flexibility as well as the beneficial effects of adaptive flexibility.

2.4 Managerial Tacit Knowledge

As discussed in Sect. 2.2, learning is the process of creating knowledge (Kolb 1984). Formal learning alone is insufficient for the development of managers. What matters is the learning that takes place on the job (Wagner and Sternberg 1987). Practical intelligence is related more to managerial success than academic intelligence is, and therefore, the ability to learn informally on the job is a critical determinant of managerial success. The need to participate in informal forms of learning, such as expatriate learning, is linked to a form of knowledge mostly associated with experts and successful people: tacit knowledge. Oxford English Dictionary (1933) described tacit knowledge as the knowledge that usually is not openly expressed or stated. Tacit knowledge is believed to be one essential factor that distinguishes successful managers from others (Armstrong and Mahmud 2008). The ability to acquire tacit knowledge informally on the job is a hallmark of managerial success (Wagner and Sternberg 1987).

2.4.1 *Nature and Characteristics of Tacit Knowledge*

The term 'tacit knowledge' evolved from multi-disciplinary studies such as the philosophy of science by Polanyi (1966), ecological psychology, and organisational behaviour (Schon 1983). It has been utilised to describe knowledge that is obtained from daily experience which has an implicit and un-codified quality. The origin of tacit knowledge is often attributed to Michael Polanyi who described it in his famous quote, 'we can know more than we can tell' (1966: 4). In Polanyi's (1966) book, he classified two types of knowledge: tacit knowledge and explicit knowledge. Anderson (1983) distinguished between procedural knowledge and declarative knowledge by referring to the former as knowledge about how to do something, and to the latter as knowledge about something. Declarative knowledge is consciously formed, controlled, and articulable, while procedural knowledge is identified as unconscious with automatic learning, which guides actions and decisions without being in our field of consciousness (Anderson 1983). Based on Anderson's work, Sternberg and Horvath (1999) defined tacit knowledge as 'knowledge that is grounded in personal experience, and is procedural rather than declarative in structure'. Wagner further defined tacit knowledge as 'Work-related practical know-how that usually is not openly expressed or stated, and that usually is not directly taught' (1993, p. 19). Sternberg and Grigorenko (2001) argued that all tacit knowledge is a subset of procedural knowledge.

Nonaka (1994) holds that there are two types of tacit knowledge: technical tacit knowledge and cognitive tacit knowledge. Technical tacit knowledge is created through actions and needs to be experienced to be learned and therefore, does not need language as the intermediary. In the technical dimension, the term 'know-how' is commonly used to describe the skills and crafts acquired in relation to mastery of work (Nonaka 1994). Expertise is associated with this technical tacit knowledge: the ability to demonstrate flawless execution of tasks yet finding difficulty in articulating the principles behind it (Baumard 1999). On the other hand, mental models, perspectives, and beliefs make up the cognitive tacit knowledge and are deeply ingrained in the mind to the extent that they exist at the subconscious level and affect how individuals perceives the world. These pre-established cognitive patterns will act as a filter to incoming information, resulting in the formation of knowledge that is unique to an individual (Baumard 1999). Cognitive tacit knowledge can be transmitted through interaction or socialization involving the use of language. Beside these two types, Baumard (1999) suggests that implicit knowledge is another form of tacit knowledge. He claims that implicit knowledge is known and can be explicated, but rarely occurs because the knowledge often lies deep in our mind.

Choo (1998), along the same line as Nonaka, classifies tacit knowledge into cognitive and technical components. Moreover, he included the individual and collective perspectives in his stance on tacit knowledge. Individual tacit knowledge is knowledge that is acquired through experience, context-specific, and action oriented. Choo, however, contended that there is also another form of tacit knowledge which he called 'collective tacit knowledge', accrued by virtue of shared practices and tacit understandings in groups that work together (pp. 118–119). Collins (2001) contends that tacit knowledge is more diverse by indicating five different tacit knowledge types: concealed knowledge, mismatched knowledge, ostensive knowledge, unrecognised knowledge, and uncognized/uncognizable knowledge. Concealed knowledge refers to knowledge that is obscured either intentionally as a secret or unintentionally when the individual did not notice the existence of it. Mismatched knowledge refers to the group level, as it occurs when different groups focus on different problems, because the groups are not observing each other's work. Ostensive knowledge is knowledge that is inexpressible through verbal language. However, it can be articulated through pointing and showing. Unrecognisable knowledge is generated through imitating critical behaviour without noticing the importance. Uncognizable knowledge is typical in language, such as human's ability to speak in their native language without awareness of how they do it.

According to Sternberg and his colleagues (Sternberg 1997; Sternberg and Horvath 1999; Sternberg et al. 2000), the concept of tacit knowledge comprises three main features: procedural, practically useful, and without others' direct assistance. Firstly, tacit knowledge is procedural. Tacit knowledge is closely connected to action. It takes the form of 'knowing-how' as opposed to 'knowing-what'. This kind of 'knowing how' is called procedural knowledge: it is the knowledge that has a precise application (Winograd 1975, cited in Sternberg et al. 2000) or it can be stated that it is condition-action pairs of a general form (Nonaka 1994; Sternberg et al. 2000). Anderson (1983) suggests that tacit knowledge is a subset of life relevant procedures found in individual experience. This type of knowledge provides guidance for individual action and behaviour even though it is hard to transfer. Second, tacit knowledge is practically useful. Tacit knowledge is a 'vehicle' that enables people to achieve valued objectives. A highly valued objective requires a higher level of knowledge for it to be successfully achieved, hence this knowledge becomes very valuable (Sternberg 1997). Third, tacit knowledge is generated without direct assistance from others. Basically, tacit knowledge is attained personally by the individual when they are able to sort out the key lessons from their experiential learning and be able to identify crucial knowledge (Sternberg et al. 2000). Normally, individuals accumulate their tacit knowledge by means of personal experience of certain circumstances, or by trial and error, and it will gradually become their own unique knowledge that cannot be imitated by others. Individuals who learn knowledge formally do not accumulate levels of knowledge that are equivalent to the levels of knowledge accumulated by individuals who learn through experience or experiential learning. For the purpose of this research, the definition of tacit knowledge will be taken to be 'knowledge that is grounded in personal experience, and is procedural rather than declarative in structure' (Sternberg and Horvath 1999; Armstrong and Mahmud 2008).

2.4.2 Tacit Knowledge and Practical Intelligence

Practical intelligence is one of the concepts that have been researched as an alternative to traditional views of intelligence. Traditional views suggest that the variety of competencies required for achievement can be integrated as general intelligence. Recently, however, several researchers contend that general intelligence presents a limited perspective of an individual's ability to thrive in a successful life. For instance, Goleman (1995) and Mayer et al. (2000) propose emotional intelligence. Sternberg (1985, 1997) indicates a concept of creative and practical intelligence.

The concept of practical intelligence emerged from the tests traditionally used to measure intelligence. These measures were essentially related to academic rather than practical ability (Wagner and Sternberg 1986). Practical intelligence refers to the individual ability to identify optimal fit between themselves and needs of environment via adapting to the situation, or choosing a new environment in the quest of personally-valued goals (Sternberg et al. 2000). It is different from other kinds of intelligence. Practical intelligence involves not just adapting to environments, but also the shaping and selection of environments. The workplace is the best place to see practical intelligence in action. Most of the crucial rules of the workplace are unspoken. A few people excel at acquiring this type of knowledge.

Sternberg and colleagues (Sternberg 1985; Wagner and Sternberg 1986) extended the distinction in order to determine which attributes would differentiate academic and practical issues. Academic issues were identified by the following attributes: (1) formulated by others, (2) well-defined, (3) providing complete information, (4) characterised by having only one correct answer, (5) characterised by having one approach to the correct answer, (6) disembodied from ordinary experience, and (7) lacking or without intrinsic interest. Conversely, practical issues (occurring with work-related problems) were identified by the following attributes: (1) unformulated or required reformulation, (2) inadequate information required for solution, (3) linked to daily experience, (4) weakly defined, (5) characterised by a variety of correct answers, each with liabilities as well as assets, (6) of personal interest, and (7) characterised by a variety of approaches for choosing problem solutions. It is logical to assume that the differences between academic and practical environments will mean that someone who is proficient in finding solutions to problems in one environment may not be able to transfer these skills to problem solving in the other environment. In addition, Sternberg and Wagner (1993) note that academic intelligence is accessed via conventional tests. In contrast to this approach, practical intelligence tests look at the relevant norms involved in the process of knowledge acquisition: informal context, commonly tacit, learned through observation and modelling, and not necessarily recognised at school.

The present study focuses on the concept of practical intelligence as it underlies the acquisition and utilisation of tacit knowledge (Wagner and Sternberg 1986; Sternberg and Horvath 1999; Sternberg et al. 2000). Tacit knowledge is one of the tools that can be used to measure the ability to learn from experience. Tacit knowledge reveals what individuals learn in everyday life that cannot be formally taught or conveyed. Scores that measure levels of practical intelligence are predictive of an ability to learn to solve practical problems at work. Nevertheless, they are less predictive of an ability to solve academic problems at school (Wagner and Sternberg 1986).

2.4.3 The Structure of Managerial Tacit Knowledge

A substantial amount of research has been undertaken into the nature of tacit knowledge in a variety of professions, such as nursing, education, medicine, accounting, law, management and so on (Armstrong and Mahmud 2008). These studies provide a valuable insight into the working of tacit knowledge in these various professions. Sternberg's work into the nature of tacit knowledge in various professions is particularly noteworthy (e.g., Sternberg et al. 1993; Sternberg et al. 2000; Sternberg and Grigorenko 2001; Sternberg and Wagner 1993; Wagner and Sternberg 1986, 1987) because it provides a framework and a sound methodological basis from which tacit knowledge can be studied.

In the business and management domain, the difference between academic and practical approaches can be clearly demonstrated. Existent research has revealed that successful managers hardly ever refer to specific rules of thought in their approaches to problem solving (McCall and Kaplan 1985). They substituted this with an action-oriented approach at the initial problem solving stage by utilising analyses and action based on personal experience. Schon (1983) suggests that a significant amount of competent managerial behaviour appears as action that is almost spontaneous, based on intuition rather than rationality. It is 'ordinarily tacit, implicit in our patterns of action' (Schon 1983). In Wagner and Sternberg's (1987) study of the role of tacit knowledge in the domain of business management, it became clear that there were significant variations in the level and content of tacit knowledge within business managers. These variations are believed to exist because the managers go through their experiences differently, and at different points in time and context. Wagner (1987) described tacit knowledge as having particular importance for managerial success and broke it down into three categories based on the content of managerial tacit knowledge:

- managing self: tacit knowledge about managing self refers to knowledge about self-motivational and self-organizational aspects of managerial performance;
- managing others: tacit knowledge about managing others refers to knowledge about managing one's subordinates and how to interact with one's peers and superiors;
- managing tasks: tacit knowledge about managing tasks refers to knowledge about how to do specific tasks well.

Managing self, others, and tasks defines the scope of managerial tacit knowledge based on the content of a situation. Managerial tacit knowledge in managing self concerns self-motivation as well as the self-organisational aspects of managerial performance. For example, what is the best way to handle a problem caused by procrastination? In this case, individuals need time management skills in order to organise, prioritise, and complete their workloads. This will minimize the problems caused by procrastination. Self-management can be perceived as the ability to increase productivity on a daily basis. Effective managing-self individuals are able to set a priority of a numbers of tasks and as a result, their time is allocated accordingly. Sometimes this means that deadlines for low-priority tasks are missed or that extra responsibility is delegated to subordinates (Sternberg et al. 2000). Managerial tacit knowledge in managing others resides in people management skills: the skills to manage subordinates, co-workers, and superiors. An example of this type of tacit knowledge can be seen in the art of persuasion: the power to convince a doubtful superior to accept a good idea. Another example is knowledge about how to assign tasks that will utilise the capabilities of a subordinate whilst downplaying their weaknesses (Wagner and Sternberg 1986). Managing others is the key to remaining on the executive fast track, because an inability to manage others is the main reason for derailment. To act openly to the ideas and opinions in a particular task is also considered highly important in managing others (Sternberg et al. 2000). Managerial tacit knowledge in managing tasks concerns performing specific managerial tasks successfully. An example of managing tasks is knowing how to communicate to others the main point in a presentation (Wagner 1987).

Wagner (1987) extended the scope of managerial tacit knowledge to also include the context and the orientation of tacit knowledge. The context of managerial tacit knowledge refers to whether the knowledge concerns short-term or long-term accomplishments; while the orientation of managerial tacit knowledge refers to whether the knowledge concerns the ideal quality or practicality. A local context is regarding a concern with the short-term accomplishment of a given task, which is limited to the task at hand; a global context, on the other hand, is regarding a

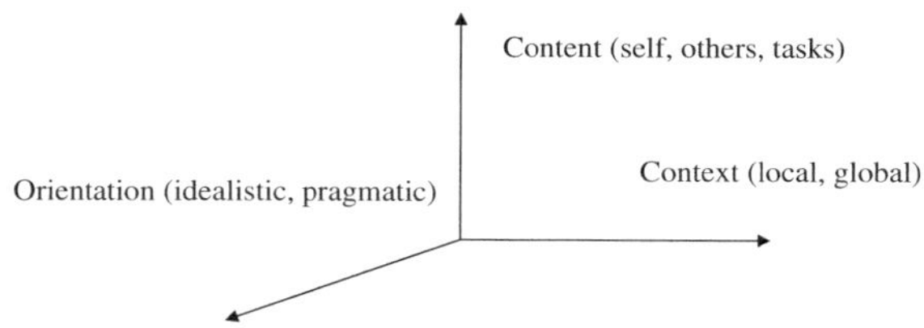

Fig. 2.7 Wagner's three-dimensional framework of managerial tacit knowledge

concern with long-term accomplishment, which focuses on how the present situation fits into the bigger picture. Managerial tacit knowledge with an idealistic orientation refers to a focus on the ideal quality of an idea; on the other hand, managerial tacit knowledge with a pragmatic orientation refers to a focus on how workable an idea is without regard to its ideal quality. This allows the managerial tacit knowledge framework to be constructed on a three-dimensional basis as illustrated in Fig. 2.7.

2.4.4 Acquisition of Managerial Tacit Knowledge

Wagner and Sternberg (1987) contend that there are three mental processes instrumental in the acquisition of managerial tacit knowledge: selective encoding, selective combination, and selective comparison. Selective encoding is the first process. It is used to filter information from the environment. In particular, selective encoding involves separating relevant information in one's experience from information that is irrelevant to one's purposes; selective combination is the second process. It is used to put together the information that is selectively encoded as relevant for one's purposes. This process involves understanding how relevant information interrelates and forms a pattern; the third process is selective comparison. It is used to relate previously known information to new information. This process involves drawing upon one's existing knowledge in order to incorporate new knowledge. Wagner and Sternberg (1987) propose that these three mental processes of acquisition of managerial tacit knowledge should be used interactively in order to maximize one's learning on the job. Managers need to make fairly continual use of all three processes in order to make sense of a new situation and to re-evaluate old situations.

Baumard (1999) holds that managerial tacit knowledge is generated in the intimacy of lived experience. The major source of tacit knowledge is experience and there exist differences between individuals in the level and content of tacit knowledge acquired (Wagner and Sternberg 1987). The differences in the level and content of managerial tacit knowledge can largely be attributed to the different ways in which people learn from experience. This is affected by both the context of the learning environment and the differences in the way individuals prefer to engage in the learning process. The present study will then investigate the source of differences in the levels of accumulated managerial tacit knowledge from these two perspectives: learning environment and individual learning preferences.

2.4.4.1 Learning Context in the Acquisition of Managerial Tacit Knowledge

Nonaka (1994) argues that the generation and accumulation of tacit knowledge is determined by the 'variety' of an individual's experience and the individual's commitment and involvement in the 'context' of the situation. Lots of existent research studies point out the differences in learning as the source of differences in the level and content of tacit knowledge. Experience alone, despite exhibiting prominence in relation to the acquisition of tacit knowledge, would not suffice. First of all, the learning process has been highlighted as one important reason why some people are less adept at acquiring knowledge from experience than others and an important part of a learning process is the learning environment. Compared with formal learning environments, Sternberg and Grigorenko (2001) suggest that informal or implicit learning environments, such as learning on an International Assignment, do not adequately support the knowledge acquisition process for some individuals. In informal learning environments, learners have to rely on their own capability to acquire knowledge from experience. Sternberg (1988) contends that formal learning environments support knowledge acquisition by facilitating the process of selective encoding, selective combination, and selective comparison, which are essential features of the learning process for many people. Informal learning environments, on the other hand, often fail to provide these features. Sternberg and Grigorenko (2001) contend that tacit knowledge is context-specific knowledge about what to do in a given situation or class of situations. Tacit knowledge is gained primarily from working on practical problems that are specific to their particular domain. The consequence of drawing on or using one's tacit knowledge is also likely to be context-dependent because tacit knowledge does not always transfer effectively from one professional context to another (Choo 1998). Tacit knowledge needs to be relevant to be useful.

Moreover, different learning contexts contain different supportive ways for individuals to acquire knowledge. To match the preferred ways of learning demanded by an external environment with that of the individual is likely to improve the acquisition of managerial tacit knowledge (Sternberg et al. 2000; Armstrong and Mahmud 2008). There is widespread evidence to suggest that when learners are involved in environments that are matched with their unique learning styles, they achieve significantly higher learning outcomes (Kolb and Kolb 2005; Armstrong and Mahmud 2008). Conversely, a mismatch between learning style and learning context is likely to impede the process of learning and knowledge acquisition. An individual with a strong orientation toward the converging learning style, for example, would tend to be less focused on people and more concerned with technology and problem solving. They would therefore be less suited to an interdependent context, such as Chinese business environment, because learning opportunities in an interdependent context would be congruent with the diverging learning style.

2.4.4.2 Individual Learning Preferences in the Acquisition of Managerial Tacit Knowledge

In addition to the context of the learning environment, individual differences in preferred ways of organizing and processing information and experience are likely to have a profound effect on the acquisition of tacit knowledge. A person's aptitude to learn is another differentiating factor (Wagner and Sternberg 1987). Sternberg et al. (2000) regard tacit knowledge as a subset of procedural knowledge depicted as paths 'Episodic Memory-Procedural Memory' and 'Personal Experience—Procedural Memory'. This knowledge, unsupported by direct instruction, may well lead to a performance advantage for the individual because 'it is likely that some individuals will fail to acquire it' (Sternberg et al. 2000: 117). Individuals differ in the way they perceive, conceptualise, organise, and process information and these differences depend on several attributes unique to the individual. People tend to learn in different ways from their experiences as a result of their pre-established learning structures, which influence the way they perceive, conceptualise, organise, and process information (Zhang 2001). In explaining the differences in the level and content of tacit knowledge across individuals who appear to show similar abilities and experiences, Kolb (1984) and Kolb and Kolb (2005) suggest that it is due to the different learning styles of individuals. Unique attributes of an individual, such as learning style, may account for these differences and this may contribute to the variations in tacit knowledge between different people.

Furthermore, all tacit knowledge is a subset of procedural knowledge and it is, therefore, unconsciously formed with automatic learning outside our field of consciousness. Being automatic and outside the field of consciousness, the acquisition of tacit knowledge depends largely on a person's preferred way of learning. People will usually learn, especially without formal instructions, in their preferred mode of learning, expressed in the notion of learning style. Learning style is believed to represent the interface between cognitive style and the external learning environment, and hence contextualizes individual differences in learning. The concept of style is used as a construct in psychology and is used for studying individual differences in learning and behaviour. Style is believed to constitute a preference to do things, irrespective of their ability to do it (Zhang 2001). Several researchers have explored the role of style in affecting learning outcomes (Zhang 2001). Zhang (2001) contend that styles can change with situations, time, and demands and therefore, it is possible to provide avenues for change to match needs or effectiveness. Therefore, we can propose that differences in learning styles will result in differences in learning outcomes, and consequently in the level of accumulated managerial tacit knowledge. In this study, the researcher will investigate the relationship between western expatriate managers' learning styles and their levels of accumulated managerial tacit knowledge as well as the effects of learning style transitions on the accumulation of managerial tacit knowledge.

2.4.5 Managerial Tacit Knowledge and Performance

Tacit knowledge tests have been found to predict performance and utilise a number of criteria in various domains. Tacit knowledge scores are found to be significantly associated with salary increases (Wagner and Sternberg 1985; Wagner 1987), performance ratings of bank managers (Wagner and Sternberg 1985). Research on tacit knowledge associated with auditors revealed that senior staff had higher levels of managerial tacit knowledge than the novice staff, and the managers with higher levels of tacit knowledge received higher performance evaluations (Tan and Libby 1997). In comparing the predictive validity of tacit knowledge tests and conventional ability tests, Wagner and Sternberg (1990) found that tacit knowledge scores of business executives explained 32 % of the variance in performance on managerial simulation beyond scores on traditional IQ test. In the case of military leaders, tacit knowledge scores accounted for 4–6 % of significance variance in leadership effectiveness beyond scores on tests of verbal intelligence. These studies provided evidence that tacit knowledge caters for variance in performance that is not accounted by traditional tests of abstract, academic intelligence. Similarly, a study conducted by Colonia-Willner (1998) found that bank managers' levels of managerial tacit knowledge significantly predicted an index of managerial skills, whereas psychometric and verbal reasoning did not. In a study conducted by Armstrong and Mahmud (2008), it was found that there is a significant association between tacit knowledge and the innovative performance of a firm.

An important criterion for evaluating the validity of managerial tacit knowledge is an ability to explain individual differences in work performance. In other words, individuals who learn successfully from personal experience will be more likely to be excellent at their work. Furthermore, managerial tacit knowledge as a component of practical intelligence should explain work performance. Sternberg and Wagner (1993) outline several major research findings on the role of managerial tacit knowledge in job performance research. Firstly, managerial tacit knowledge will increase when job experience increases provided that the person uses the experience to acquire and use tacit knowledge. Secondly, managerial tacit knowledge is not significantly correlated to IQ. Thirdly, tacit knowledge was the best single predictor in performance simulations. Sternberg and Wagner (1985) provide three samples of evidence regarding tacit knowledge and real world pursuits: (1) academic psychologists versus graduate and undergraduate students with a major in psychology; (2) business managers versus graduate and undergraduate students with a major in business; (3) local bank managers. They found that tacit knowledge moderately predicts job performance such as salary, performance appraisal ratings, and number of publications in the research.

Moreover, tacit knowledge is difficult to imitate, communicate, and transfer; therefore, it becomes the asset that underlies sustainable competitive advantage. This is because tacit knowledge can become the asset that enables an organisation to remain superior to its competitors. Tacit knowledge is a 'differential ability' that is diverse across organisations, exclusive, and imperfectly imitable (Conner 1994). Baumard (1999) argues that organisations normally neglect tacit knowledge. As a result of recognising that tacit knowledge is the source of competitive advantage, the organisation should retain the tacit knowledge of its own employees. Knowledge in the organisation should be readily transferred within the organisation in order for the organisation to be competitive. Knowledge that cannot be spread will remain the property of employees and this will restrict the benefit or value gained by the organisation. However, knowledge that is spread inter-organisation is not regarded as the source of competitive advantage. As a result, the underlying core competency of the firm, organizational tacit knowledge, is the key to competitive advantage and requires effective transmission within the organisation.

2.4.6 Measuring Managerial Tacit Knowledge

The three categories of managing self, others, and tasks has become the core feature in the development of the Tacit Knowledge Inventory for Managers (TKIM). Wagner and Sternberg (1986) combined two research methods: the critical-incident technique and the simulation approach, and developed the tacit knowledge inventory for managers. The critical-incident technique requires asking participants to describe several incidents they handled particularly well and several they handled particularly poorly. The simulation approach requires observing participants when they handle tasks that simulate job performance. Wagner and Sternberg's (1986) approach of developing TKIM differs from one based on the critical-incident technique in that they do not assume that participants can and will relate incidents that are in some way critical. Rather than that, Wagner and Sternberg (1986) asked participants to describe typical situations and possible responses to them, and then adopt a variety of item-discrimination procedures to identify important items statistically. One characteristic that Wagner and Sternberg (1986) shared with the simulation approach is that they resemble the tasks encountered on the job.

Wagner and Sternberg (1985) describe their approach in developing the tacit knowledge inventory for managers (TKIM) as follows. First, they interviewed experienced and highly successful managers by asking them to describe work-related situations/incidents, which they had experienced and had handled either particularly well or poorly (Wagner and Sternberg 1985), incidents that can influence a task's success or failure allowing identification of competencies required by a particular job. Critical incident technique and work on managerial job competency formed the basis for elicitation of these incidents and identification of work-related situations to use as scenarios (Wagner 1987).

Table 2.1 List of constructs in TKIM

Question	Construct	Definition	Items
Part A	Managing oneself	Knowledge about self-motivation and self-organizational aspects of performance in work related situation	30
Part B	Managing tasks	Knowledge of how to do specific work related tasks well	30
Part C	Managing others	Knowledge about managing supervision, subordinates or interactions with peers	31

These successful managers or managerial experts were also asked about their responses to the incidents. Wagner and Stemberg (1985) then carefully identified these incidents to determine which of the responses were based on knowledge that was tacit in nature and learned from personal experience, which could not be formally acquired (Sternberg and Grigorenko 2001). Key responses were then identified through item discrimination procedures. They then assembled these scenarios, with each scenario associated with alternative possible responses for dealing with that problem. The situations simulate specific incidents in the workplace, incidents that require use of tacit knowledge in order to solve (Sternberg and Grigorenko 2001). Acting as observable indicators of tacit knowledge, these incidents can help mitigate the problems of articulating tacit knowledge in the respondents. The methodology does not require that individuals articulate their decision processes; it only requires that they rate possible actions to scenarios. The measures developed using this method define and investigate tacit knowledge unique to the management domain. A list of sub-construct and details of the Tacit Knowledge Inventory for Managers (TKIM) are shown in Table 2.1.

2.5 Expatriate Learning

Expatriate learning refers to how expatriates learn and develop based on their international assignments. Since international assignments provide intensive environmental change and intercultural experiences, expatriate learning on international assignments becomes an important approach and organizational intervention for manager development, especially in the area of global management ability. This study draws on Kolb's (1984) experiential learning theory (ELT) and cross-cultural research to illustrate a process model of how expatriates learn and develop based on their international assignment experiences.

The research adopts the ELT framework as the basis of an expatriate learning model for three reasons. First, ELT is an adult learning theory which highlights the critical role experience plays in affecting learning and change. This fits quite well with the main characteristic of expatriate learning. Expatriates work and live in an environment that 'forces' them to experience various uncertainties and complexities. These intensive international experiences are expatriates' learning sources and wealth. Second, ELT emphasizes learning is the interaction between individuals and their environments. This is consistent with the context of expatriate learning. Expatriate learning is built on the interaction between the expatriate and the outside environment during his/her international assignment. Third, ELT emphasizes changes in learning. This fits well with the developmental objective of expatriate assignments. Expatriates learn from their international assignment experiences to develop global management ability and become qualified global managers. They recreate themselves in response to external changes to gain a new appreciation of the world. Therefore, this research proposes that experiential learning theory (ELT) is a robust and effective lens through which to view expatriate learning and development.

2.5.1 Expatriate Learning Process

Expatriate learning is a continuous process in a dynamic cycle, which consists of every learning experience during the international assignment. This study integrates four streams of research: international assignment and cross-cultural research, cognitive dissonance studies, knowledge acquisition and management research, and experiential learning theory (ELT), to propose that expatriate learning processes can be portrayed as four learning phases in a dynamic learning cycle based on ELT. These four learning phases are (1) exposure to diversity and dissonance experience (concrete experience), (2) self-reflection (reflective observation), (3) integration across diverse cultures and markets (abstract conceptualization), and (4) modification and self-development (active experimentation). The researcher will now elaborate further on these four phases.

2.5.1.1 Exposure to Diversity and Dissonance Experience

Exposure to diversity and dissonance experience is the first phase on the expatriate learning cycle. Expatriates work and live in cross-cultural environments that are full of novelties and diversities (Mendenhall and Oddou 1985; Shaffer et al. 2006). In order to successfully complete their international assignments, they need to actively learn different cultural and business norms as well as develop positive contacts with host nationals in the host country. They have to learn and execute local appropriate behaviours to reduce adaptive stress. As a result, expatriates will experience several cross-cultural and global-local dissonances. Some negative arousal and discomfort feelings will then arise during international assignments (Maertz Jr. et al. 2004).

Scher and Cooper (1989) describe that dissonance is aroused whenever behaviour is inconsistent with societal normative standards for competent or moral behaviour, creating aversive consequences. In their model, these societal standards are internalized or otherwise used as evaluative standards in judging one's own behaviour. Further, the dissonance is motivational in that it impels the individual to attempt to reduce and eliminate it (Maertz Jr. et al. 2004). During international assignments, expatriates undergo two primary kinds of dissonance: one is cultural dissonance due to cultural and national diversity and the other is strategic dissonance due to global integration and local responsiveness. Maertz Jr. et al. (2004) defined cultural dissonance as: anticipating or currently perceiving inconsistencies between one's behaviours, executed or condoned in order to conform to the host culture situation, and one's VABNs (values, attitudes, beliefs, and behavioural norms). On the other hand, strategic dissonance refers to: managing complex operations and integrating geographically distant and strategically diverse businesses while simultaneously responding to local conditions.

2.5.1.2 Self-reflection

After expatriates seek and grasp every concrete international experience, they move on to the second phase of the expatriate learning cycle: self-reflection or articulation of current mindsets. Our current mindsets shape our observations and interpretations of the world around us, which in turn affect whether or not our mindsets change or remain unaltered. Unless this iterative process allows for new learning, it is easy to get trapped in our old mental models (Nonaka 1998). A powerful way to reduce the likelihood of this entrapment is to articulate one's current mindsets.

Reflective observation is the process that helps people to describe the situation objectively and cultivate an articulation of own current mindsets (Kolb 1984). This phase of expatriate learning cycle occurs when expatriates think about experiences and reflect critically on their assumptions and beliefs. Doing so requires accepting the possibility that our view of the world is just one of many alternative interpretations of reality and allows us to consider different perspectives or views of the situation. When expatriates reflect on their international experiences by gathering and analyzing information, it becomes possible to change the mindsets that guide their future actions. Maertz Jr. et al. (2004) support this phase of expatriate learning from a cognitive perspective. They claimed that expatriates will use different kinds of cognitive dissonance reduction methods to maintain the self-concept against threat from cognitive dissonance experiences during international assignments. Expatriates who regularly adopt perceptual modification, which search for and reflect on the deeper attribution and empathetic understanding, as the method of cognitive dissonance reduction are supposed to be better at achieving integrative development.

2.5.1.3 Integration Across Diverse Cultures and Markets

After expatriates reflect on their international experiences by gathering and analyzing information, they move on to the third phase of the expatriate learning cycle: integration across diverse cultures and markets. The third stage emphasizes the importance of building general theories using scientific, as opposed to intuitive, approaches. This stage requires learners to distil their reflections into more general concepts that can guide their future actions, and emphasizes thinking, rather than feeling (Kolb 1984). Research in cognitive psychology has shown that experts conceptualize problems more efficiently and effectively because they have more organized knowledge structures with stronger linkages among domain-related concepts. In contrast, novices are less efficient because their knowledge representations tend to be based on salient surface elements. In addition, novices are often less effective in their knowledge acquisition because of their lack of pre-organized schemas that provides efficient classification of knowledge. Integration across diverse cultures and markets enable expatriates to translate their insights from a particular experience into more general concepts and interpretations that can be applied to future challenges and other cultural and business contexts. Integrating across diverse cultures and markets, expatriates will have more organized and elaborated knowledge structures that facilitate their information processing as well as identification of relevant principles.

Hocking et al. (2007) proposed that expatriates can develop integrative capacity to become qualified global managers through a cumulative understanding of both corporate practice and local environment contexts during international assignments. They claimed that integrative capacity can be cultivated through a two-phase process of cross-border knowledge adaptation. The first phase requires that expatriate managers funnel corporate knowledge gained from their former experience and modify it to fit their specific host-country environment; the second phase involves a reinterpretation of locally accessed knowledge and its subsequent expansion to fit a broader corporate contextual framework. In other words, the conversion of context-specific knowledge into context-generic knowledge enriches expatriates' integrative capacity, which can enable expatriates' next international assignment experience to be more readily understood and assimilated. Levy et al. (2007) argued that expatriates with higher cognitive complexity will be more accurate and effective in developing general ideas and conceptual interpretations of culture based on their international assignments.

2.5.1.4 Modification and Self-development

After expatriates integrate reflections into more general concepts and interpretations across diverse cultures and markets, they move on to the fourth phase of the expatriate learning cycle: test and modification of changed mindsets and further development of self. This stage both completes the cycle of expatriate learning and ensures that the cycle begins anew by assisting the creation of new experiences. During this phase of the expatriate learning cycle, expatriates may consciously plan for opportunities to verify their insights (for example, whether an authoritarian leadership style or a participative leadership style is more effective in this new environment) and then carry out their plan (give different directions to subordinates). Expatriates therefore gain experiences based on real interactions with others

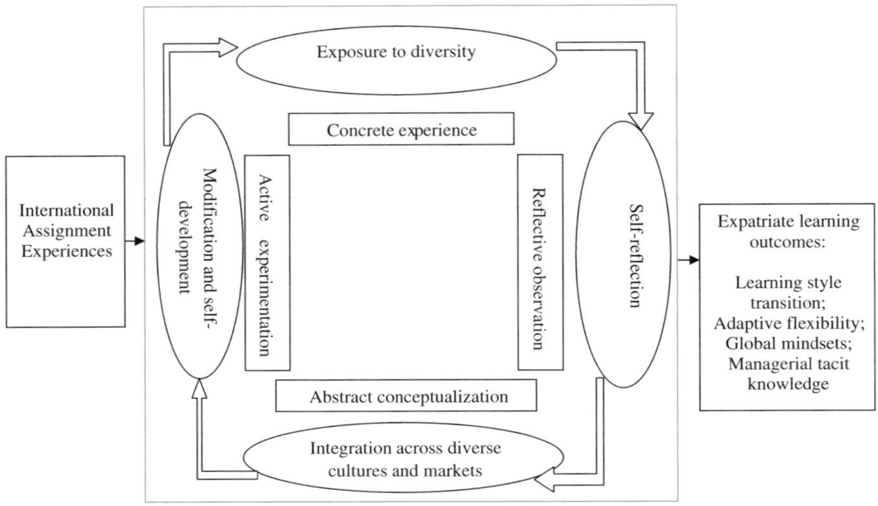

Fig. 2.8 Expatriate learning process model

and then gather self-correcting and self-development. Ng et al. (2009) claimed that active experimentation facilitates development of a wide range of flexible leadership behaviours for expatriate managers. Figure 2.8 illustrates the expatriate learning process model. In Fig. 2.8, expatriates learn in a dynamic cycle based on their international assignment experiences and then obtain several learning outcomes. Expatriate learning outcomes will be discussed respectively in Sect. 2.5.2.

2.5.2 Expatriate Learning Outcomes

Learning, defined as the process of creating knowledge based on the transformation of experience, is a multifaceted construct with implications for multiple learning outcomes. In thinking about implications of international assignment experiences on expatriate learning, this study identifies expatriate learning outcomes in four aspects: learning style transition, managerial tacit knowledge, adaptive flexibility, and global mindsets.

2.5.2.1 Learning Style Transition

(a) Concrete experience as primary learning mode for expatriate learning

Kolb (1984) proposed that individuals with an orientation toward concrete experience learning mode are open to new experiences, emphasize feeling rather than thinking, and function well in unstructured situations. Yamazaki and Kayes (2004) conducted a literature review on expatriate adaptation and suggested that concrete experience is a primary learning skill for successful expatriation because it is related to valuing another culture and to developing positive interactions with the host nationals. Yamazaki and Kayes (2007) conducted an exploratory study of how Japanese expatriates adapt to working in the United States over time. Their research suggested that Japanese managers become more concrete in their learning styles over time spent in the USA. They also suggested that expatriate adaptation requires learning in the concrete mode above the other three learning modes and expatriates as foreign nationals in the host country require more concrete learning than the host nationals. Ng et al. (2009) proposed that expatriates with a preference for concrete experience learning mode will actively seek cross-cultural experiences during their international assignments, which is important for leaders to translate their international assignment experiences into learning outcomes that are critical for global leadership development. Shaffer et al. (2006) suggested that expatriates with a learning goal orientation will actively seek intercultural experiences during their international assignments.

Western expatriates confront huge cultural and business differences in China. It is important for them to value Chinese culture and actively build up positive contacts with local Chinese people (colleagues inside their organization, colleagues outside their organization, friends in their daily life and so on) to gain successful expatriation. Expatriates with longer international assignment tenures have greater degrees of cross-cultural involvement, thus improving the amount and quality of concrete international experiences they could learn from. Li and Scullion (2010) argued that local knowledge in emerging markets, such as China, has a significant special nature: undiffused, highly tacit, and fast-changing, and that very nature determines the need for intensive socialized activities in these markets. Hocking et al. (2007) emphasize that local knowledge access is a significant contributor to expatriate learning. Therefore, this study proposes a second hypothesis that the concrete experience mode of western expatriate learning is positively related to the length of international assignment tenure in China.

Hypothesis 2a The longer western expatriate managers have engaged in their International assignments in China, the more they will show their learning preferences for concrete experience over abstract conceptualization.

(b) Cross-cultural impacts on learning styles

As discussed in section in 2.2.2, culture is an important environmental characteristic that has a great influence on learning styles and learning styles will change according to the environmental change. Moreover, the longer the time that individuals have spent in a certain environment that accentuates a particular learning style, the more they tend to specialize even more in this learning style (Kolb 1984; Hayes and Allinson 1988).

This study is based on the assumption that typical Chinese learning styles have a preference for reflective observation over active experimentation, which is different from Westerners (as discussed in 2.2.2). Auyeung and Sands (1996) postulated that students from Chinese cultures are significantly more reflective than are Western students based on their research of testing the relationship between individualism and collectivism, RO and AE learning modes. Western expatriates tend to differ in the degree of learning orientation that is accentuated in China. The environmental differences may cause Western expatriates' learning styles to be shifted towards the ones matched with the demands produced by Chinese business environments. The transition of learning styles will occur in accordance with the amount of continuous time the Western expatriates have spent in China. Therefore, this study proposes the second hypothesis that the reflective observation mode of Western expatriate learning is positively related to the length of international assignment tenure in China.

Hypothesis 2b The longer western expatriate managers have engaged in their International assignments in China, the more they will show their learning preferences for reflective observation over active experimentation.

Hypothesis 2c The longer western expatriate managers have engaged in their International assignments in China, the more balancing their learning styles will be.

2.5.2.2 Managerial Tacit Knowledge

Nonaka (1994) argues that the generation and accumulation of tacit knowledge is determined by the 'variety' of an individual's experiences and the individual's commitment and involvement in the 'context' of the situation (pp. 21–22). Sternberg et al. (2000) refer to tacit knowledge as experience based on the knowledge required for solving practical problems (pp. 104–105). Baumard (1999) argues that managerial tacit knowledge is generated in the intimacy of lived experience.

The growing emphasis on international assignment experiential approaches to manager development can be attributed to the importance accrued to international experience. Existent research demonstrates that firms led by CEOs with international experience perform better financially. In addition, global managers themselves find international assignments beneficial for their personal and professional development. In research conducted by Dickmann and Doherty (2008), most managers reported that living and working abroad was the most powerful experience in developing their career capital. The role of experience in the acquisition of tacit knowledge has been widely acknowledged within the literature on tacit knowledge. However, previous studies have revealed mixed results on the relationship between length of experience and tacit knowledge (Armstrong and Mahmud 2008; Colonia-Willner 1998; Wagner 1987; Wagner and Sternberg 1985,

1986). It has been argued that learning from experience results in a form of knowledge that is tacit in nature (Nonaka and Takeuchi 1995; Nonaka 1994). If learning from experience should lead to the accumulation of tacit knowledge, therefore, it follows that the longer the length of experience a person has, the more the opportunity they have to learn from it, resulting in a higher level of tacit knowledge acquired. This gives rise to the following hypotheses that there is a significant relationship between the lengths of western expatriate managers' international assignment experience and their levels of accumulated managerial tacit knowledge. In this study, the researcher investigates western expatriate managers' accumulation of managerial tacit knowledge in two aspects: managing self and managing others. The study proposes the hypotheses regarding how Western expatriate managers accumulate managerial tacit knowledge during their international assignments.

Hypothesis 3a The longer western expatriate managers have engaged in their International assignments in China, the greater their levels of accumulated managerial tacit knowledge in managing self.

Hypothesis 3b The longer western expatriate managers have engaged in their International assignments in China, the greater their levels of accumulated managerial tacit knowledge in managing others.

2.5.2.3 Adaptive Flexibility

As discussed in Sect. 2.3.4, adaptive flexibility describes how an individual learns to adapt to changing circumstances over time and it is an indicator of the level of individual development. Thus, if individuals show systematic variability in their response to different environmental demands, we can infer they own higher levels of adaptive flexibility and individual development. Yamazaki and Kayes (2007) proposed that expatriates use different modes of adaptation and develop greater adaptive flexibility to adapt to a new culture. International assignments are full of challenges and uncertainties, especially in a host country with significant diversities. The complex and ever-changing global environment requires international managers to be flexible. As a result, expatriates need, and are forced, to develop their adaptive flexibility to obtain successful expatriation. Therefore, this study proposes the hypothesis that expatriate's adaptive flexibility is positively related to the length of international assignment tenure.

Hypothesis 4 Duration of western expatriate managers' engagement in international assignments in China will positively influence their adjustment to the host culture via adaptive flexibility.

2.5.2.4 Global Mindsets

Expatriates on international assignments are expected to broaden the horizon and foster global mindsets through working and living in a distinct culture and system. A number of disciplines have attempted to define global mindset, resulting in lots of definitions, which is the mark of a relatively young research field. The vast majority of existent studies conceptualize global mindsets in relation to two salient aspects of the global environment: (1) cultural and national diversity and/or (2) strategic variety and complexity associated with globalization (Levy et al. 2007).

(a) The definition of global mindset

The core properties of global mindsets are described in three relatively distinct perspectives: attitudinal perspective, behavioural perspective, and cognitive perspective (Levy et al. 2007). Studies within the attitudinal perspective describe global mindsets using terms such as 'attitude', 'state of mind', and 'orientation'. Perlmutter's (1969) ground-breaking tripartite typology of managerial mindsets in MNCs serves as a conceptual anchor for the attitudinal perspective. Perlmutter and his colleagues (1969) offer a typology of MNCs that is explicitly based on the mindsets of senior executives. He originally distinguished among three primary attitudes or states of mind toward managing a multinational enterprise: ethnocentric, polycentric, and geocentric. Perlmutter's notion of geocentrism serves as an underlying construct for many of the contemporary conceptualizations of global mindsets that focus on the challenge of overcoming ingrained ethnocentrism and transcending nationally entrenched perceptions (Maznevski and Lane 2004). For example, Bouquet (2005) defines global mindsets as attention to global strategic issues, arguing that attention is the core element and a primary manifestation of global mindsets. He finds empirical support for the hypothesized relationships that the firm's decision environment influences attention structures, which, in turn, affect top management team (TMT) attention to global strategic issues. Studies within the behavioural perspective define global mindsets in behavioural or competency-related ability. Beechler and Javidan (2007) defined the critical components of global mindsets as intellectual capital, psychological capital, and social capital. Even though all of these three capitals are regarding ability and competence, Beechler and Javidan (2007) mentioned that cognitive attributes are also in the properties of global mindsets.

Studies within the cognitive perspective define the core properties of global mindsets in cognitive structure and cognitive complexity. Most of them conceptualize global mindsets both in the context of cultural and strategic diversity (Levy et al. 2007). Rhinesmith (1992) described global mindsets as entailing high levels of cognitive capabilities, especially scanning and information-processing capabilities, as well as the ability to balance competing realities and demands and to appreciate cultural diversity. Govindarajan and Gupta (2001) conceptualized global mindsets as a knowledge structure characterized by both high differentiation and high integration. Arora et al. (2004) described global mindsets as the tension between 'thinking globally' and 'acting locally'. Arora et al. (2004) found in their empirical study of 65 managers in the textile industry that managers are better in conceptualization (thinking globally) than in contextualization (acting locally). Levy et al. (2007) emphasized that cognitive properties are the most fundamental building blocks of global mindsets. Elaborating on their definition, global mindsets are characterized by three complementary aspects: an openness to and awareness of multiple spheres of meaning and action, complex representation and articulation of cultural and strategic dynamics, and mediation and integration of ideals and actions oriented both to the global and local.

Obviously, this diversity of terms and perspectives on global mindsets presents a considerable challenge for theoretical integration in this field. This study agrees with Levy et al.'s (2007) perspective that cognitive properties are the most fundamental components of global mindsets, and emphasizes that cognitive properties of global mindsets refer to individual higher level of cognitive structure and cognitive complexity.

(b) Expatriates cultivate global mindsets during international assignments

Expatriate assignments are the most common ways that MNCs adopt to develop managers' global mindsets (Govindarajan and Gupta 2001; Gupta and Govindarajan 2002; Levy et al. 2007). Govindarajan and Gupta (2001) proposed that expatriation can be used to cultivate managers' global mindsets. Arora et al. (2004) presented evidence to suggest that international assignment experience has a statistically significant impact on managers' global mindsets. Nummela et al. (2004) through their empirical findings offer tangential evidence on the hypothesis that top management team's (TMT) international work experience is positively related to global mindsets.

2.5.2.5 The Relationships Among Expatriate Learning Outcomes

(a) Learning style and managerial tacit knowledge

Tacit knowledge is believed to be a product of learning from experience that affects performance in real-world settings (Nonaka and Takeuchi 1995). It is recognised as an essential element of expertise and has been shown to be important for success of individuals (Nestor-Baker 1999) and for competitive advantage in organisations (Prahalad and Hamel 1990). Previous authors (e.g. Baumard 1999) attribute the origin of the construct to the science philosopher Polanyi who captured the meaning of tacit knowledge in his famous remark "we can know more than we can tell" (1966, p. 4). Managerial tacit knowledge is believed to be generated in the intimacy of lived personal experience (Baumard 1999; Sternberg and Horvath 1999), guides actions and decisions without being in our field of consciousness (Anderson 1983) and is believed to be an essential factor that distinguishes successful managers from others (Armstrong and Mahmud 2008; Argyris 1999; Wager and Sternberg 1987). Whilst studies have consistently demonstrated differences in level and content of tacit knowledge between expert and novice groups (Wagner et al. 1999; Patel et al.

1999; Tan and Libby 1997; Nestor-Baker 1999; Williams 1991), few have accounted for why or how these differences occur. We are informed, however, that differences can be attributed to the context of the learning environment and differences in the way individuals prefer to engage in the learning process (Sternberg et al. 2000).

Peoples national culture (Yamazaki 2005; Yamazaki and Kayes 2004), work environment (Choo 1998; Sternberg and Grigorenko 2001) and individual learning styles (Kolb and Kolb 2005; Armstrong and Mahmud 2008) have all been shown to influence the acquisition of tacit knowledge. When peoples learning styles are matched with their work environment it has been demonstrated that they achieve significantly more learning outcomes in an educational context (Dunn and Griggs 2003) and higher levels of managerial tacit knowledge in a management context (Armstrong and Mahmud 2008). Conversely, a mismatch between learning style and work context is likely to impede the process of learning and knowledge acquisition. Elaborating further on this person-culture congruence theory, individuals with a strong orientation toward the converging learning style would rather deal with technical tasks and problems than with social and interpersonal issues (Kolb 1984). This style is more suited to Yamazaki's (2005) definition of a low context culture (e.g. USA). This is opposite to the diverging learning style associated with a preference for working in groups to gather information, listening with an open mind, and receiving personalised feedback (Kolb 1984). This style is more suited to Yamazaki's (2005) definition of a high context culture (e.g. China). This leads to the following hypothesis:

Hypothesis 5a Western expatriate managers' learning styles will differentiate between levels of managerial tacit knowledge accumulated during their international assignments in China.

The category of managerial tacit knowledge labelled managing others (Wagner 1987) refers to knowledge about interacting and communicating effectively with one's subordinates, peers and superiors. Success in interpersonal interactions and communications of this nature is consistent with characteristics associated with the CE mode of grasping experience according to Kolb's (1984) experiential learning theory (ELT). ELT suggests that people with CE learning preferences: have broad cultural interests; are interested in people; rely heavily on people for information rather than on their own technical abilities to solve problems. They have also been described as being more adept at establishing personal relationships, communicating effectively, and helping others (Kolb et al. 2001). Yamazaki (2005) contends that in high context cultures (e.g. China) people rely on CE abilities to acquire tacit knowledge that serves to distinguish covert cues for effective communication and successful interpersonal relationships. This leads to the following hypothesis:

Hypothesis 5b Western expatriate managers with learning preferences for concrete experience over abstract conceptualisation accumulate higher levels of managerial tacit knowledge related to managing others during their international assignments in China.

The category of managerial tacit knowledge labelled managing self (Wagner 1987) refers to knowledge about self-motivational and self-organisational aspects of managerial performance. Acquisition of tacit knowledge associated with self depends on the ability to reflect on one's own behaviours in order to understand a wide range of information, see things from different perspectives, and develop an understanding of internal incompatibilities between specific behaviours and expected performance (Sternberg and Grigorenko 2001; Sternberg et al. 2000). Success in reflecting on one's own behaviours of this nature is consistent with characteristics associated with the RO mode of transforming experience according to Kolb's (1984) experiential learning theory. ELT suggests that people with RO learning preferences: learn by reflecting, making careful observations before making judgements; look inward for meaning and view things from different perspectives. In Yamazaki's (2005) definition of high context cultures (e.g. China), it has been suggested that people rely on Reflective Observation abilities for transforming experiences (Kolb and Kolb 2005; Yamazaki 2005; Fridland 2002). This leads to the following hypothesis:

Hypothesis 5c Western expatriate managers with learning preferences for reflective observation over active experimentation accumulate higher levels of managerial tacit knowledge related to managing self during their international assignments in China.

2. Learning style and adaptive flexibility

Kolb (1984) hypothesised that learning styles are determined by the interplay between people and their environments. As a consequence learning styles have been shown to differ from one culture to another (Yamazaki 2005), and expatriate managers' learning styles have been shown to change over a period of time in response to cultural demands (Yamazaki and Kayes 2007). Propensity for changes of this nature, however, will depend on the extent to which individuals are able to learn to adapt to changing circumstances over time-otherwise known as 'adaptive flexibility' (Boyatzis and Kolb 1993; Kolb 1984).

Flexibility of a person's learning style is related to the degree to which one integrates the dual dialectics of the learning process—conceptualizing/experiencing (AC-CE) and acting/reflecting (AE-OR) (Kolb 1984). Kolb (1984) hypothesised that individuals with balanced learning profiles on these dimensions will be more sophisticated (adaptively flexible) learners than those with specialised learning styles. Mainemelis et al. (2002) provided empirical evidence of this and concluded that 'the more balanced individuals are on the dual dialectics of learning, the more they will show adaptive flexibility' (p3). Whilst they confirmed this for both dimensions of the learning process, their results were stronger for the conceptualizing/experiencing dimension than the acting/reflecting dimension. Adaptive flexibility then, refers to the degree to which one changes learning style to manage competing demands and deal with environmental complexity. This leads to the following hypotheses:

Hypothesis 6a Western expatriate managers with learning preference for concrete experience over abstract conceptualization develop higher levels of adaptive flexibility during their International assignments in China.

Hypothesis 6b Western expatriate managers with learning preference for reflective observation over active experimentation develop higher levels of adaptive flexibility during their International assignments in China.

Hypothesis 6c Western expatriate managers with balanced learning styles demonstrate higher levels of adaptive flexibility during their International assignments in China.

2.5.3 Expatriate Learning and Expatriate Adjustment

Understanding how expatriates adapt to new cultural circumstances appears to be very important for MNCs and their expatriates. This study will contribute to such understanding in light of learning perspectives. The successful adaptation of expatriates hinges on how well they learn from experiences in foreign operations (Ratiu 1983; Ng et al. 2009). Expatriates' learning from experience produces acquisition of essential skills and knowledge demanded for effective managerial behaviour in numerous transitional situations. According to the qualitative study of Ratiu (1983), expatriates' way of learning from cross-cultural experiences results in discrimination between ordinary managers and outstanding managers who perform well in intercultural environments. Shaffer et al. (2003) contend that well-adjusted expatriates will have greater reserves of personal resources (like time, effort, and emotional investment) available to spend on the behaviours that facilitate their job performance and learning. Selmer (2006) contends that there is a positive relationship between an expatriate's learning ability and his/her extent of adjustment. If an individual cannot learn how to adjust in a novel cultural context, relevant pieces of information are likely to be unidentified or their importance overlooked. On the other hand, well-adjusted expatriates, attuned to the local socio-cultural environment, may be able to identify relevant knowledge and correctly assess its importance for various business decisions (Selmer 2006). Furuya et al. (2009) contend that learning on international assignments is influenced directly by three antecedent factors: organizational support from the firm, intercultural personality characteristics of the expatriate, and the self-adjustment encountered by the expatriate during the overseas experience. They propose that international assignments provide great opportunity for expatriate learning and the nature of the assignment given and how it is framed within the organization context will affect what is learned. The organization's attitude toward its international operations (e.g., the company maintains a positive attitude about being a global company; the company emphasizes the importance of global work experience) may broadly frame how managers view the expatriate assignment and what they are expected to take away from such assignments. Furuya et al. (2009) examined 305 repatriates, who had been recently repatriated to the home office after a 1 to 2 year first-time overseas assignment, and they found a positive relationship between expatriate self-adjustment and their global management competency learning. They further propose that expatriate learning would lead to heightened employee job motivation and to higher levels of general work performance.

Yamazaki's (2005) recent theoretical study about expatriate adaptation argues that there may be different learning strategies for effective adaptation in accordance with their home countries. Hocking et al. (2004)' empirical studies regarding the differentials between assignment purposes and assignment outcomes argues that expatriate learning is an inevitable emergent outcome of the expatriate knowledge transfer process, which indicates that expatriates place a greater emphasis than the company on the relevance of their self-learning as an assignment purpose. These studies have directed our attention to the importance of experiential learning for the successful adaptation and high performance of expatriates. While the great importance of this area of expatriate study is beginning to be understood, we do not know empirically much about what kinds of learning strategies expatriates tend to adopt for cross-cultural adaptation in intercultural business contexts. Though it is commonly held that expatriates engage in extensive learning while on assignment, there is scant empirical research on what they have learned or on what factors may affect their learning (Furuya et al. 2009).

From the preceding discussions, it can be postulated that western expatriate managers with learning preferences that matched with the host culture will adapt better in the host country; adaptive flexibility will be an important component of successful cross- cultural adjustment; and levels of managerial tacit knowledge accumulated in the host culture will positively influence their adjustment to international assignments in the host culture, which points to a mediation effect of managerial tacit knowledge. Thus, the present research hypothesises the following:

Hypothesis 7a Western expatriate managers with strong learning preferences for concrete experience will adjust better to their international assignment in China than those with a strong learning preference for abstract conceptualization.

Hypothesis 7b Western expatriate managers with strong learning preferences for reflective observation will adjust better to their international assignment in China than those with a strong learning preference for active experimentation.

Hypothesis 8 Western expatriate managers' who arrive with higher levels of adaptive flexibility will adjust better to their international assignment in China.

Hypothesis 9 Learning styles will positively influence expatriate managers' adjustment to the host culture via levels of accumulated managerial tacit knowledge.

2.6 Research Framework and Hypotheses

This section integrates all the hypotheses and the exploratory question derived from the above literature review. Whole seventeen research hypotheses concern five components as follows: the length of international assignment tenure in the host country, learning style, adaptive flexibility, managerial tacit knowledge, and expatriate adjustment in the host country. Theoretical connections among these five components are organized structurally in a model as depicted in Fig. 2.9. In this model, the arrow shows the influential direction between the components.

All seventeen research hypotheses are integrated below:

- Hypothesis 1: Duration of expatriate managers' international experiences in the host culture will positively influence their adjustment to the current international assignment.
- Hypothesis 2a: The longer western expatriate managers have engaged in their International assignments in China, the more they will show their learning preferences for concrete experience over abstract conceptualization.
- Hypothesis 2b: The longer western expatriate managers have engaged in their International assignments in China, the more they will show their learning preferences for reflective observation over active experimentation.
- Hypothesis 2c: The longer western expatriate managers have engaged in their International assignments in China, the more balancing their learning styles will be.
- Hypothesis 3a: The longer western expatriate managers have engaged in their International assignments in China, the greater their levels of accumulated managerial tacit knowledge in managing self.

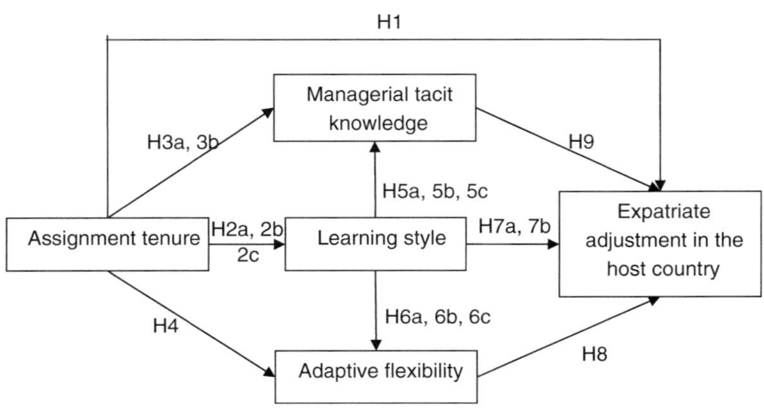

Fig. 2.9 Research framework

- Hypothesis 3b: The longer western expatriate managers have engaged in their International assignments in China, the greater their levels of accumulated managerial tacit knowledge in managing others.
- Hypothesis 4: Duration of western expatriate managers' engagement in international assignments in China will positively influence their adjustment to the host culture via adaptive flexibility.
- Hypothesis 5a: Western expatriate managers' learning styles will differentiate between levels of managerial tacit knowledge accumulated during their international assignments in China.
- Hypothesis 5b: Western expatriate managers with learning preference for reflective observation over active experimentation accumulate greater levels of managerial tacit knowledge related to managing self during their International assignments in China.
- Hypothesis 5c: Western expatriate managers with learning preference for concrete experience over abstract conceptualization accumulate greater levels of managerial tacit knowledge related to managing others during their International assignments in China.
- Hypothesis 6a: Western expatriate managers with learning preference for concrete experience over abstract conceptualization develop higher levels of adaptive flexibility during their International assignments in China.
- Hypothesis 6b: Western expatriate managers with learning preference for reflective observation over active experimentation develop higher levels of adaptive flexibility during their International assignments in China.
- Hypothesis 6c: Western expatriate managers with balanced learning styles demonstrate higher levels of adaptive flexibility during their International assignments in China.
- Hypothesis 7a: Western expatriate managers with strong learning preferences for concrete experience will adjust better to their international assignment in China than those with a strong learning preference for abstract conceptualization.
- Hypothesis 7b: Western expatriate managers with strong learning preferences for reflective observation will adjust better to their international assignment in China than those with a strong learning preference for active experimentation.
- Hypothesis 8: Western expatriate managers' who arrive with higher levels of adaptive flexibility will adjust better to their international assignment in China.
- Hypothesis 9: Learning styles will positively influence expatriate managers' adjustment to the host culture via levels of accumulated managerial tacit knowledge.

One exploratory question is described as follows:

Exploratory Question 1: To what extent do Western expatriate managers differ from host Chinese managers with regard to learning styles and levels of accumulated managerial tacit knowledge?

Table 2.2 Depiction of these parallelisms between research questions and hypotheses

Hypotheses	Research question	Derived section
H1	Research question (1)	2.2.3
H2a, H2b, H2c	Research question (2)	2.5.2.1
H3a, H3b	Research question (2)	2.5.2.2
H4	Research question (2)	2.5.2.3
H5a, H5b, H5c	Research question (3)	2.5.2.5
H6a, H6b, H6c	Research question (3)	2.5.2.5
H7a, H7b	Research question (1)	2.5.3
H8	Research question (1)	2.5.3
H9	Research question (1)	2.5.3

These hypotheses and the exploratory question are designed to answer the three research questions discussed in Chap. 1: (1) How do Western expatriate managers adapt when working in China? (2) What do Western expatriate managers learn from their international assignments in China? (3) How do Western expatriate managers learn from their international assignments in China? Table 2.2 depicts the parallelisms between research questions and hypotheses.

References

Anderson, J. (1983). *The architecture of cognition*. Cambridge, MA: Harvard University Presures.

Anderson, J. A. (1988). Cognitive styles and multicultural populations. *Journal of Teacher Education, 39*(1), 2–9.

Argyris, C. (1999). Tacit knowledge and management. In R. J. Sternberg & J. A. Horvath (Eds.), *Tacit knowledge in professional practice: Researcher and practitioner perspectives*. L. Erlbaum: Mahwah, NJ.

Armstrong, S. J., & Mahmud, A. (2008). Experiential learning and the acquisition of managerial tacit knowledge. *Academy of Management Learning and Education, 7*(2), 189–208.

Arora, A., Jaju, A., Kefalas, A. G., & Perenich, T. (2004). An exploratory analysis of global managerial mindsets: a case of US textile and apparel industry. *Journal of International Management, 10*(3), 393–411.

Auyeung, P., & Sands, J. (1996). A cross-cultural study of the learning style of accounting students. *Accounting and Finance, 36*, 261–274.

Bandura, A. (1977). *Social Learning Theory*. Englewood Cliffs, NJ: Prentice Hall.

Barmeyer, C. I. (2004). Learning styles and their impact on cross-cultural training: An international comparison in France, Germany and Quebec. *International Journal of Intercultural Relations, 28*, 577–594.

Baumard, Paul. (1999). *Tacit knowledge in the organization*. London: Sage.

Beechler, S., & Javidan, M. (2007). Leading with a global mindset. In M. Javidan, R. Steers, & M. Hitt (Eds.), *The global mindset (advances in international management)* (pp. 131–170). JAI Presures: Oxford, UK.

Bhaskar-Shrinivas, P., Harrison, D. A., Shaffer, M. A., & Luk, D. M. (2005). Input-based and time-based models of international adjustment: Meta-analytic evidence and theoretical extensions. *Academy of Management Journal, 482*, 25–281.

Black, J. S. (1988). Work role transitions: A study of American expatriate managers in Japan. *Journal of International Business Studies, 19*, 277–294.

Black, J. S., & Gregersen, H. B. (1991). Antecedentstocross-culturaladjustmentfor expatriates in Pacific Rim assignments. *Human Relations, 44*(5), 497–515.

Black, J. S., & Mendenhall, M. (1991). The U-curve adjustment hypothesis revisited: A review and theoretical framework. *Journal of International Business Studies, 22*, 225–247.

Black, J. S., & Stephens, G. K. (1989). The influence of the spouse on American expatriate adjustment in overseas assignments. *Journal of Management, 15*, 529–544.

Black, J. S., Mendenhall, M., & Oddou, G. (1991). Toward a comprehensive model of international adjustment: An integration of multiple theoretical perspectives. *Academy of Management Review, 16*, 291–317.

Bouquet, C. A. (2005). *Building global mindsets: An attention-based perspective*. New York: Palgrave Macmillan.

Boyatzis, R. E., & Kolb, D. A. (1993). *Adaptive Style Inventory: Self Scored Inventory and Interpretation Booklet.* Boston, MA: TRG Hay/McBer, Training Resources Group.

Boyatzis, R. E., & Mainemelis, C. (2000). Learning styles and adaptive flexibility: Testing experiential learning theory. *Management Learning*.

Brookfield GMAC Global Relocations Services. (2005). *Global relocation trends: 2005 survey report*. New Jersey: GMAC.

Caligiuri, P. M. (1997). Assessing expatriate success: Beyond just "being there." In Z. Aycan (Ed.), *New approaches to employee management* (Vol. 4—*Expatriate management: Theory and research*, pp. 117–140). Stamford, CT: JAI Presures.

Chen, M.-J. (2001). *Inside Chinese business: A GUIDE FOR MANAGERS WORLDWIDE*. Boston, MA: Harvard Business School Presures.

Choo, C. (1998). *The knowing organization: How organizations use information to construct meaning, create knowledge, and make decisions*. New York: Oxford University Presures.

Church, A. T. (1982). Sojourner adjustment. *Psychological Bulletin, 9*, 540–572.

Collins, H. M. (Feb. 2001). Tacit knowledge. *Trust and the Q of Sapphire, Social Studies of Science*, *31*(1), 71–85.

Collings, D. G., Scullion, H., & Morley, M. J. (2007). Changing patterns of global staffing in the multinational enterprise: Challenges to the conventional expatriate assignment and emerging alternatives. *Journal of World Business, 42*, 198–213.

Colonia-Willner, R. (1998). Practical intelligence at work: Relationship between aging and cognitive efficiency among managers in bank environment. *Psychology and Aging, 13*(1), 45–57.

Conner, K. R. (1994). *The resource-based challenge to the industry-structure perspective*. Annual Meeting of the Academy of Management, Dallas: Best Paper Proceedings.

Curry, L. (1983). An organization of learning style theory and constructs. In L. Curry (Ed.), *Learning style in continuing medical education*. Ottawa: Canadian Medical Association.

DeCiantis, T., & Kirton, J. (1996). An examination of Kolb's learning style. *The Modern American College*. San Fransisco: Jossey Bass.

De Vita, G. (2001). Learning styles, culture and inclusive instruction in the multicultural classroom: a business and management perspective. *Innovations in Education and Teaching International, 38*(2), 165–174.

Dickmann, M., & Doherty, N. (2008). Exploring the career capital impact of international assignments within distinct organizational contexts. *British Journal of Management., 19*, 145–161.

Dunn, R., & Griggs, S. A. (2003). *Synthesis of the Dunn and Dunn Learning-Style Model Research: Who, what, when, where, and so what?*. New York: St John's University Presures.

Edstrom, A., & Galbraith, J. R. (1977). Alternative Policies for International Transfers of Managers. *Management International Review, 17*(2), 11–22.

Fridland, G. H. (2002). *Adult learning styles and cultural background: A comparison of the learning style preferences of American teachers of English as a second language and Chinese teachers of English as a foreign language*. Unpublished doctoral dissertation, University of Memphis, TN.

Furuya, N., Stevens, M. J., Bird, A., Oddou, G., & Mendenhall, M. E. (2009). Managing the learning and transfer of global management competence: Antecedents and outcomes of Japanese repatriation effectiveness. *Journal of International Business Studies*, *40*(2), 200–215.

Geiger, M. A., & Pinto, J. K. (1991). Changes to learning style preference during a three-year longitudinal study. *Psychological Reports*, *69*, 755–762.

Govindarajan, V., & Gupta, A. K. (2001). *The quest for global dominance: Transforming global presence into global competitive advantage*. San Francisco: Jossey-Bass.

Grainger, R. J., & Nankervis, A. R. (2001). Expatriation practices in the global business environment. *Research and Practice in Human Resource Management, 9*(2), 77–92.

Gregersen, H. B., & Black, J. S. (1992). Antecedents to commitment to a parent company and a foreign operation. *Academy of Management Journal, 35*, 65–90.

Gupta, A. K., & Govindarajan, V. (2002). Cultivating a global mindset. *Academy of Management Executive, 16*(1), 116–126.

Guzzo, R. A., Noonan, K. A., & Elron, E. (1994). Expatriate managers and psychological contract. *Journal of Applied Psychology*, *79*, 617–626.

Hall, E. T. (1976). *Beyond culture*. Garden City, NY: Anchor Presures/Doubleday.

Hall, E. T. (1977). *Beyond culture*. Garden City, NY: Anchor Presures/Doubleday.

Harzing, A. W. (2001). Of bears bees and spiders: The role of expatriates in controlling foreign subsidiaries. *Journal of World Business, 26*, 366–379.

Hayes, J., & Allinson, C. W. (1988). Cultural differences in the learning styles of managers. *Management International Review, 28*, 75–80.

Hechanova, R., Beehr, T. A., & Christiansen, N. D. (2003). Antecedents and consequences of employees' adjustment to overseas assignment: A meta analytic review. *Applied Psychology: An International Review*, *52*, 213–236.

Hocking, J. B., Brown, M., & Harzing, A.-W. (2004). A knowledge transfer perspective of strategic assignment purposes and their path-dependent outcomes. *International Journal of Human Resource Management*, *15*, 565–586.

Hocking, J. B., Brown, M., & Harzing, A.-W. (2007). Balancing global and local strategic contexts: Expatriate knowledge transfer, applications, and learning with a transnational organization. *Human Resource Management*, *46*(4), 513–533.

Hofstede, G. H. (1997). *Culture and organization: Software of mind*. New York: McGraw Hill.

Hofstede, G. H. (2010). *Culture and Organization: Software of Mind*. New York: McGraw Hill.

Hoppe, M. H. (1990). *A comparative study of country elites: International differences in work related values and learning and their implications for management training and development*. Unpublished doctoral dissertation, University of North Carolina at Chapel Hill, NC.

Hung, C. L. (1994). Business Mindsets and Styles of the Chinese in the People's Republic of China, Hong Kong, and Taiwan. *The International Executive*, *36*(2), 203–221.

Jackson, T. (1995). European management learning: Across-cultural interpretation of Kolb's learning cycle. *Journal of Management Development, 14*(6), 42–50.

Katz, N. (1988). Individual learning style: Israeli norms and cross-cultural equivalence of Kolb's Learning Style Inventory. *Journal of Cross-Cultural Psychology, 19*(3), 361–379.

Klein, T., & Lee, Y. (2006). Developing global leadership capabilities and global mindset: A review. *Handbook of Research in Human Resource Management*, 197–222.

Kolb, D. (1981). Learning styles and disciplinery differences. In A.W. Chickering & Associates. *The Modern American College*. San Fransisco: Jossey Bass.

Kolb, D. A. (1984). *Experiential learning: Experience as the source of learning and development*. Englewood Cliffs, NJ: Prentice-Hall.

Kolb, D. (1986). Learning styles and disciplinery differences. In A. W. Chickering, & Associates. *The Modern American College*. San Fransisco: Jossey Bass.

Kolb, D. A. (1999). *Learning Style Inventory, version 3: Technical specifications*. TRG Hay/McBer, Training Resources Group. 116 Huntington Avenue, Boston, MA02116, trg_mcber@haygroup.com.

Kolb, D. A., Boyatzis, R., & Mainemelis, C. (2001). Experiential learning theory: Previous research and new directions. In R. Sternberg & L. Zhang (Eds.), *Perspectives on cognitive learning, and thinking styles* (pp. 228–247). Mahwah, NJ: Erlbaum.

Kolb, D. A., & Fry, R. (1975). Toward an applied theory of experiential learning. In C. Cooper (Ed.), *Theories of group processes* (pp. 33–57). New York: Wiley.

Kolb, A. Y., & Kolb, D. A. (2005). Learning styles and learning spaces: Enhancing experiential learning in higher education. *Academy of Management Learning and Education*, *4*(2), 193–212.

Kolb, A. Y., & Kolb, D. A. (2009). The learning way: Meta-cognitive aspects of experiential learning. *Simulation & Gaming, 40*(3), 297–327.

Levy, O., Beechler, S., Taylor, S., & Boyacigiller, N. (2007). What we talk about when we talk about global mindset: Managerial cognition in Multinational Corporations. *Journal of International Business Studies, 38*(2), 231–258.

Li, S., & Scullion, H. (2010). Developing the local competence of expatriate managers for emerging markets: A knowledge-based approach. *Journal of World Business*, *45*, 190–196.

Liu, C. H., & Lee, H. W. (2008). A proposed model of expatriates in multinational corporations. *Cross-Cultural Management, 15*(2), 176–193.

Maertz, C. P. Jr., Hassan, A., & Magnusson, P. (2004). When learning is not enough: A process model of expatriate adjustment as cultural cognitive dissonance reduction. *Organizational Behaviour and Human Decision Processes*, *108*, 66–78.

Mainemelis, C., Boyatzis, R. E., & Kolb, D. A. (2002). Learning styles and adaptive flexibility: Testing experiential learning theory. *Management Learning, 33*(1), 5–33.

Markus, H. R., & Kitayama, S. (1991). Culture and the self: Implications for cognition, emotion, and motivation. *Psychological Review, 98*, 224–253.

Mayer, J. D., Salovey, P., & Caruso, D. (2000). Competing models of emotional intelligence. In R. J. Sternberg (Ed.), *Handbook of intelligence* (pp. 396–420). NY: Cambridge University Presures.

Maznevski, M. L., & Lane, H. W. (2004). Shaping the global mindset: Designing educational experiences for effective global thinking and action. In N. Boyacigiller, R. M. Goodman, & M. Phillips (Eds.), *Crossing cultures: Insights from master teachers* (pp. 171–184). London: Routledge.

McCall, M. W., & Kaplan, R. E. (1985). *Whatever it takes: Decision makers at work.* Englewood Cliffs, NJ: Prentice-Hall.

McGinley, J. (2008). Expatriate adjustment within a social context: Examination of a sample in Russia. *Journal of Social, Evolutionary, and Cultural Psychology, 2*(2), 56–68.

McMurray, D. (1998). Learning styles and organizational behavior in Japanese EFL classrooms. *Journal of Fukui Prefecture University, 13*, 29–43.

Mendenhall, M., & Oddou, G. (1985). The dimensions of expatriate acculturation: A review. *Academy of Management Review, 10*, 39–48.

Mol, S. T., Born, M. P., Willemsen, M. E., & Van der Molen, H. T. (2005). Predicting expatriate job performance for selection purposes: A quantitative review. *Journalk of Cross-Cultural Psychology*, *35*(5), 590–620.

National foreign trade council. (2006). *National foreign trade council: 2006 survey report.* New Jersey: National foreign trade council.

Nestor-Baker, N. (1999). *Tacit knowledge in the superintendency: An exploratory analysis.* (Doctoral dissertation, The Ohio State University). University Microfilms International Dissertation Services, AAT 9941397.

Ng, K. Y., Dyne, L. V., & Ang, S. (2009). From experience to experiential learning: Cultural intelligence as a learning capability for global leader development. *Academy of Management Learning and Education*, *8*(4), 511–526.

Nonaka, I. (1994). The concept of 'ba': Building a foundation for knowledge creation. *California Management Review*, *40*(3), 40–54.

Nonaka, I. (1998). The concept of 'ba': Building a foundation for knowledge creation. *California Management Review, 40*(3), 40–54.

Nonaka, I., & Takeuchi, H. (1995). *The knowledge-creating company*. Oxford: Oxford University Presures.

Nummela, N., Saarenketo, S., & Puumalainen, K. (2004). A global mindset: a prerequisite for successful internationalization. *Canadian Journal of Administrative Sciences, 21*(1), 51–64.

Okpara, O., & Kabongo, D. (2010). Cross-cultural training and expatriate adjustment: A study of western expatriates in Nigeria. *Journal of World Business*, *46*(2011), 22–30.

Ones, D. S., & Viswesvaran, C. (1997). Personality determinants in the prediction of aspects of expatriate job success. In D. M. Saunder & Z. Aycan (Eds.), *New approaches to employee management* (Vol. 4, pp. 63–92). Greenwich, CT: JAI Presures.

Patel, V., Arocha, J., & Kaufman, D. (1999). Expertise and tacit knowledge in medicine. In R. Sternberg & J. Horvath (Eds.), *Tacit knowledge in professional practice: Researcher and practitioner perspectives*. Mahwah, NJ: Lawrence Erlbaum.

Perlmutter, H. (1969). The tortuous evolution of the multinational corporation. *Columbia Journal of World Business, 4*(1), 9–18.

Pires, G., & Stanton, J. (2005). Ethnicity and acculturation in a culturally diverse country: Identifying ethnic market segments. *Journal of Multilingual and Multi-Cultural development, 21*(1), 42–57.

Polanyi, M. (1966). *The tacit dimension*. London: Routledge & Kegan Paul Ltd.

Prahalad, C., & Hamel, G. (1990). The core competence of the corporation. *Harvard Business Review, 68*, 79–91.

Pratt, D. D. (1991). Conceptions of self within China and the United States. *International Journal of Intercultural Relations, 15*, 285–310.

Ratiu, I. (1983). Thinking internationally: A comparison of how international executives learn. *International Studies of Management and Organization, 13*(1–2), 139–150.

Reynolds, M. (1997). Learning styles: A critique. *Management Learning*, *28*(2), 115–133.

Rhinesmith, S. H. (1992). Global mindsets for global managers. *Training & Development, 46*(10), 63–69.

Roberts, K., Kossek, E., & Ozeki, C. (1998). Managing the global workforce: Challenges and strategies. *Academy of Management Executive, 12*(4), 93–106.

Scher, S. J., & Cooper, J. (1989). Motivational basis of dissonance: The singular role of behavioural consequences. *Journal of Personality and Social Psychology, 56*, 899–906.

Schon, D. (1983). *The reflective practitioner: How professional thinks in action*. NY: Basic Book Inc.

Searle, W., & Ward, C. (1990). The prediction of psychological and socio-cultural adjustment during cross-cultural transitions. *International Journal of Intercultural Relations, 14*, 449–464.

Selmer, J. (2002). Practice makes perfect? *International Experience and Expatriate Adjustment, Management International Review*, *42*(1), 71–87.

Selmer, J. (2004). Psychological barriers to adjustment of Western business expatriates in China: Newcomers vs. Long stayers. *International Journal of Human Resource Management, 15*(4), 794–813.

Selmer, J. (2006). Cultural novelty and adjustment: Western business expatriates in China. *International Journal of Human Resource Management, 17*(7), 1209–1222.

Selmer, J., & Shiu, L. S. C. (1999). Coming Home? Adjustment of Hong Kong Chinese expatriate business managers assigned to the People's Republic of China. *International Journal of Intercultural Relations, 23*(3), 447–463.

Shaffer, M. A., & Harrison, D. A. (2001). Forgotten partners: Developing and testing a model of spouse adjustment to international assignments. *Journal of Applied Psychology, 86*, 238–254.

Shaffer, M. A., Harrison, D. A., & Gilley, K. M. (1999). Dimensions, determinants, and differences in the expatriate adjustment process. *Journal of International Business Studies, 30*, 557–582.

Shaffer, M. A., Ferzandi, L., Harrison, D. A., Gregersen, H. B., & Black, J. S. (2003). *You can take it with you: Individual differences and expatriate effectiveness*. Seattle: Paper presented at the annual meeting of the Academy of Management.

Shaffer, M. A., Harrison, D, A., Gregersen, H., Black, J. S., & Ferzandi, L. A. (2006). You can take it with you: Individual differences and expatriate effectiveness. *Journal of Applied Psychology, 91*, 109–125.

Simth, D. M., & Kolb, D. A. (1985). *Learning style inventory: User's guide*. Boston, MA: Hay/Mcber.

Sparrow, P., Brewster, C., & Harris, H. (2004). *Globalizing human resource management*. London: Routledge.

Stahl, G. K., & Bjorkman, I. (Eds.). (2006). *Handbook of research in international human resource management*. Cheltenham, UK: Edward Elgar.

Sternberg, R. (1985). *Beyond IQ: A triarchic of human intelligence*. New York: Cambridge University Presures.

Sternberg, R. (1988). Mental-self government: A theory of intellectual styles and their development. *Human Development, 31*, 197–224.

Sternberg, R. (1997). Managerial intelligence: Why IQ isn't enough. *Journal of Management, 23*(3), 475–493.

Sternberg, R. J., & Grigorenko E. L. (2001). *Practical Intelligence in Everyday Life*. New York: Cambridge University Press.

Sternberg, R., & Horvath, J. (Eds.). (1999). *Tacit knowledge in professional practice: Researcher and practitioner perspectives*. Mahwah, NJ: Lawrence Erlbaum.

Sternberg, R., & Wagner, R. (1993). The gocentric view of intelligence and job performance is wrong. *Current Directions in Psychological Science, 2*, 1–4.

Sternberg, R. J., Wagner, R. K., & Okagaki, L. (1993). Practical intelligence: The nature and role of tacit knowledge in work and at school. In H. Reese & J. Puckett (Eds.), *Advances in lifespan development* (pp. 205–227). Hillsdale, NJ: Lawrence Erlbaum Associates Inc.

Sternberg, R. J., Forsythe, G. B., Hedlund, J., Horvath, J. A., Wagner, R. K., Williams, W. M., et al. (2000). *Practical Intelligence in Everyday Life*. New York: Cambridge University Presures.

Takeuchi, R., Tesluk, P. E., Yun, S., & Lepak, D. P. (2005). An integrative view of international experience. *Academy of Management Journal, 48*(1), 85–101.

Tan, J. A. C., Hartel, C. E. J., Panipucci, D., & Strybosch, V. E. (2005). The effect of emotions in cross-cultural expatriate differences. *Cross Cultural Management, 12*(2), 4–15.

Tan, H., & Libby, R. (1997). Tacit managerial versus technical knowledge as determinants of adult expertise in the field. *Journal of Accounting Research, 35*(1), 97–113.

Tharenou, P., & Harvey, M. (2008). Examining the overseas staffing options utilized by Australian headquartered multinational corporations. *International Journal of Human Resource Management, 17*, 1095–1114.

Torbiorn, J. (1988). *The Lessons of Experience: How Successful Executives Develop on the Job*. NY: Lexington Book.

Triandis, H. C. (1995). *Individualism and collectivism*. Boulder, CO: Westview Presures.

Tung, R. L. (1982). Selection and training procedures of U.S., European and Japanese multinationals. *California Management Review, 25*, 57–71.

Wagner, R. K. (1987). Tacit knowledge in everyday intelligence behaviour. *Journal of Personality and Social Psychology, 52*(6), 301–312.

Wagner, R. K., & Sternberg, R. J. (1985). Practical intelligence in real-world pursuits: The role of tacit knowledge. *Journal of Personality and Social Psychology, 49*(2), 436–458.

Wagner, R. K., & Sternberg, R. J. (1986). Tacit knowledge and intelligence in the everyday world. In R. Sternberg & R. Wagner (Eds.), *Practical intelligence: Nature and origins of competence in the everyday world*. New York: Cambridge University Presures.

Wagner, R. K., & Sternberg, R. J. (1987). Tacit knowledge in managerial success. *Journal of Business and Psychology, 1*(4), 301–312.

Wagner, R. K., & Sternberg, R. J. (1990). Street smarts. In K. E. Clark & M. B. Clark (Eds.), *Measures of leadership* (pp. 493–504). West Orange, N.J.: Leadership Library of America.

Wagner, R., Sujan, H., Sujan, M., Sternberg, R., & Raashotte, C. (1999). Tacit knowledge in sales. In R. Sternberg & J. Horvath (Eds.), *Tacit knowledge in professional practice: Researcher and practitioner perspectives*. Mahwah, NJ: Lawrence Erlbaum.
Ward, C., & Kennedy, A. (1992). Locus of control, mood disturbance and social difficulty during cross-cultural transitions. *International Journal of Intercultural Relations, 16*, 175–194.
Ward, C., & Searle, W. (1991). The impact of value discrepancies and cultural identity on psychological and socio-cultural adjustment of sojoumers. *International Journal of Intercultural Relations, 15*, 209–225.
Williams, W. (1991). *Tacit knowledge and the successful executive* (Doctoral dissertation, Yale University, 1991). University Microfilms International Dissertation Services, AAT9136207.
Yamazaki, Y. (2005). Learning styles and typologies of cultural differences: A theoretical and empirical comparison. *International Journal of Intercultural Relations, 29*(2005), 521–548.
Yamazaki, Y., & Kayes, D. C. (2004). An experiential approach to cross-cultural learning: A review of competencies for successful expatriate adaptation. *Academy of Management Learning and Education, 3*(4), 362–379.
Yamazaki, Y., & Kayes, D. C. (2007). Expatriate learning: exploring how Japanese managers adapt in the United States. *International Journal of Human Resource Management, 18*(8), 1373–1395.
Yuen, C., & Lee, S. N. (1994). Applicability of the learning style inventory in an Asian context and its predictive value. *Educational and Psychological Measurement, 54*(2), 541–549.
Zhang, L. F. (2001). Do thinking styles contribute to academic achievement beyond self-rated abilities? *The Journal of Psychology, 35*(6), 621–637.
Zull, J. E. (2002). *The art of changing the brain: Enriching teaching by exploring the biology of learning*. Sterling, VA: Stylus.

Chapter 3
Research Design and Methodology

The purpose of this research is to explore the relationship between expatriate learning, expatriate adaptation, and international assignment experience, and to verify the relationships between the variables described. Thus, this chapter outlines the research methodology adopted in order to answer the research questions and contribute to the knowledge gap as discussed in the literature review. This chapter explains the design and methodology of the study. It consists of research design, population and sampling, research instruments, and analysis methods. This research is considered as primarily an explanatory-exploratory study, as it explores and establishes causal relationships between variables.

3.1 Research Design

Research design focuses upon turning research objectives and questions into a research project. It consists of research philosophy, research paradigm, research strategy, and research methods.

3.1.1 Research Philosophy and Paradigm

Research philosophy relates to the development of knowledge and the nature of that knowledge, it is precisely what the researcher is doing when embarking on research-developing knowledge in a particular field. The research philosophy the researcher adopts contains important assumptions about the way in which he/she views the world. These assumptions will underpin the researcher's research strategy and the methods chosen as part of that strategy.

3.1.1.1 Assumptions About the Nature of Social Science

All theories of organisations are based upon a philosophy of science and a theory of society. Before we adopt our research philosophy, we should examine the

Y. Li, *Expatriate Manager's Adaption and Knowledge Acquisition*,
DOI 10.1007/978-981-10-0053-9_3

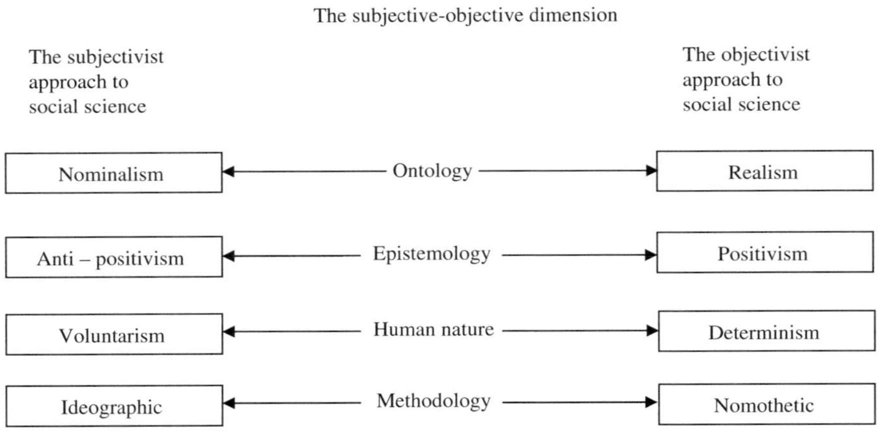

Fig. 3.1 A scheme for analyzing assumptions about the nature of social science

philosophical assumptions which under write different approaches to social science. It is convenient to conceptualise social science in terms of four sets of assumptions related to ontology, epistemology, human nature, and methodology. Figure 3.1 depicts these four sets of assumptions as the subjective-objective dimension.

First, there are assumptions of an ontological nature which concern the very essence of the phenomena under investigation. Ontology raises questions of the assumptions researchers have about the way the world operates and the commitment held to particular views. The nominalist represents the position that the social world external to individual cognition is made up of nothing more than names, concepts and labels which are used to structure reality; the realism, on the other hand, postulates that the social world external to individual cognition is a real world made up of hard, tangible and relatively immutable structures. This study adopts the perspectives of realism.

Secondly, there are assumptions of an epistemological nature which concern the grounds of knowledge. Epistemology raises questions of what researchers think constitutes acceptable knowledge in a field of study. Positivist epistemology seeks to explain and predict what happens in the social world by searching for regularities and casual relationships between its constituent elements, it is in essence based upon the traditional approaches which dominate the natural sciences. For the anti-positivist epistemology, the social world is essentially relativistic and can only be understood from the point of view of the individuals who are directly involved in the activities which are to be studied. This study adopts the perspectives of positivism.

Thirdly, there are assumptions of human nature which concern the relationship between human beings and their environment. Determinism, at one extreme, regards a person and his/her activities as being completely determined by the situation or environment in which he/she is located. Voluntarism, at another extreme, postulates a person is completely autonomous and free-willed. Insofar as social science theories are concerned to understand human activities, they must incline implicitly or explicitly to one or the other of these points of view, or adopt an intermediate standpoint which allows for the influence of both situational and voluntary factors in accounting for the activities of human beings. This study adopts an intermediate standpoint about human nature to include both situational and voluntary factors in explaining the activities of human beings.

The three sets of assumptions outlined above have direct implications for a methodological nature. Each one has important consequences for the way in which researchers attempt to investigate and obtain knowledge about the social world. The ideographic approach to social science is based on the view that one can only understand the social world by obtaining firsthand knowledge of the subject under investigation. It thus places considerable stress upon getting close to one's subject and exploring its detailed background and life history. The nomothetic approach to social science, on the other hand, places emphasis on the importance of basing research upon systematic protocol and technique. Nomothetic methodology adopts approaches and methods which are employed in the natural sciences. Therefore it is preoccupied with the construction of scientific tests and the use of quantitative techniques for the analysis of data. Following the above three sets of employed assumptions, this study adopts the nomothetic methodology. Overall, it can be concluded that this study is conducted in the objective dimension to social science.

3.1.1.2 Research Philosophy

Understanding the assumptions about the nature of social science is a primary way of thinking about research philosophy. Based on the research 'onion' model introduced by Saunders et al. (2009) as shown in Table 3.1, there are four main

Table 3.1 The research 'onion'

Layer	Approaches
1. Research philosophies	**Positivism**, realism, interpretivism, pragmatism
2. Research approaches	**Deductive**, inductive
3. Research strategies	Experiment, **survey**, case study, action research, grounded theory, Ethnography, archival research
4. Choices	Mono method, **mixed methods**, multi method
5. Time horizons	**Cross sectional**, longitudinal
6. Techniques and procedures	**Data collection and data analysis**

Source Saunders et al. (2009: 108)

research philosophies in management research in layer 1: Positivism, Realism, Interpretivism, and Pragmatism.

Pragmatism holds that the most important determinant of the epistemology, ontology, and axiology adopted is the research question. Interpretivism is an epistemology which advocates that it is necessary for the researcher to understand the differences between humans in our role as social actors. The essence of realism is that what the senses show us as reality is the truth: objects have an existence independent of the mind. It is similar to positivism in that it assumes a scientific approach to the development of knowledge. Positivism relates to the philosophical stance of the natural scientist. It entails working with an observable social reality and the end product can be law-like generalisations that are similar to those in the physical and natural sciences (Saunders et al. 2009). The Positivism research philosophy is employed in this study, shown as bold in the Table 3.1.

Axiology is a branch of philosophy that studies judgements about value. It refers to the researcher's view of the role of values in research. The role that the researcher's own values play in all stages of the research process is of great importance to the credibility of his/her research. Being clear of one's own value position can help in deciding what is appropriate ethically and arguing one's position in the event of queries about decisions that have been taken (Saunders et al. 2009). This study, regarded as positivist philosophy, claims that the process of research is value free from researcher and the object of study would be unaffected by research activities. On the other hand, interpretivist researchers believe that research approach is the reflection of one's own values and the researcher is involved with what is being researched. The comparison of these four research philosophies in the area of axiology and data collection techniques most often used in management research is shown in Table 3.2.

Table 3.2 Comparison of the four research philosophies

	Axiology	Data collection techniques most often used
Positivism	Research is undertaken in a value-free way, the researcher is independent of the data and maintains an objective stance	Highly structured, large samples, measurement, quantitative, but can use qualitative
Realism	Research is value laden; the researcher is biased by world views, cultural experiences and upbringings. These will impact on the research	Methods chosen must fit the subject matter, quantitative or qualitative
Interpretivism	Research is value bound, the researcher is part of what is being researched, cannot be separated and so will be subjective	Small samples, in-depth investigations, qualitative
Pragmatism	Values play a large role in interpreting results, the researcher adopting both objective and subjective points of view	Mixed or multiple method designs, quantitative and qualitative

Source Saunders et al. (2009: 119)

3.1.1.3 Research Paradigm

The aim of this study is to test and modify a theory, therefore the deductive approach is employed in this study. An inductive approach is where the result of the analysis would formulate a theory, and thus a deductive approach relates more to positivism and an inductive approach is attached more to interpretivism. A deductive approach possesses several important characteristics and advantages. First, deduction is the search to explain the causal relationships between variables. Second, researchers can develop hypotheses and controls to allow the testing of these hypotheses. Researchers can also adopt a highly structured methodology to facilitate replication, which is an important issue to ensure reliability. Third, deductive analysis needs to be operationalized in a way that enables facts to be measured quantitatively. The final characteristic of a deductive approach is generalisation. In order to be able to generalise statistically about regularities in human social behaviour, it is necessary to select samples with sufficient numerical size. In this study, the results will be generalized to understand the nature of expatriates learning during their international assignments.

Deductive research will progress through five sequential stages:

1. Deducing a hypothesis, a testable proposition about the relationship between two or more concepts or variables, from the theory;
2. Expressing the hypothesis in operational terms, the measurement of the concepts or variables, which propose a relationship between two specific concepts or variables;
3. Testing this operational hypothesis;
4. Examining the specific outcome of the inquiry. It will either tend to confirm the theory or indicate the need for its modification;
5. If necessary, modifying the theory in the light of the findings.

3.1.2 Research Strategy and Methods

3.1.2.1 Research Strategy

The main research strategies are experiment, survey, case study, action research, grounded theory, ethnography, and archival research as shown in Table 3.3 (Saunders et al. 2009). This study adopts survey strategy as the research strategy. The survey strategy is usually associated with the deductive approach. It is a popular and common strategy in business and management research and is most frequently used to answer who, what, where, how much and how many questions. Therefore, the survey strategy tends to be used for explanatory and exploratory research. The differences between these research strategies are shown in Table 3.3.

Table 3.3 Different research strategies

Research strategy	Form of research question	Control over behavioural events?	Focuses on contemporary events?
Experiment	How, why	Yes	Yes
Survey	Who, what, where, how many, how much	No	Yes
Archival research	Who, what, where, how many, how much	No	Yes/no
History	How, why	No	No
Case study	How, why	No	Yes

Besides, grounded theory is referred as ‘theory building’ through a combination of induction and deduction which emphasizes developing and building new theory. Ethnography is rooted firmly in the inductive approach whose purpose is to describe and explain the social world the research subjects inhabit in the way in which they would describe and explain it.

The technique of survey research gives an opportunity to introduce and clarify the research to respondents. The advantages of survey methodology are described below:

1. This method helps to focus on the specific issue by defining and detailing its various characteristic;
2. The result of survey is quantifiable and therefore responds to statistical treatment, resulting in precision and accuracy in the data collected;
3. Using statistical inference allows the researcher to generalize the findings from a sample of respondents to a larger populations thus permitting more global statements;
4. The survey method is fast and straightforward compared to many other research methods. As a result researchers or practitioners act in a relatively quick and intellectually respectable manner.

Thus, using a survey strategy can offer researchers more control over the research process and, when sampling is used, it is possible to generate findings that are representative of the whole population at a lower cost than collecting the data for the whole population. On the other hand, when researchers choose survey strategy, they need to spend time ensuring that the sample is representative, designing and piloting the data collection instrument and the study has a good response rate.

3.1.2.2 Research Methods

In business and management research, the terms quantitative and qualitative are used widely to differentiate both data collection techniques and data analysis procedures. Quantitative is predominantly used as a synonym for any data collection technique (such as a questionnaire) or data analysis procedure (such as graphs or statistics) that generates or uses numerical data. In contrast, qualitative is used predominantly as a synonym for any data collection technique (such as an interview) or data analysis procedure (such as categorising data) that generates or uses non-numerical data. Quantitative and qualitative data collection techniques and analysis procedures each have their own strengths and weakness (Saunders et al. 2009).

Research method choices include mono method and multiple methods. Mono method choice means using a single data collection technique and corresponding analysis procedures. On the other hand, multiple methods choice means using more than one data collection technique and analysis procedures to answer the research questions. Multiple methods choice is increasingly advocated within business and management research, where single researches study may use quantitative and qualitative techniques and procedures in combination as well as use primary and secondary data. Previous research posits that multiple methods are useful as they provide better opportunities to answer the research questions and to better evaluate the extent to which the research findings can be trusted and inferred.

This study is a multiple methods research or a mixed-model research, more precisely. In the aspect of data collection techniques, this study collects quantitative data by questionnaire instrument and collects qualitative data by semi-structured individual interviews. In the aspect of data analysis procedures, both quantitative and qualitative data are analysed quantitatively in this study. There are especially two reasons for choosing mixed-model method design in this study: triangulation and aid interpretation. In this study, triangulation refers to use of two independent sources of data collection techniques, questionnaire and semi-structured interviews, to corroborate research findings within a study. Regarding aid interpretation, this study uses semi-structured interviews to support and explain relationships between quantitative variables. All in all, a multiple methods approach enables us to produce richness and provides a deeper understanding of data and investigation of this research.

3.1.2.3 Time Horizons

Because of time constraints, a cross-sectional time horizon is therefore considered most appropriate for this study. Cross-sectional research is the study of a particular phenomenon or phenomena at a particular time. Cross-sectional studies often employ the survey strategy and seek to explain how factors are related in different organizations such as relationships between different variables. However, the study adopts a pseudo longitudinal research method that examines Western expatriates with different lengths of assignment tenure to better understand how expatriates learn and develop over time.

3.2 Population and Sampling

3.2.1 Target Population

The full set of cases from which a sample is taken is called target population. The purpose of this study is to examine how Western expatriate managers adapt, learn and develop when working in China as well as how Western expatriate managers differ from host Chinese managers in China. For this purpose, the target population of this research consists of two parts: Western expatriate managers and host Chinese managers. Western expatriate managers are confined only to Western managers who have been transferred from western countries (Western Europe or North America) to China for international assignments. Western businesspersons with short business trips to China or the Western workers who were hired as local staff in China are excluded. Host Chinese managers are Western expatriate managers' Chinese counterparts in China.

3.2.2 Sampling

3.2.2.1 Sampling Method

In this study, the need to sample is because it is impracticable to survey the entire population and the budget and time constraints prevent this research from surveying the entire population. The sampling techniques can be divided into two types: probability sampling and non-probability sampling. In probability sampling, the probability of each case being selected from the population is known and is usually equal for all cases. This means that it is possible to answer research questions and to achieve objectives that require estimating statistically the characteristics of the population from the sample. Probability sampling is often associated with survey and experimental research strategies (Saunders et al. 2009). On the other hand, in non-probability sampling, the probability of each case being selected from the total population is not known and it is impossible to answer research questions or to address objectives that require making statistical inferences about the characteristics of the population from the sample. This study adopts probability sampling method in association with a survey-based research strategy.

According to Saunders et al. (2009), the process of probability sampling can be divided into four stages: (1) identify a suitable sampling frame based on the research questions; (2) decide a suitable sample size; (3) select the most appropriate sampling technique and select the sample; (4) check that the sample is representative of the population. In the first stage, the sampling frame refers to a complete list of all the cases in the population from which the research sample will be drawn. In the second stage, the larger the sample's size the lower the likely error in generalising to the population. Probability sampling is therefore a compromise between the accuracy of the results and the amount of time and money invested in collecting, checking and analysing the data. Statisticians have shown that a sample size of 30 or more will usually result in a sampling distribution for the mean that is very close to a normal distribution. This provides an advice of a minimum number of 30 for statistical analyses and a useful rule of thumb for the smallest number in each category within the overall sample. Besides, for most business and management research, researchers are content to estimate the population's characteristics at 95 % certainty to within ±3–5 % of its true values (Saunders et al. 2009). In the third stage, five main techniques can be used to select a probability sample: simple random sampling, systematic sampling, stratified random sampling, cluster sampling, and multi-stage sampling.

3.2.2.2 Sampling Procedures

The survey includes self-administered questionnaires and semi-structured interviews. Data was collected in western MNCs' subsidiaries in China. The directory of MNCs in China (published by the Chinese government) was used to guide the identification and selection of the research samples. This research chose western MNCs which have subsidiaries in China. Data collection was concentrated during 16 weeks from the middle of February to the beginning of June 2012. Data collection in China was focused in Beijing and Shanghai in order to provide for this research a sufficient number of samples that are relatively homogeneous in terms of business lines.

The data collection strategy had three phases: (1) an initial contact and visit; (2) a confirmation; (3) data collection on visit. First, the researcher phoned and emailed the manager chosen to be in charge of the survey distribution to make an appointment with them. Then the researcher visited them to explain this research in a face-to-face conversation in China. In agreement with participation in this research, they received the necessary number of survey packets for their colleagues. The survey packet contains a cover letter, a set of instruments, and a return envelope. We also provided the manager the link to the electronic version of the questionnaire in case some expatriate managers prefer to complete the questionnaire online. Details regarding the electronic version of the questionnaire are discussed in Sect. 3.3.2. At the meeting, a due date for filled survey collection was set up tentatively for from 1 to 2 weeks later. A survey packet and also the link to the electronic questionnaire were then distributed to their western expatriate managers in their firms. In this phase, the researcher visited 28 western MNCs, and 18 of them agreed to participate in this research and another 10 organizations declined. Second, the researchers visited or phoned the same managers prior to the tentative due date for the collection to confirm that the collection date are still convenient for them and for interview. The collection date was adjusted if necessary. Third, the researchers visited them again on the due date to receive the sealed envelopes including filled questionnaire and conducted semi-structured interviews with some expatriate managers.

A total of 200 western expatriate managers of 18 western MNCs received the survey packet through the internal distribution system in the organization. Of the

200 expatriates, 121 expatriate managers completed the questionnaire. The response rate was 60.5 %. Babbie (1973) views a response rate of 60 % as good. The relative high response rate may be due to the following three reasons. The first reason is the acquisition of agreement from each western firm, promoting its western expatriate managers to participate in this study. The involvement of corporations may serve to generate a better return rate of survey response. Secondly, the CEO of one MNC and most managers whom I met valued this research and clearly understood how to complete these questionnaires. Their affirmative attitudes and positive involvement had a great influence on the response rate as well as the quality of filled research questionnaires. Some senior managers mentioned that they actually received questions from their expatriate managers and answered them properly. The third reason may be the feedback system about the result of respondents' learning styles, levels of accumulated managerial tacit knowledge, and adaptive styles upon their request. If respondents want to get a report of their results, they were able to receive an individual electronic report free of charge. At the end of our data collection, 73 % of the participants requested their results. This feedback service appeared to motivate expatriate managers to participate in our study.

In this research, we also sought to examine if there were significant empirical differences between western expatriate managers and host Chinese managers working in the same MNCs in terms of the ways they adapt to managerial responsibilities within MNCs. To explore this question we returned to the western MNCs that participated in the study and asked 12 of the medium to large organizations that supported our previous research to participate in our second study. Eight western MNCs agreed to participate in our second study. Sixty-six percent of the western expatriate managers that participated in our previous study come from these 8 western MNCs. The participating organizations were administered a Chinese version of a revised demographic questionnaire, the Chinese version of Learning style inventory, and the Chinese version of Tacit knowledge inventory for managers. They were also provided the link to the electronic version of the Chinese questionnaire. Details regarding the electronic version of the Chinese questionnaire are discussed in Sect. 3.3.2. In this phase, we only targeted host Chinese managers. Of the 240 Chinese managers that received our survey packets, 133 returned completed questionnaires, for a response rate of 55.4 %.

3.2.3 Research Samples

The purpose of this study was to investigate how western expatriate managers acquire new knowledge, learn, adapt, and develop when working in the cross-cultural environment of Chinese business settings. We also investigated how western expatriate managers with substantial work experience in China differ from host Chinese managers working in the same MNCs in terms of learning styles and levels of managerial tacit knowledge. Therefore, our research sample includes two parts: 121 western expatriate managers and 133 host Chinese managers.

3.2.3.1 Western Expatriate Managers

The first part of our research sample consists of 121 western expatriate managers who belong to the 18 western MNCs that agreed to participate in this research. The 18 western MNCs had their own various attributes that conditioned the 121 samples as one aspect of demographic characteristics such as type of industry, the number of employees, etc. In addition, individual western expatriate managers have their own attributes such as age, gender, the level of educational achievement, etc. The demographic characteristics of the sample are therefore described as two separate components according to corporate attributes and individual attributes.

(a) Demographic characteristics dependent on corporate attributes
Data collection was conducted through the cooperation of western MNCs mostly located in Beijing, China. The primary lines of their business are manufacturing industry and IT (Information Technology). Thirty-seven percent of the sample (western expatriate managers) works for 6 IT firms, 36 % works for 8 Manufacturing firms, 15 % works for 3 Finance firms, and 12 % works for 1 Logistics firm. A total employment size of the western MNCs ranges from 60 to 2000 employees: 21 % of the sample works for small size companies of 1–99, 22 % of the sample works for middle size companies of 100–999, and 57 % of the sample works for relatively large companies of 1000–2000. The number of western expatriates in 18 western MNCs range from 3 to 36. 17 percent of the sample works for the MNCs with 8 or less western expatriates, 73 % of the sample works for the MNCs with 10–17, and 11 % works for the MNC with 36. 5 firms are establishes with the foreign and China joint venture at 50 % of capital ratio; 31 % of the sample are employed in these 5 firms accordingly. Sixty-nine percent of the sample is employed in western based MNCs. Table 3.4 illustrates the demographic characteristics of the sample in accordance with the corporate attributes as follows.

(b) Demographic characteristics dependent on individual attributes
The other demographic characteristics of the sample are dependent upon individual attributes. Eighty-seven percent of the sample is male, while 13 % is female. Ages of the sample are varied in the range from 20's to 50's. The group of 20's is 6.6 %; that of 30–39 is 58.7 %; that of 40–49 is 31.4 %; and that of 50–60 is 3.3 %. The majority of the sample belongs to the two groups of 30–39 and 40–49, which occupied 90.1 % in total. The mean score of the length of time the western expatriate managers have spent in China is 36.5 months (approximately 3 years) with the standard deviation of 6.34. The value of this standard deviation suggests that the length of the time tends to be varied among the 121 western expatriate managers. Eighteen percent of the sample have spent one year or less in China; 35 % of the sample have spent over 1–3 years; 30 % over 3–5 years; and 17 % over five years. The number of western expatriate managers who have previous overseas assignment experiences is 42 (34.7 %), while that of those without previous overseas assignment experience is 79 (65.3 %). 26 (21.5 %) western expatriate managers have one previous overseas assignment experience; 14 (11.6 %) western

Table 3.4 Demographic characteristics of the sample dependent on corporate attributes

	Corporate base (N = 18)		Individual base (N = 121)	
	No. of western MNCs	(%)	No. of western expatriates	(%)
Type of industry				
Manufacturing	8	44	44	36
Logistics	1	5	14	12
IT	6	33	45	37
Finance	3	17	18	15
Total employees				
60–99	6	33	25	21
100–999	10	56	69	57
1000–2000	2	11	27	22
No. of western expatriates				
1–8	5	28	20	17
10–17	12	67	88	73
20–40	1	5	13	11
Firm structure				
Western-China joint venture	5	28	37	31
Western based	13	72	84	69

expatriate managers have two international assignment before; and 2 western expatriate managers (1.7 %) have three previous international assignment experiences. Eighty-nine (73.6 %) western expatriate managers have no experience of overseas studies.

In western MNCs' subsidiaries in China, hierarchical job position seems to be fairly varied among the western expatriate managers: 4.1 % of the sample is engaged as CEO or president; 21.5 % as senior managers; 62 % as middle managers; and 12.4 % as junior managers. Furthermore, organizational job functions also have variations among the western expatriate managers: 17.4 % of the sample is Human Resource Management/general administration; 24.8 % is operations/production; 18.2 % is sales and marketing; 24 % is engineering/design; and 10.7 % is finance/accounting. Table 3.5 illustrates all the demographic characteristics of the sample based on the discussed individual attributes.

3.2.3.2 Host Chinese Managers

The second part of our research sample consists of 133 host Chinese managers who belong to the 8 western MNCs that participated in our previous research. 66 % of western expatriate managers participated in the study belong to these 8 western MNCs. The demographic characteristics of host Chinese managers are also described as two separate components according to corporate attributes and individual attributes.

Table 3.5 Demographic characteristics of the sample dependent on individual attributes

	Frequency	%
Nationality		
UK/Ireland	43	35.5
USA	36	29.8
Canada	26	21.5
Australian	11	9.1
Other	5	4.1
Gender		
Male	105	86.8
Female	16	13.2
Age		
20–29	8	6.6
30–39	71	58.7
40–49	38	31.4
50–60	4	3.3
Over 60	0	0
International family (parents or spouse come from different country)		
No	102	84.3
Yes, Not from Greater China	10	8.3
Yes, from Greater China	9	7.4
Length of time spent in China		
1 year or less	22	18
1 to 3 years	42	35
3 to 5 years	36	30
over 5 years	21	17
Overseas assignment experience		
Experience	42	34.7
No experience	79	65.3
Overseas study experience		
No	89	73.6
Yes	32	26.4
Educational achievement		
Master	51	42.1
Bachelor	69	57
other	1	0.8
Job position		
CEO/president	5	4.1
Senior manager	26	21.5
Middle manager	75	62
Junior manager	15	12.4

(continued)

Table 3.5 (continued)

	Frequency	%
Function area		
HRM/general administration	21	17.4
Operations/production	30	24.8
Sales and marketing	22	18.2
Engineering/design	29	24
Finance/accounting	13	10.7
Other	6	5

(a) Demographic characteristics dependent on corporate attributes
The lines of their business are manufacturing industry, IT (Information Technology), and Logistics. Fifty percent of the sample (host Chinese managers) works for 4 Manufacturing firms, 37.5 % works for 3 IT firms, and 12.5 % works for 1 Logistics firm. The 8 western MNCs are medium to large organizations: 75 % of the sample works for middle size companies of 100–999, and 25 % of the sample works for relatively large companies of 1000–2000. The number of western expatriates in 8 western MNCs ranges from 7 to 36. 12.5 % of the sample works for the MNCs with 7 western expatriates, 75 % of the sample works for the MNCs with 10–17 western expatriates, and 12.5 % works for the MNC with 36. Three firms are establishes with the foreign and China joint venture at 50 % of capital ratio; 66.9 % of the sample are employed in these 3 firms accordingly. Thirty-three percent of the sample is employed in western based MNCs. Table 3.6 illustrates the demographic characteristics of the sample in accordance with the corporate attributes as follows.

Table 3.6 Demographic characteristics of the sample dependent on corporate attributes

	Corporate base (N = 8)		Individual base (N = 133)	
	No. of western MNCs	(%)	No. of Chinese managers	(%)
Type of industry				
Manufacturing	4	50	45	33.8
Logistics	1	12.5	55	41.4
IT	3	37.5	33	24.8
Total employees				
100–999	6	75	58	43.6
1000–2000	2	25	75	56.4
No. of expatriates				
1–8	1	12.5	18	13.5
10–17	6	75	92	69.2
20–40	1	12.5	23	17.3
Firm structure				
Western-China	3	37.5	89	66.9
Western based	5	62.5	44	33.1

(b) Demographic characteristics dependent on individual attributes
The other demographic characteristics of the sample are dependent upon individual attributes. Sixty-four percent of the sample is male, while 36 % is female. Ages of the sample are varied in the range from 20's to 50's. The group of 20–29 is 5.3 %; that of 30–39 is 73.7 %; that of 40–49 is 20.3 %; and that of 50–60 is 0.8 %. The majority of the sample belongs to the two groups of 30–39 and 40–49, which occupied 94 % in total. 124 (93.2 %) host Chinese managers have no experience of overseas studies. All host Chinese managers have no previous international assignment experience. 62.4 % of the sample is engaged as junior managers; 35.3 % as middle managers; and 2.3 % as senior managers.

Furthermore, 18.8 % of the sample has been in a managerial role for less than 3 years; 24.1 % of the sample with 3–5 years; 31.6 % of the sample with 5–10 years; and 25.6 % of the sample over 10 years. With regard to host Chinese managers' overall working experience in western MNCs, 25.6 % of the sample has been working in western MNCs for less than 5 years; 29.3 % of the sample for 5–10 years; 26.3 % of the sample for 10–15 years; and 18.8 % of the sample for over 15 years. Table 3.7 illustrates all the demographic characteristics of the sample based on the discussed individual attributes.

3.3 Research Instruments

The survey of this study consists of an in-depth questionnaire targeted at Western expatriate managers in China.

The questionnaire includes four assessment measures which include: Kolb's (1999) Learning Styles Inventory, Kolb's (1999) Adaptive Styles Inventory, Sternberg et al. (2000) Tacit Knowledge Inventory for Managers, and Black et al.'s (1989) Expatriate Adjustment Scale. List of sub-construct and details of the questionnaire are shown in Table 3.8.

3.3.1 Learning Style Inventory (LSI)

Kolb (1999) describes the development of the Learning Style Inventory (LSI). It is noted that the LSI was first developed in the 1971 and first published in 1976 (Kolb 1999). The major criticism of this inventory at that time (e.g. Mainemelis et al. 2002) concerned the internal consistency of the scales and the scales' test-retest reliability. These criticisms led to the development of the second version of LSI: the LSI-II in 1986. Internal consistency of LSI was reported to be improved, however, critics continued to report problems with test-retest reliability. The most recent

Table 3.7 Demographic characteristics of the sample dependent on individual attributes

	Frequency	%
Nationality		
Chinese	133	100
Gender		
Male	85	63.9
Female	48	36.1
Age		
20–29	7	5.3
30–39	98	73.7
40–49	27	20.3
50–60	1	0.8
Over 60	0	0
Overseas assignment experience		
No experience	133	100
Overseas study experience		
No	124	93.2
Yes	9	6.8
Time in a managerial role		
1 year or less	25	18.8
1 to 3 years	32	24.1
3 to 5 years	42	31.6
Over 5 years	34	25.6
Time in western MNCs		
5 years or less	34	25.6
5 to 10 years	39	29.3
10 to 15 years	35	26.3
Over 15 years	25	18.8
Educational achievement		
Master	36	27.1
Bachelor	80	60.2
Other	17	12.8
Job position		
Senior manager	3	2.3
Middle manager	47	35.3
Junior manager	83	62.4
Function area		
HRM/general administration	3	2.3
Operations/production	46	34.6
Sales and marketing	44	33.1
Engineering/design	19	14.3
Finance/accounting	17	12.8
Other	4	3

Table 3.8 List of constructs in the questionnaire

Questions	Construct	References	Items
Part 1	Learning style inventory	Geiger et al. (1993), Kolb (1999)	12
Part 2	Adaptive style inventory	Kolb (1984)	48
Part 3	Tacit knowledge inventory for managers	Sternberg et al. (2000)	61
Part 4	Expatriate adjustment scale	Black and colleagues (Black and Stephens 1989)	14

version, the Learning Styles Inventory-III (LSI-III), was released in 1999 and it was stated that 'randomizing the order of the LSI-II items has resulted in dramatic improvements in its test-retest reliability' (Kolb 1999). Kolb's (1999) Learning Styles Inventory-III was administered in this study. The Learning Styles Inventory received very positive evaluation from undergraduate students because it helped to find ways of improving their own learning in different learning situations (Loo 1999). Whilst earlier criticisms such as reported encountering problems in mapping the factor structure of the learning style inventory to the hypothesized dimensions, subsequent developments of the instrument (Kolb 1999) have now overcome these limitations. The LSI is now one of the most frequently used instruments to assess learning styles (Mainemelis et al. 2002; Armstrong and Mahmud 2008) and has been widely used to examine learning styles in cross-cultural settings (e.g., Katz 1988; Hoppe 1990; Yuen and Lee 1994; Auyeung and Sands 1996; Fridland 2002; Yamazaki and Kayes 2007 etc.). Because of the LSI's usefulness and empirical reliability and validity in operation (Katz 1988), cross-cultural researchers adopt the LSI for learning style studies.

Kolb's standard LSI (1999) is based on the forced-choice method and ipsative scaling and the justification for this lies in the need to maximize differences within the measure (Geiger et al. 1993) because the LSI is intended to measure an individual's preference in learning, rather than ability to learn. However, criticisms of some of the previous studies using the LSI have been levelled at the deficiency and limitations of ipsative measures. Forced-choice rating was developed by Sisson (Kolb 1984) in an effort to overcome the problems associated with the free-choice method: social desirability, leniency, and acquiescent response sets. Another important contribution of the forced-choice method is that it reflects the hierarchal nature of values and the dialectical dynamics involved in learning and life in general. The forced-choice method can overcome problems of the free-choice method, but it may also create new psychometric difficulties. Forced-choice instruments often provide ipsative measures. Ipsative measures produce nominal data, and previous researchers have often proceeded to correlate these scores with normative data. This is known to be controversial and limits the nature of the methods that can be used to determine an instrument's validity, and compare it with other instruments (Armstrong and Mahmud 2008). Attempts to create and study a normative form of the LSI were first undertaken by Geiger et al. (1993). Geiger et al. (1993) converted the 12 items on the standard LSI into an independent, randomly ordered 48-item questionnaire. Each item was scored on a 7-point Likert scale. Statistical procedures in several previous studies to compare the ipsative and normative forms of the LSI revealed strong support for the same learning style preferences theorized by Kolb in both measures.

According to Greer and Dunlap (1997), the main issue with ipsative measure is its use of cross-subject comparison. Kolb's learning style inventory offers little correlation or comparative strength between one person and another and therefore, it is difficult to predict the performance of others in relation to the scores of an individual (Geiger et al. 1993). Geiger et al. (1993) contend that the learning style inventory's use of cross-subject comparison also presents a problem with using factor analysis to determine internal construct validity. He found some ambiguity in the factor structure of the learning style inventory (Geiger et al. 1992). Loo (1999) found that the test-retest stability of Kolb's learning style inventory was poor over a 10-week period. Truluck and Courtenay (1999) found that older individuals above the age of 65 demonstrated an age-related trend to become more reflective in the learning environment. They further argue that Kolb's learning style inventory does not take the impact of age into consideration which therefore, contributes to the ongoing psychometric issues.

In the LSI, the four scale scores (CE, RO, AC, and AE) are clearly ipsative. However, the two dimensional scores AC-CE and AE-RO are not ipsative. When the dimension AC-CE takes a particular value, the dimension AE-RO can take two to four different values and the score on one dimension does not determine the score on the other. It should be noted that learning styles in the LSI are determined on the basis of the two non-ipsative dimensional scores and not the four ipsative scale scores (Mainemelis et al. 2002). The LSI was developed to test the construct validity of experiential learning theory. Construct validation is not focused on an outcome criterion but on the theory or construct that the test measures. Here the emphasis is on the pattern of convergent and discriminate theoretical predictions made by the theory (Mainemelis et al. 2002).

3.3.1.1 Scoring the LSI

Kolb's standard LSI (1999) is composed of 12 questions, each of which asks people to complete a sentence by ranking four choices (A, B, C, and D) that correspond to the four learning modes encompassed by Experiential Learning Theory. For example, the first question in the LSI is 'When I learn', and the four choices to be ranked are 'A: I like to deal with my feelings'; 'B: I like to think about ideas'; 'C: I like to be doing things'; and 'D: I like to watch and listen'. These four items reflect, in turn, the concrete experience mode, the abstract conceptualization mode, the active experimentation mode, and the reflective observation mode of learning. The respondent then ranks the four endings for each question according to how well he/she thinks each ending fits with how he/she would go about learning something. 'Most like you' is ranked a 4, 'more like you' is ranked a 3, 'less like you' is ranked a 2, and 'least like you' is ranked a 1. A sample item from the LSI is presented for information below:

1. When I learn:	I like to deal with my feelings ________	I like to think about ideas ________
	I like to be doing things ________	I like to watch and listen ________

The sum of responses for each mode is determined and represents the degree to which a person relies on that mode of learning. After the summation of the scores for each learning mode (CE, RO, AC, and AE), the subtraction of CE from AC and that of RO from AE determine the two dimensional scores: AC-CE and AE-RO. A combination of two values of AC-CE and AE-RO determines which of the four learning styles the individual prefers to use. The four learning styles, as discussed in the section 'experiential learning', are the diverging, the converging, the assimilating, and the accommodating learning styles. Four scores, CE, RO, AC, and AE, measure an individual's preference for the four modes, and two dimensional scores, AC-CE and AE-RO, indicate that an individual's relative preference for one pole or the other of the two dialectics: conceptualizing-experiencing and acting-reflecting. According to the cut-off points of the two learning dimensions, AC-CE and AE-RO, as the LSI normative scores present by Kolb (1999) and Smith and Kolb (1985), Fig. 3.2 illustrates the divide of the four learning styles.

In the present research, the study also calculates two other scores that measure the degree to which an individual is balanced in their preference for AC-CE and AE-RO. The balancing learning profile on the two experiential learning dimensions

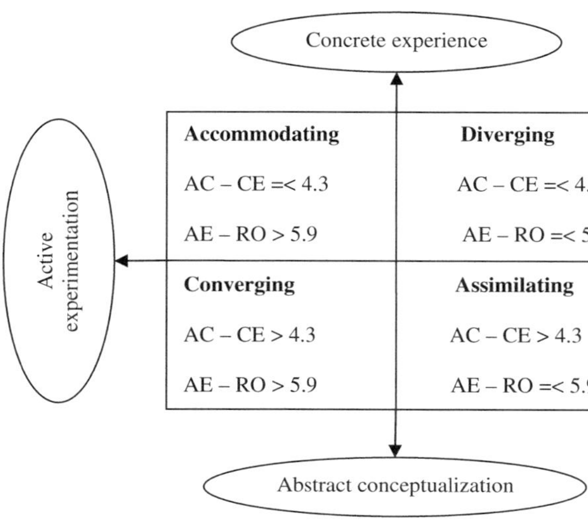

Fig. 3.2 The two cut-off points (AC-CE and AE-RO) of the four learning styles

is computed as the absolute value of the two dimensional scores (AC-CE and AE-RO). For example, individuals scoring equally in AC and CE can be said to be balancing on this learning dimension. Their absolute value of AC-CE score reflects an inverse score of this balance. In particular, a low score indicates a balancing profile, whereas a high score indicates a learning style specializing in either end of the dialectical dimension. These two scores representing the balancing learning style were first applied by Mainemelis et al. (2002). The assumption is that the more balancing a person is in his/her dialectic preference, the more he/she will experience a creative tension or attraction to both poles opening a wider space for flexible adaptation. A search of the 1004 studies listed in the Bibliography of research on Experiential learning theory and the LSI found that only three studies examining the balancing learning style. Goldman (1972, cited in Mainemelis et al. 2002) in a study of MIT seniors found a significant relationship between a balancing learning style and cumulative grade point average. Weathersby (1977, cited in Mainemelis et al. 2002) examined a large sample of adult learners at Goddard College and she indentified a style that balancing the experiencing-conceptualizing learning dimension. She further proposes that this learning style represents s higher level of adult development. More recently, Mainemelis et al. (2002) investigated the differences between balancing and specialized learning styles in a sample of 198 MBA students. Their results illustrated that participants with balancing learning styles own greater levels of adaptive flexibility and adaptive flexibility in learning style is predictive of highly integrated and complex levels of adult development.

In summary, eight variables were calculated from the LSI: raw scores for each of the four learning modes (CE, RO, AC, and AE), two measures of the two dimensions in Experiential learning theory (AC-CE and AE-RO), and to assess the balancing learning style, the absolute value of these two dimensional scores (ABS (AC-CE) and ABS (AE-RO)).

3.3.2 *Adaptive Style Inventory (ASI)*

Adaptive flexibility is a derivative of the developmental dimension of the experiential learning theory. It purports to measure the extent to which a person flexibly modifies his/her behaviours as a function of the interaction between his/her internal structures and the environment. The Adaptive Style Inventory (ASI) was created to assess individual adaptive flexibility (Kolb 1984; Boyatzis and Kolb 1993). The Learning Style Inventory and the Adaptive Style Inventory have been designed to be theoretically commensurate while methodologically diverse in order to reduce spurious common method variance among them (Mainemelis et al. 2002). To accomplish ASI, there requires two conditions to be met. First, a holistic system of environmental demands that samples the person's actual and potential life space is required. As Scott (1966, cited in Kolb 1984) argued that adaptive flexibility is meaningful only if there is some situation or circumstance being adapted to.

Second, the dimensions of personal-response flexibility and situation demand should be defined in commensurate terms. Flexibility of response should be measured along a dimension so that situation/person matches or mismatches can be identified that are related to the situation responded to. Experiential learning theory provides a framework within which these conditions can be met (Kolb 1984).

The adaptive style inventory instrument is divided into four situations that the respondent has to 'adapt' to. These situations correspond to the four learning styles: diverging situations, assimilating situations, converging situations, and accommodating situations. The ASI uses a 48-item, paired comparison method to rank learning preferences for the four learning modes in eight personalized learning contexts. Individuals are asked to think of personal examples for each of eight situations which describe four learning contexts (two situations per context): valuing ('when I consider my feelings' and 'When I try to see the world as another person sees it'), thinking ('When systematically analyzing something' and 'When developing an idea'), deciding ('When deciding between two alternatives' and 'When evaluating an opportunity'), and acting ('When I start to do something new' and 'When I try to complete a task on time'). For each of the eight situations, individuals are provided with six paired sentences, which compare each learning mode with the other three. For example, one situation question and the six pairs of choices for it are shown below:

Situation 1. When I start to do something new:

Pair 1: Choose A or B:

A. I rely on my feelings to guide me. (Concrete experience)
B. I set priorities. (Abstract conceptualization)

Pair 2: Choose C or D:

C. I try out different ways of doing it. (Active experimentation)
D. I observe the situation. (Reflective observation)

Pair 3: Choose E or F:

E. I rely on my feelings to guide me. (Concrete experience)
F. I observe the situation. (Reflective observation)

Pair 4: Choose G or H:

G. I rely on my feelings to guide me. (Concrete experience)
H. I try out different ways of doing it. (Active experimentation)

Pair 5: Choose I or J:

I. I set priorities. (Abstract conceptualization)
J. I observe the situation. (Reflective observation)

Pair 6: Choose K or L:

K. I set priorities. (Abstract conceptualization)
L. I try out different ways of doing it. (Active experimentation)

Individuals are asked to choose from each pair the sentence that is more like what they would actually do in that situation. The respondents, in effect, are reporting how they respond behaviourally in certain kinds of situations. The items in the ASI are randomly distributed to encourage the respondents to consider each situation in isolation from the others. Like the LSI, the ASI assesses preferences for the four scales (CE, RO, AC, and AE) and two dimensions (AC-CE and AE-RO), but it also measures adaptive flexibility in learning-the degree to which individuals change their learning style to respond to different learning situations in their life. Individuals with high adaptive flexibility are more self-directed, have richer life structures characterized by many life contexts with many connections between them, and experience less conflict in their lives. The adaptive style inventory thus yields an adaptive profile for the four different learning style environments and an average adaptive profile across all four situations.

Besides the adaptive flexibility scores, the adaptive style inventory can also be portrayed in a way that shows one's adaptive orientations as five points on a two dimensional learning space. One point represents average responses across all situations, i.e. total adaptive flexibility score. Other four points portray how the person responded in each of the four kinds of situations. Arrows are then drawn from the total score to each of the situational scores. These arrows indicate the direction of the person's response to each kind of situation. The amount of adaptive flexibility from situation to situation is indicated by the length of the arrows. Figure 3.3 presents an example of one respondent's geometric adaptive flexibility score on ASI.

In Fig. 3.3, this respondent has a total score well within the Diverging quadrant indicating a strong tendency to respond to all situations in a concrete and reflective mode. Each of the situational pressures was responded to in terms other than the pressures of the environment (relative to the total score), except in Converging situations. In Diverging situations, the respondent responds in very concrete ways but also responds in slightly more active ways than his overall response. The response to Diverging situations would be interpreted as more appropriate to Accommodating situations. Admittedly, the response in terms of the total grid is still in the Diverging quadrant which makes the response consonant with the situational pressures. However, the reference point for each respondent is not the theoretical centre of the grid, but their own total score. In Accommodating situations, the respondent responds in a more abstract way and in a relatively reflective way, contrary to the Accommodating situational pressures which demands a concrete and active response. In Assimilating situations, the respondent responds in a reflective way as would be demanded by the situation, but also responds in a concrete way which is contrary to the Assimilating situational pressures. Finally, the respondent responds to Converging situations in ways appropriate to the Converging situational pressures.

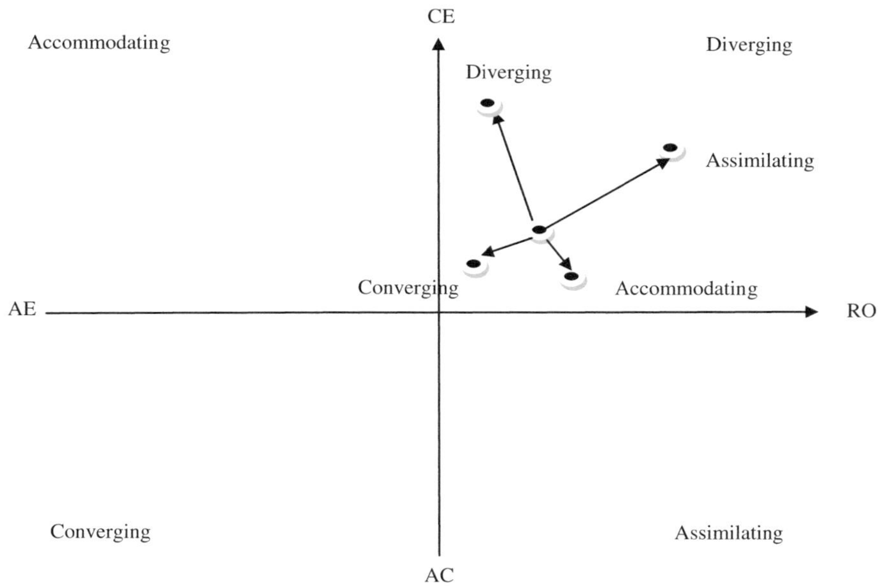

Fig. 3.3 Geometric adaptive flexibility score on ASI

3.3.2.1 Scoring the ASI

Formulas were devised to assess the level of adaptive flexibility quantitatively in the adaptive style inventory (Kolb 1984; Boyatzis and Kolb 1993). They determine how much the respondent varied his/her adaptive orientation from situation to situation. Five such variables were created: concrete experience adaptive flexibility, adaptive flexibility on CE, (CEAF), reflective observation adaptive flexibility, adaptive flexibility on RO, (ROAF), abstract conceptualization adaptive flexibility, adaptive flexibility on AC, (ACAF), active experimentation adaptive flexibility, adaptive flexibility on AE, (AEAF), and total adaptive flexibility (TAF). For example, AEAF means the extent to which people vary their active experimentation orientation across the four situations. The TAF is the sum of CEAF, ROAF, ACAF, and AEAF. Formulas to compute the adaptive flexibility on Concrete Experience in Converging situation (deciding situation) are first described as follows:

$$AF^{cn}_{ce} = ABS\left(T_{ce}/4 - t^{cn}_{ce}\right)$$

- Where 'AF' is Adaptive Flexibility
- Where 'cn' is convering situation (deciding situations)
- Where 'ce' is concrete experience adaptive responses
- Where 'ABS' is the absolute value

- Where 'T' is the total score
- Where 't' is the total score with a situation
- Where the number 4 divides the total score to be comparable to the total score within each situation

Similarly, formulas to compute the adaptive flexibility on Concrete Experience in three other situations and the total adaptive flexibility on Concrete Experience are described below:

$$\begin{aligned}
AF_{ce}^{as} &= ABS\left(T_{ce}/4 - t_{ce}^{as}\right)\\
AF_{ce}^{dv} &= ABS\left(T_{ce}/4 - t_{ce}^{dv}\right)\\
AF_{ce}^{ac} &= ABS\left(T_{ce}/4 - t_{ce}^{ac}\right)\\
AF_{ce}^{t} &= AF_{ce}^{cn} + AF_{ce}^{as} + AF_{ce}^{dv} + AF_{ce}^{ac}
\end{aligned}$$

- Where 'as' is assimilating situations (thinking situations)
- Where 'dv' is diverging situations (valuing situations)
- Where 'ac' is accommodating situations (acting situations)
- Where 't' is the total score with a situation

This set of formulas expresureses the difference between the total score of a respondent in terms of Concrete Experience mode responses and the sub-scores for the same mode within each separate kind of situation. Then, we'd have to compute the adaptive flexibility on RO, AC, and AE in four learning situations respectively. Formulas to compute the adaptive flexibility on Reflective Observation in four situations are described below:

$$\begin{aligned}
AF_{ro}^{cn} &= ABS\left(T_{ro}/4 - t_{ro}^{cn}\right)\\
AF_{ro}^{as} &= ABS\left(T_{ce}/4 - t_{ro}^{as}\right)\\
AF_{ro}^{dv} &= ABS\left(T_{ce}/4 - t_{ro}^{dv}\right)\\
AF_{ro}^{ac} &= ABS\left(T_{ce}/4 - t_{ro}^{ac}\right)\\
AF_{ro}^{t} &= AF_{ro}^{cn} + AF_{ro}^{as} + AF_{ro}^{dv} + AF_{ro}^{ac}
\end{aligned}$$

Formulas to compute the adaptive flexibility on Abstract Conceptualization in four situations are described below:

$$\begin{aligned}
AF_{ac}^{cn} &= ABS\left(T_{ac}/4 - t_{ac}^{cn}\right)\\
AF_{ac}^{as} &= ABS\left(T_{ac}/4 - t_{ac}^{as}\right)\\
AF_{ac}^{dv} &= ABS\left(T_{ac}/4 - t_{ac}^{dv}\right)\\
AF_{ac}^{ac} &= ABS\left(T_{ac}/4 - t_{ac}^{ac}\right)\\
AF_{ac}^{t} &= AF_{ac}^{cn} + AF_{ac}^{as} + AF_{ac}^{dv} + AF_{ac}^{ac}
\end{aligned}$$

Formulas to compute the adaptive flexibility on Active Experimentation in four situations are described below:

$$
\begin{aligned}
AF_{ae}^{cn} &= ABS\left(T_{ae}/4 - t_{ae}^{cn}\right) \\
AF_{ae}^{as} &= ABS\left(T_{ae}/4 - t_{ae}^{as}\right) \\
AF_{ae}^{dv} &= ABS\left(T_{ae}/4 - t_{ae}^{dv}\right) \\
AF_{ae}^{ac} &= ABS\left(T_{ae}/4 - t_{ae}^{ac}\right) \\
AF_{ae}^{t} &= AF_{ae}^{cn} + AF_{ae}^{as} + AF_{ae}^{dv} + AF_{ae}^{ac}
\end{aligned}
$$

Finally, a grand total score (AF^t) was conceived which combined all of the totals for the mode adaptive flexibility scores.

$$AF^t = AF_{ae}^t + AF_{ae}^t + AF_{ae}^t + AF_{ae}^t$$

Adaptive flexibility in each adaptive mode would be expected to be relatively independent of adaptive flexibility in the other three adaptive modes. If any relationship exists among the different adaptive flexibility scores, it would be that the distribution of adaptive flexibility would be shared rather equally among all four adaptive modes. In addition, adaptive flexibility on each dimension, abstract-concrete and active-reflective, is positively related, i.e. adaptive flexibility on AC relates positively to adaptive flexibility on CE and adaptive flexibility on AE relates positively to adaptive flexibility on RO. This suggests that as a person is flexible in one adaptive mode, he/she tends to be adaptively flexible in the dialectically related adaptive mode. On the other hand, adaptive flexibility in a mode from one dimension does not relate to adaptive flexibility in a mode from another dimension, i.e. adaptive flexibility in the abstract-concrete dimension does not relate to adaptive flexibility in the active-reflective dimension. Moreover, it should be noted that these scores do not take into account the direction of the person's adaptation to a given situation demand but simply the degree of variation in adaptive modes from situation to situation, since adaptive flexibility is composed of both movement toward the presures of a situation and movement in other directions (Kolb 1984).

In summary, five variables were calculated from the ASI: adaptive flexibility on each of the four learning modes (CE, RO, AC, and AE): CEAF, ROAF, ACAF, and AEAF and total adaptive flexibility: TAF.

3.3.2.2 Comparing the Results of the ASI with the LSI

After respondents have completed the LSI and the ASI, it should be useful to compare his/her overall learning style preferences from the ASI with those of the LSI. When comparing the respondent's responses from the ASI with the LSI, the shapes of the two profiles should be similar. The respondent's dominant preference for a particular quadrant or for two quadrants should appear the same

(Kolb 1984; Boyatzis and Kolb 1993). If they do not, there are two possible explanations. First, if the respondent has taken the LSI a long time ago (e.g. several months) before he/she takes the ASI, it is possible that the respondent's learning style has changed. It would be better that the respondent takes the LSI again and compares the results with his/her previous assessment. A second possibility may result from the different structure of the two inventories (Kolb 1984). The LSI assesses overall preferences regardless of the settings. The ASI requires the respondent to respond to his/her approach to learning based upon eight specific settings. If the respondent has a strong overall learning preference, it is conceivable that the respondent completed the LSI thinking about only one or two types of learning situations. The ASI forces the respondent to respond to four major types of learning situations, not merely the ones the respondent may choose on his/her own. In this case, the LSI probably reflects the respondent's overall learning preference while the ASI offers information about the respondent's reactions to a variety of situations.

Learning flexibilities and inflexibilities can be determined by examining the respondent's pattern of responses to the ASI. These patterns illustrate the combinations of styles which the respondent prefers (Boyatzis and Kolb 1993). If the respondent's scores, i.e. adaptive flexibility, on CE, RO, AC, and AE near, this suggests that his/her even bias or flexibility toward using all four learning styles equally throughout all four situations. On the other hand, if the respondent's scores on CE, RO, AC, and AE vary, for example, 20 for CE and 18 for RO but 6 for AC and 4 for AE, this suggests that in various learning situations, the respondent demonstrates a flexibility regarding Concrete Experience and Reflective Observation. It also suggests that in these learning situations, the respondent resists using, or demonstrates an inflexibility regarding Abstract Conceptualization and Active Experimentation. These patterns also represent the types of learning situations the respondent finds interesting or boring. In other words, the respondent learns better in some situations than others (Boyatzis and Kolb 1993).

In addition to overall flexibility and inflexibility, it is important to analyze a respondent's response to the stimulus, or pressures, of the learning situations, i.e. the directionality of adaptability. By examining a respondent's profiles of the four learning situations, we can determine not only whether the respondent's learning style changes from one situation to the next, but also how different situations elicit different approaches to adapting. The respondent can respond by using the learning styles demanded by the situation, or by implementing alternative styles. Either approach can be effective, depending upon whether he/she chooses to respond to what the circumstances call for, or opt to change the situation by using s different set of learning styles (Boyatzis and Kolb 1993). Research in Adaptive learning styles has shown that moving toward the needs of the situation reflects adaptability to the immediate situation; moving away from the pressures represents integrative flexibility (Kolb 1984; Boyatzis and Kolb 1993). Each of these has benefits. For example, a person could approach an acting situation by responding to its immediate demand (AE and CE), or he/she may choose to confront the situation from a thinking perspective (AC and RO), generating several theories on how the situation could be resolved, as opposed to jumping in with an experimental 'hands-on' approach.

Finally, when we look at a respondent's answering profile, we can identify styles he/she uses or avoids regardless of the situational demand, i.e. overuse and underuse of learning styles. An overused style may represent a 'strength' that the respondent has developed over a period of time, conceivably under different circumstances, such as in a prior job or in an educational setting. The respondent's skill in using this style may lead him/her to turn to it when a less developed style is required or would be more productive. Over-reliance on a particular style, however, may prevent the development of a currently 'weaker' style, thus diminishing the opportunity for practice, competence, and increased confidence in its use. A respondent's answering profile may indicate or confirm an awareness that certain situations are more difficult for him/her to adapt to successfully. In other words, the respondent may be competent in the use of the style suggested for a particular situation, but responds by using an alternative style. This phenomenon sometimes occurs through misinterpreting a situation, or as a result of a strong environmental influence to overlook the best approach (Boyatzis and Kolb 1993). This adaptive strategy, while effective in the short run, may have long-term consequences that make its value questionable (Kolb 1984).

3.3.3 Tacit Knowledge Inventory for Managers (TKIM)

TKIM is purported to measure knowledge acquired through managerial experience and is made up of 9 scenarios, 3 scenarios for each of the three categories of managerial tacit knowledge. Each scenario comes with around 10 possible solution options. For every possible solution option available, respondents need to rate it based on a Likert Scale from 1 to 7 ('1' refers to extremely bad, '4' refers to neither good nor bad, and '7' refers to extremely good). The scenarios depicted in the TKIM will elicit different responses from different individuals. Theoretically, experts are expected to respond differently from novices due to the content and organization of their tacit knowledge. Empirical research has shown that the TKIM is able to predict success in managers. Performance on the TKIM differentiates individuals on the basis of amount of managerial experience and is related to criteria of managerial success. A sample scenario and its solution options from the TKIM are presented for information below:

Situation 1

You are an executive vice-president in the marketing division of Sherman Electronics, a company that sells audio and video supplies. You have been with Sherman Electronics since finishing college, having spent 13 years in a managerial role in human resources and two years in your present position.

Sherman Electronics has been losing market share for its products steadily over the past five years. Sherman's strength in the past has been introducing new products before its competition, but now its product line seems to be three steps behind the leaders in a rapidly changing market. A strategy of focusing on more stable segments of the market has been aborted because of fierce competition from large overseas companies.

You believe that your lack of knowledge about the latest audio and video products and technology limits your effectiveness. Your schedule is very busy, but you think it is important to catch up on, and keep up with, innovation that affects your industry.

Rate the quality of the following strategies for becoming more knowledgeable about new products and technology on a 1- to 7- point scale						
1	2	3	4	5	6	7
Extremely bad			**Neither good nor bad**			**Extremely good**
1. Ask for a leave of absence to pursue an advanced technical degree						
2. Order a news clipping service (news clipping services provide news from a large number of sources on a given topic)						
3. Subscribe to several technical journals relevant to your manufacturing operations						
4. Subscribes to several consumer-oriented magazines that cover your products						
5. Begin attending trade shows of products in your industry						
6. Ask to sit in on weekly discussions of new product ideas held by the Research and Development division						
7. Attend a series of technical presentations by research scientists from outside the company who are brought in by the Manufacturing Operations division						
8. Hire a staff member whose primary responsibility is to keep you abreast of current trends in your industry						
9. Ask the Engineering division to prepare monthly summary reports of innovative products						
10. Ask for weekly presentations for you and your staff on technical issues by staff in the Research and Development and Manufacturing Operations divisions						

3.3.3.1 Scoring the TKIM

Wagner and Sternberg (1985) first developed the Tacit Knowledge Inventory for Managers (TKIM) by using the critical incident technique and the simulation approach. They defined the scope of managerial tacit knowledge based on the content of a situation. Sternberg et al. (2000) further revised the TKIM by slightly modifying its expresuresion. While an instrument, such as this, can never access the entire spectrum of managerial tacit knowledge, it does, nevertheless, define important aspects against which the learning associated with its acquisition can be explored. The scenarios depicted in the TKIM are designed to elicit different responses from different individuals. Theoretically, successful managers are expected to respond differently from novices due to the content and organization of their tacit knowledge (Wagner and Sternberg 1985). The scenarios presented in the TKIM are work-related situations, each followed by a series of items that are relevant to handling that situation. The instructions given for completing the TKIM requested that respondents briefly scan all of the items and then rate the quality of each item on a Likert Scale from 1 to 7 provided. Instructions to respondents also stressed that there were no 'correct' answers, only different ways to respond to each situation.

The scoring method employed by Wagner (1987) has been recognized for its ability to allow for meaningful comparisons between groups (Sternberg et al. 2000). Before scoring began, respondents' ratings were first transformed. Wagner (1987) observed tacit knowledge scores generated by the prototype method are affected by individual differences in respondents' use of the entire scale. He claimed that because tacit knowledge scores are based on deviation from an expert profile, they would vary with the extent to which a respondent used the entire rating scale. He therefore suggested that the raw data on the tacit knowledge inventory should be transformed by 'standardizing the standard deviation of ratings across response items for subject to the common value of 1.5' (Wagner 1987: 1241). As a result, every entry was transformed to a standardized standard deviation of '1.5' in the present research using the formula below:

$$\left(\left(\left(X_{ij} - X_i\right)/sd_i\right) \times 1.5\right)$$

- Where 'i' is the respondent (for western expatriate managers, i = 1–121; for Chinese managers, i = 1–133)
- Where 'j' is the sequence number of the response items/solution option (j = 1–51)
- Where 'X_i' is the mean across each respondent's response items
- Where 'sd_i' is the standard deviation across each respondent's response items

Armstrong and Mahmud (2008) described the TKIM's scoring instruction in the following detail. First, researchers/test administrators are instructed to develop their own expert/successful group. The mean ratings for each item, i.e. solution option for the scenario, in the measurement are calculated for the expert group in order to form a successful manager's profile. It should be noted that the ratings from the expert group also need to be transformed to a standardized standard deviation of '1.5'. Then, respondent's scores on the TKIM are derived by subtracting their answer for each item from the expert profile for that item. This generates difference scores between the respondents and the expert profile (Sternberg et al. 2000) that can produce either positive or negative values. Some previous researchers (Wagner 1987) have chosen to square these difference scores to remove the polarity, while others have argued that the squaring tends to inflate the value and this affects further calculations (Kerr 1991; Armstrong and Mahmud 2008). Kerr (1991) suggests for the use of absolute values for studies such as those that adopt expert-novice comparisons. The present study adopted the use of absolute values to remove the tacit knowledge scores' polarity.

Values for each of the work-related situations, i.e. scenarios, in the inventory were then summated in order to arrive at a score for each of the three contexts of managing self, managing others, and managing tasks. Summating the scores for each of these sub-scales yields a total score for managerial tacit knowledge. Armstrong and Mahmud's (2008) approach was then adopted where the summated scores for each situation (scenario) were divided by the number of items representing that situation, in order to provide an average value. Averaging was necessary to facilitate meaningful comparisons between the three contexts of managerial tacit knowledge because they were not made up of the same number of items. In summary, nine variables were calculated from the TKIM in the present study: the score for scenario 1, the score for scenario 2, the score for scenario 3, the score for scenario 4, the score for scenario 5, the score for scenario 6, managerial tacit knowledge in managing self, managerial tacit knowledge in managing others, and total managerial tacit knowledge.

3.3.3.2 Criteria for Selecting the Expert Group

The Tacit Knowledge Inventory for Managers (TKIM) requires the identification of an expert profile. A group of expert/successful managers were needed to create a profile against which the research sample could be compared to. This is a fundamental requirement of TKIM adopted in the study. The prototypical scoring system of TKIM requires scores from the respondents to be compared against the scores of the expert/successful managers' profile (Armstrong and Mahmud 2008). Respondents with TKIM scores close to the scores of the expert profile are deemed to have a higher level of accumulated managerial tacit knowledge. Wagner (1987) used the term 'prototype/prototypical' to describe the quantification of tacit knowledge by 'comparing a subject's response item ratings to a prototype derived from the mean response item ratings of an expert group'. Therefore, the term prototype refers to a mean rating of the expert group. Theoretically, expert managers are expected to respond differently to 'lower level' managers on each test item due to the content and organization of their tacit knowledge. Many previous studies have been conducted on comparing the responses of different groups of people to scenarios depicted in TKIM against scores obtained from an expert group within that particular field, such as bank managers, managers in Malaysian public sector (Armstrong and Mahmud 2008; Wagner and Stemberg 1985). This is referred to as the 'expert–novice' comparison method.

With regard to the criteria for selecting the expert group, previous studies of tacit knowledge in the professions have identified expert managers as those who are senior, highly successful, and very experienced managers (Kerr 1991). Existent research has also shown that tacit knowledge is context-specific (Sternberg and Grigorenko 2001) and has a certain lifespan. This means that tacit knowledge which brought success to individuals within a given work context may not be a suitable indicator of successful management in a different context or in a different time-frame. The selection criteria adopted in the present research for the expert group builds on those adopted in previous studies. Our expert group consists of 25 successful global managers who are currently assigned in China. The study selects the expert group, successful global managers, by considering only those who comply with strict criteria laid out below and within the same work context as the participants being studied (i.e., within international assignments in China) as well as within a limited frame of time. Other important criteria were that:

- First, they must have very high status in western MNCs' subsidiaries in China. All managers in our expert group have job title as one of Chief Executive Officer (CEO); Chief Operations Officer (COO); Chief Financial Officer (CFO); Chief Information Officer (CIO); Human Resource Director (HRD); Operations Director (OD); Marketing Director (MD).
- Second, they must have significant length of service at a senior position. In our expert group, the lengths of service at a senior position range from 8 to 19 years and average at about 13 years.
- Third, they must have experienced at least two international assignments, except the current one in China. In our expert group, the amount of international assignments experienced range from 2 to 7 and average at near to 4 times.
- Fourth, they must have been assigned in China for more than 5 years. In our expert group, the lengths of international assignment experience in China range from 6 to 20 years and average at about 14 years.

3.3.4 Expatriate Adjustment Scale (EAS)

Expatriate adjustment has been conceptualized as multi-dimensional. The expatriate adjustment scale assesses three dimensions of expatriate adjustment and consists of 14 items: 7 items for general adjustment, 4 items for interaction/socialization adjustment, and 3 items for work adjustment. The general adjustment items examined such things as the expatriates' adjustment to living conditions, housing, and food. The interaction adjustment items investigated the expatriates' adjustment to socializing with host country nationals. The work adjustment items examined the expatriates' adjustment to the requirements of the new job position. For each item, respondents indicate their own degree of adjustment on a 5-point scale. Rating anchors range from '1 (very unadjusted)' to '5 (very well adjusted)'. For example, one item asks expatriates to rate their own degree of adaptation to a number of specific general living conditions. This item from the EAS is presented for information below:

1. Living conditions in general	1	2	3	4	5

Although this widely used scale has been criticized for being merely a statistical construct with elements that are not well-defined or discrete, this measurement has been consistently validated (Selmer 2006). Furthermore, it has been found to be structurally equivalent with a good fit when applied on culturally dissimilar samples providing evidence of its construct validity.

3.3.4.1 Scoring the EAS

The expatriate adjustment scale assesses three dimensions of expatriate adjustment and consists of 14 items: 7 items for general adjustment, 4 items for interaction adjustment, and 3 items for work adjustment. The items for general adjustment are: item 1: living conditions in general; item 3: food; item 4: shopping; item 6: entertainment/recreation facilities and opportunities; item 7: health care facilities. It should be noted that item 2 and item 5 in general adjustment are removed base on the results of SEM analysis in Chap. 4. The four items for socialization adjustment are: item 8: socializing with host nationals; item 9: interacting with host nationals on a day-to-day basis; item 10: interacting with host nationals outside of work; item 11: speaking with host nationals. The three items for work adjustment are: item 12: specific job responsibilities; item 13: performance standards and expectations; item 14: supervisory responsibilities.

Values for each of the three dimensions in the EAS are first summated in order to arrive at a score for each of the three dimensions of expatriate adjustment: general adjustment, socialization adjustment, and work adjustment. The summated scores for each dimension were divided by the number of items representing that dimension, in order to provide an average value. Averaging was necessary to facilitate meaningful comparisons between the three dimensions because they were not made up of the same number of items. Finally, summating the scores for each of these subscales yields a total score for cross-cultural adjustment. In summary, four variables were calculated from the EAS: general adjustment, socialization adjustment, work adjustment, and overall adjustment.

3.3.5 Demographic Questionnaires

3.3.5.1 Demographic Questionnaire for Western Expatriate Managers

Research participants (western expatriate managers) in the present study were asked to provide information about ten items such as: (1) nationality; (2) gender; (3) age; (4) international family: whether any member of his/her family (parents or spouse) come from different countries; (5) the length of the current assignment (how many months); (6) their experience of previous overseas assignments (No. of previous assignment and overall duration); (7) the experience of studies abroad or the acquisition of degrees from overseas schools; (8) the highest level of educational achievement; (9) hierarchical job positions; (10) organizational job functions. The above 10 items are illustrated in the Appendix as the demographic questionnaire in English for western expatriate managers and are described as following variables in detail.

1. Nationality: the first question is related to nationality: which country the respondent's passport was issued from. All western expatriate managers need to indicate their nationalities.
2. Gender: the second question is related to gender. It describes a categorical variable of Male or Female.
3. Age: the third demographic question asks western expatriates to choose an appropriate box showing their ages as five levels, each of which describes a 10-year interval, except the 60's.
4. International family: the fourth question is regarding whether any member of the expatriate's family (parents or spouse) comes from different countries. Western expatriate managers are asked to choose one of the following three categories: No, Yes but not from Greater China, and Yes and from Greater China.
5. Length of time spent in China: the fifth question that western expatriate need to answer is to state how long they have been assigned in China for their present overseas assignment. This item is calculated as a total of months.
6. Previous overseas assignment experience: the sixth question asks of western expatriate managers is how many overseas assignments they have experience except their current assignment. Because 65 % of the sample did not have overseas assignment experience, the results of this question were translated into a categorical variable: those with overseas assignment experience in the past versus those without such experience.

7. Overseas study experience: the seventh question describes a categorical variable of No or Yes.
8. Educational achievement: the eighth question asks western expatriate managers to choose an appropriate box showing their highest levels of educational achievement as four levels: PhD, Master, Bachelor, and Others.
9. Hierarchical job positions: the ninth question is related to hierarchical job positions in their organizations. Western expatriate managers are asked to choose one of five hierarchical job positions: the president/CEO, a senior manager, a middle manager, a junior manager, and others. As a result, hierarchical job positions were categorized as four levels: the president/CEO, a senior manager, a middle manager, and a junior manager.
10. Organizational job functions: the tenth question asks western expatriate managers to choose one of six job functions: Human Resource Management/general administration, operations/production, sales/marketing, engineering/design, finance/accounting, and others.

3.3.5.2 Demographic Questionnaire for Host Chinese Managers

Research participants (host Chinese managers) in the present study were asked to provide information about nine items such as: (1) gender; (2) age; (3) their experience of previous overseas assignments [No. of previous assignment and overall duration (how many months)]; (4) the experience of studies abroad or the acquisition of degrees from overseas schools; (5) the highest level of educational achievement; (6) hierarchical job positions; (7) the length of time in a managerial role; (8) organizational job functions; (9) the total length of time working in western MNCs including the current one and previous working experience in western MNCs. The above 9 items are illustrated in Appendix as the demographic questionnaire in Chinese for host Chinese managers and are described as following variables in detail.

1. Gender: the first question is related to gender. It describes a categorical variable of Male or Female.
2. Age: the second demographic question asks local Chinese expatriates to choose an appropriate box showing their ages as five levels, each of which describes a 10-year interval, except the 60's.
3. Previous overseas assignment experience: the third question asks of Chinese managers is how many previous overseas assignments they have experienced. All host Chinese managers participated in the present study had no previous international assignment experience.
4. Overseas study experience: the fourth question describes a categorical variable of No or Yes.

5. Educational achievement: the fifth question asks local Chinese managers to choose an appropriate box showing their highest levels of educational achievement as four levels: PhD, Master, Bachelor, and Others.
6. Hierarchical job positions: the sixth question is related to hierarchical job positions in their organizations. Host Chinese managers are asked to choose one of six hierarchical job positions: the president/CEO, a senior manager, a middle manager, a junior manager, an ordinary employee, and others. As a result, hierarchical job positions were categorized as three levels: a senior manager, a middle manager, and a junior manager.
7. Length of time in a managerial role: the seventh question that host Chinese managers need to answer is to state how long they have been in managerial roles. They are asked to choose one of the following five levels: less than one year, 1–3 years, 3–5 years, 5–10 years, and above 10 years.
8. Organizational job functions: the eighth question asks host Chinese managers to choose one of nine job functions: Operations, Human Resource Management, Finance, General administration, Marketing, Sales, IT, Customer service, and others. As a result, organizational job functions were categorized as six levels: Human Resource Management/general administration, operations/production, sales/marketing, engineering/design, finance/accounting, and others.
9. Total length of time working in western MNCs: the ninth question that host Chinese managers need to answer is to state how long they have been working in western MNCs. They are asked to choose one of the following five levels: less than three years, 3–5 years, 5–10 years, 10–15 years, and above 15 years.

3.3.6 Translation Procedures of Research Instruments

The sample of this study is composed of western expatriate managers and host Chinese managers. The official language is Chinese in China. Therefore, the present study needs to administer instruments that are translated into Chinese for host Chinese managers' better understanding of the meaning of each question. Chinese instruments also help local Chinese managers take less time to answer than foreign language ones. For these reasons, the assessment measure of the TKIM for Chinese managers was translated into Chinese. It should be noted that the present study did not need to translate the LSI into Chinese, because the LSI has its own official Chinese version. The Chinese version of the LSI has been conducted in several previous research studies (e.g. Yuen and Lee 1994; Auyeung and Sands 1996; Fridland 2002). The researcher first contacted the contact person of Kolb's Hay Group to apply for the electronic copy of the Chinese version of the LSI and the permission to use it for academic purposes. The researcher then filled the application form accordingly and submitted it online to Hay Group. Hay Group then approved the application for the present study and returned the electronic copy of the Chinese version of the LSI.

For cross-cultural research, Brislin et al. (1973) recommended three techniques to translate the research instrument into other languages that yields equivalence of its original version. These techniques include: comparing the meaning between the original and translated version, comparing the meaning between the original and back-translated version, and using a test-retest method by which to statistically analyze the data of both versions collected from a sample of bilinguals. These recommended techniques were also used in Armstrong and Mahmud's (2008) study about managerial tacit knowledge of Malaysian managers to translate the TKIM into Malay.

With regard to the TKIM, the researcher used all the three techniques in the translation process. The expresuresions in the TKIM are relatively straightforward so that the inventory will allow respondents to understand and answer the questionnaire with ease. For this reason, the translation process of the TKIM focused on the two methods of comparing the meaning between the English and Chinese version and comparing the meaning between the original English and back-translated version. The process of making the Chinese version of the TKIM had three steps. The first phase represents the comparing of meaning between two language versions. It included the translation of the researcher and a professional translator between Chinese and English, David, and a meeting with Dr. Zurina Hamid, who has extensive knowledge of the TKIM. David is an experienced translator with a Master degree of translation and has successfully translated many English works into Chinese. Dr. Zurina Hamid completed her doctoral research in managerial tacit knowledge in 2012 and adopted the TKIM as one of the research instruments during her field studies in Malaysia. In the meeting with David and Dr. Zurina Hamid, we compared each item of both versions thoroughly. The discussion focused on three points: correct words, natural tones, and elimination of socially desirable words and phrases, and then resulted in a revision of the Chinese version of TKIM.

The second phase refers to the test-retest method of statistical analysis. For this test, the researcher first administered this revised version of TKIM to 30 Chinese bilinguals that consist of 10 undergraduate students and 20 business managers, then followed by the English version of TKIM five days later. This administrative interval was recommended by Yamazaki's (2005) cross-cultural study. The test-retest analysis about collected data involves Pearson's correlation and paired-sample t-test as statistical techniques. Results of the test-retest analysis showed that correlation coefficients of the nine variables in the TKIM ranged from 0.93 to 0.84 with a significance level of 0.01 at two-tailed. Each coefficient represents a given scenario as follows: 0.89 of scenario 1, 0.84 of scenario 2, 0.92 of scenario 3, 0.89 of scenario 4, 0.90 of scenario 5, 0.91 of scenario 6, 0.87 of managerial tacit knowledge in managing self, 0.90 of managerial tacit knowledge in managing others, and 0.88 of total managerial tacit knowledge. The paired-sample t-test of the TKIM scores showed no significant difference between each pair of the English and Chinese version. Table 3.9 displays the results of the Pearson's correlation and Table 3.10 illustrate the results of the paired sample t-test.

Table 3.9 Results of the Pearson's correlation between English and Chinese translated TKIM

English TKIM	Chinese translated TKIM								
	S1	S2	S3	S4	S5	S6	Self	Others	Total
S1	0.89**								
S2		0.84**							
S3			0.92**						
S4				0.89**					
S5					0.90**				
S6						0.91**			
Self							0.87**		
Others								0.90**	
Total									0.88**

N = 30 Chinese bilinguals
**: $p < 0.01$ (two-tailed)

Table 3.10 Results of the paired sample t-test of English and Chinese translated TKIM

		Mean	S.D.	Significant levels English versus Chinese
S1	English	0.608	10.14	0.665
	Chinese	0.592	10.21	
S2	English	0.448	9.31	0.489
	Chinese	0.460	9.07	
S3	English	0.610	9.33	0.495
	Chinese	0.618	9.38	
S4	English	0.601	6.89	0.551
	Chinese	0.592	7.01	
S5	English	0.532	11.05	0.607
	Chinese	0.559	11.45	
S6	English	0.588	7.92	0.663
	Chinese	0.569	8.31	
Self	English	0.580	10.84	0.561
	Chinese	0.577	10.29	
Others	English	0.549	7.72	0.461
	Chinese	0.561	8.12	
Total	English	1.129	12.41	0.477
	Chinese	1.223	12.84	

N = 30 Chinese bilinguals

In addition, after the test-retest, the researcher had an interview with three participants so that the researcher could know whether there was any expressions that were difficult for them to understand. Their views were very useful to reshape the content of the Chinese TKIM and its instruction in Chinese as well. The final phase was to compare the meaning between the original and back-translated version in English. Another professional translator between Chinese and English, Deng Dong, who did not know the TKIM in English and the purpose of the job, was simply asked to translate the reshaped Chinese version into English. Then, languages used in the back-translated English version were reviewed in a meeting with Professor Steve Armstrong, my PhD supervisor. There was no discrepancy between the original and back-translated TKIM in English. The latest Chinese version that is consistent with the back-translated TKIM was discussed again with David and Dr. Zurina Hamid for a final confirmation of this translation. Appendix D-2 illustrates the Chinese version of TKIM that was adopted for this study.

3.3.7 Reliability and Validity

3.3.7.1 Reliability

Reliability analysis is used to evaluate the stability and consistency of the measurement items in each latent construct (Saunders et al. 2009). This research uses Cronbach alpha analyses to measure the reliability and confidence of the question.

(a) Learning style inventory (LSI)
Kolb's (1999) Learning Style Inventory (LSI) was employed to examine individuals' learning styles. This is one of the most frequently used instruments to assess learning styles (Yamazakin and Kayes 2007) and has been widely used to examine learning in cross-cultural settings (Yamazaki 2005). Previous studies have demonstrated strong test-retest reliabilities with coefficients for the four learning modes reaching 0.91–0.99 (Yamazaki and Kayes 2007) and high internal consistencies for the four primary scores of between alpha = 0.72–0.80. Internal reliability figures in the present study were: alpha = 0.74 (RO); alpha = 0.77 (CE); alpha = 0.72 (AC); and alpha = 0.73 (AE).

(b) Adaptive style inventory (ASI)
Boyatzis and Kolb's (1993) Adaptive Style Inventory (ASI) was used to measure the extent to which subjects' learning styles change depending on the demands of different situations—referred to as adaptive flexibility. The ASI is divided into four situations that the respondent has to 'adapt' to. These situations correspond to the four learning styles: diverging situations, assimilating situations, converging

situations, and accommodating situations. Internal reliability of the ASI in the present study was: alpha = 0.79.

(c) Tacit Knowledge Inventory for Managers (TKIM)
Wagner and Sternberg's (1985) Tacit Knowledge Inventory for Managers (TKIM) was administered to all subjects in order to determine their levels of accumulated managerial tacit knowledge (LAMTK)—believed to be critical for predicting performance (Forsythe et al. 1998). A brief explanation, together with sample items for the TKIM is given in Appendix A together with the scoring regime. Theoretically, expert/successful managers are expected to respond differently to novices due to the content and organization of their tacit knowledge. The majority of previous studies have focussed on comparing the responses of different groups of people such as business students and business managers to scenarios depicted in the TKIM against scores obtained from a successful group (e.g. business experts) within that particular field, referred to as the "expert-novice comparison". Internal reliability figures in the present study were: alpha = 0.82 (Managing self); alpha = 0.85 (Managing others); and alpha = 0.88 (Overall levels of managerial tacit knowledge).

(d) Expatriate adjustment scale
The present research used the scale developed by Black and Stephens (1989) which uses 14 item statements to measure managers' self-estimated level of adjustment. Respondents indicated how well adjusted they were to their respective host locations in China on a scale ranging from 1 = 'not adjusted very well' to 5 = 'very well adjusted'. This instrument has been consistently validated and has been found to be structurally equivalent with a good fit when applied to culturally dissimilar samples (Selmer 2006). The three sub-scales of general adjustment, interaction adjustment, and work adjustment have consistently demonstrated high internal reliability (e.g. Black and Stephens 1989; Selmer 2002, 2006). Reliability of the three dimensions in the present study was: alpha = 0.89; alpha = 0.81; and alpha = 0.90 respectively.

3.3.7.2 Validity

The validity of a measurement instrument can be measured by the degree to which the instrument measures accurately what it is supposed to measure. Validity is important to make sure that data collected are representing the intention of the research. The importance of understanding of validity has a direct effect on the research findings. If the study lacks construct validity, the findings are meaningless, destroying also the internal and external validity of the findings. The validity of instruments used in this research has been tested in various studies. The tacit knowledge inventory has been used in tests for over 20 years. The Tacit Knowledge Inventory for Managers (TKIM) by Wagner and Sternberg (1985) is a test of tacit knowledge or practical know how (Wagner 1987). This inventory is used purposely to identify individuals whose tacit knowledge indicates the potential for successful performance in managerial or executive careers (Wagner and Sternberg 1991). This inventory presents respondents with scenarios that require them to choose alternative actions from a list of solutions. Wagner and Sternberg's inventory (1991) has been tested in five studies to examine the criterion related validity of their tacit knowledge measures in academic and business settings. They found moderate correlation between their measure and a variety of criteria and some of them were considered as job performance measures.

Experiential learning theory (ELT) research is highly interdisciplinary and addressing learning and educational issues in many fields. An analysis of the 1004 entries in the 1999 bibliography shows 207 studies in management, 430 in education, 104 in information science, 101 in psychology, 72 in medicine, 63 in nursing, 22 in accounting and 5 in law.

3.4 Ethical Considerations

This research deals with human participants for sampling and data collection. Hence, following appropriate research ethics is important. According to Bryman and Bell (2007), ethical considerations include four important principles: (1) Researchers must not bring any sort of harm to participants; (2) researchers must protect participants from invasion of privacy; (3) researchers must conduct their studies without any sort of deception; (4) researchers must protect participants' data. This research has closely followed Hull University Business School's procedures and regulations for ensuring ethical research and the research was formally approved by the Business School's ethics committee. The directory of MNCs in China (published by the Chinese government) was used to guide the identification and selection of the research samples. This research chose western MNCs which have subsidiaries in China. The researcher first phoned and emailed the manager chosen to be in charge of the survey distribution to make an appointment with them. Then the researcher visited them to explain the nature of the research in a face-to-face conversation. According to Fisher and Downes (2008), a major ethical dilemma in management research when negotiating with organizations, is securing the right to privacy, access to personal records and confidential information, and informant consent. This research took account of all of these issues.

During data collection, the participants' rights, especially their right not to answer the questionnaire was respected in all cases. Participants' privacy was given high priority. To avoid any concerns the participants might have with regard to deception the researcher explained very clearly the research purpose and what data the researcher wanted from them. This study also comprised semi-structured interviews with senior managers. To ensure that the researcher interviewed these managers in an ethical way, an early appointment was made to explain to participants that they had the right to accept or decline the request to be interviewed, or to withdraw from the interview process at any time. After data collection, participants' data was protected by maintaining anonymity. The researcher changed their names into codes and all data was saved in digital files and secured by passwords. Privacy of participants' information was maintained and therefore, nobody else could recognise participants or data sources.

Appendix A: A Cover Letter to Western Expatriates

Dear Sir/Madam,

I am a PhD student from the University of Hull in the UK conducting research into ways in which expatriate managers learn, adapt, and develop when faced with completing overseas assignments. Very little is currently known about this subject and we would be grateful if you would help us with this research by completing the online survey.

The survey will take approximately **35 min** to complete and results will be kept strictly confidential. If you would like to receive individual feedback we will provide you with a report as soon as the data has been processed. This report, which we believe will be beneficial to both your personal development and future career activities, will contain feedback on the following:

- ☐ The way you learn and how you deal with ideas and day-to-day situations (learning style)
- ☐ The way you adapt to different situations (adaptive style)

Please provide your email address below if you want to receive the result report (or attach a business card).

☐ Email address: ....

We are acutely aware of how valuable you time is but your participation in this research would be highly appreciated.

Thank you in anticipation.

Yours faithfully,

Yan Li, PhD Candidate (yan.li@2010.hull.ac.uk; +86 18273180701)

Professor Steve Armstrong, Supervisor (s.j.armstrong@hull.ac.uk)

Appendix B: Respondent Profile

1) Nationality: ________________________________

2) Your gender:

   □male □female

3) Your age

   □20-29 □30-39 □40-49 □50-60 □over 60

4) Your marital status:

   □married □single

5) If married, has your family accompanied you on this assignment?

   □yes □no

   If yes, how has your family adapted to China?

   □not at all □badly □undecided □well □very well

6) When did you begin your current assignment in China?

   ______________(Year) ______________(Month)

7) How many previous overseas assignments have you experienced and what is the overall total duration?

   No. of previous assignments:_______ Overall duration (months):_________

8) Have you ever studied outside of your home country?

   □No □Yes (Where: ________________________)

9) What is your highest level of educational achievement?

   □PhD □Master □Bachelor □Others ________________________

10) What is your job function in your organization? Please check one of the followings.

   □President/CEO □senior manager □middle manager

   □junior manager □other: __________________(job function)

11) Please describe the functional area of your work (e.g. human resource management, operations, sales & marketing, engineering etc.): ___________________________

   ____

Appendix C: Learning Style Inventory

Below are 12 sentences with a choice of endings. **Rank** the endings for each sentence according to how well you think each one fits with how you would go about learning something. Try to recall some recent situations where you had to learn something new, such as in your job. Then, using the spaces provided, rank a "**4**" for the sentence ending that describes how you learn best, down to a "**1**" for the sentence ending that seems least like the way you learn.

Please rank all the endings for each sentence unit.

Example of completed sentence set:

1.When I learn:	I am happy___*2*______	I am fast ___*1*___
	I am logical ___*4*___	I am careful __*3*___

Remember:

4------------------→3	------------------→2	----------------→1	
Most like you	More like you	Less like you	Least like you

1. When I learn:	I like to deal with my feelings __________	I like to think about ideas ____________
	I like to be doing things ____________	I like to watch and listen ____________
2. I learn best when:	I listen and watch carefully ____________	I rely on logical thinking ____________
	I trust my hunches and feelings____________	I work hard to get things done____________
3. When I am learning:	I tend to reason things out ______________	I am responsible about things__________
	I am quiet and reserved ______________	I have strong feelings and reactions________
4. I learn by:	Feeling____________	Doing____________
	Watching____________	Thinking____________
5. When I learn:	I am open to new experiences________	I look at all sides of issues__________

	I like to analyze things, break them down into their parts_______________	I like to try things out_____________
6. When I am learning:	I am an observing person ____________________	I am an active person __________________
	I am an intuitive person ____________________	I am a logical person __________________
7. I learn best from:	Observation_________	Personal relationships __________________
	Rational theories______	A chance to try out and practice________
8. When I learn:	I like to see results from my work____________	I like ideas and theories __________________
	I take my time before acting_______________	I feel personally involved in things___________
9. I learn best when:	I rely on my observations ____________________	I rely on my feelings __________________
	I can try things out for myself_______________	I rely on my ideas __________________
10. When I am learning:	I am a reserved person _____________________	I am an accepting person ___________________
	I am a responsible person _____________________	I am a rational person ___________________
11.When I learn:	I get involved__________	I like to observe______
	I evaluate things________	I like to be active_____
12. I learn best when:	I analyze ideas__________	I am receptive and open-minded_________
	I am careful____________	I am practical_________

4-----------------→*3*	-----------------→*2*	-----------------→*1*	
Most like you	More like you	Less like you	Least like you

Appendix D: Tacit Knowledge Inventory for Managers

"Tacit knowledge" can be understood as work related know-how that is acquired through experience and not directly taught. This task presents work-related situations, each followed by a series of items that are relevant to handling that situation. For each situation, briefly scan all of the items and then rate the quality of each item on the 1 (extremely bad) to 7 (extremely good) scale provided. Try to use the entire scale when you respond, although it is not necessary that you do so for each situation. For example, you may decide that none of the items listed for a particular question is good, or you may decide that they all are. There are, of course, no "correct" answers.

Please respond to every item, and when you have finished, check to be sure you have not inadvertently omitted a response.

Situation 1

You are an executive vice-president in the marketing division of Sherman Electronics, a company that sells audio and video supplies. You have been with Sherman Electronics since finishing college, having spent 13 years in a managerial role in human resources and two years in your present position.

Sherman Electronics has been losing market share for its products steadily over the past five years. Sherman's strength in the past has been introducing new products before its competition, but now its product line seems to be three steps behind the leaders in a rapidly changing market. A strategy of focusing on more stable segments of the market has been aborted because of fierce competition from large overseas companies.

Rate the quality of the following strategies for becoming more knowledgeable about new products and technology on a 1- to 7- point scale						
1	2	3	4	5	6	7
Extremely bad			**Neither good nor bad**			**Extremely good**
1. Ask for a leave of absence to pursue an advanced technical degree						
2. Order a news clipping service (news clipping services provide news from a large number of sources on a given topic)						
3. Subscribe to several technical journals relevant to your manufacturing operations						
4. Subscribes to several consumer-oriented magazines that cover your products						
5. Begin attending trade shows of products in your industry						

(continued)

(continued)

6. Ask to sit in on weekly discussions of new product ideas held by the Research and Development division
7. Attend a series of technical presentations by research scientists from outside the company who are brought in by the Manufacturing Operations division
8. Hire a staff member whose primary responsibility is to keep you abreast of current trends in your industry
9. Ask the Engineering division to prepare monthly summary reports of innovative products
10. Ask for weekly presentations for you and your staff on technical issues by staff in the Research and Development and Manufacturing Operations divisions

Situation 2

An employee who reports to one of your subordinates has asked to talk with you about waste, poor management practices, and possible violations of both departmental policy and the law on the part of your subordinate. You have been in your present position only a year, but in that time you have had no indications of trouble about the subordinate in question. Neither you nor your department has an "open door" policy, so it is expected that employees should take their concerns to their immediate supervisors before bringing a matter to the attention of anyone else.

Rate the quality of the following things you are considering doing in this situation on a 1- to 7- point scale						
1	**2**	**3**	**4**	**5**	**6**	**7**
Extremely bad			**Neither good nor bad**			**Extremely good**
11. Refuse to meet with the employee unless the individual first discusses the matter with your subordinate						
12. Meet with the employee but only with your subordinate present						
13. Schedule a meeting with the employee and then with your subordinate to get both sides of the story						
14. Meet with the employee and then investigate the allegations if an investigation appears warranted before talking with your subordinate						
15. Find out more information about the employee, if you can, before making any decisions						
16. Refuse to meet with the employee and inform your subordinate that the employee has attempted to sidestep the chain of command						

(continued)

(continued)

17. Meet with your subordinate first before deciding whether to meet with the employee
18. Reprimand the employee for ignoring the chain of command
19. Ask a senior colleague whom you respect for advice about what to do in this situation
20. Turn the matter over to an assistant

Situation 3

You have just completed your most important project ever, which involved automating the department's warehouses. You have worked many evenings and weekend days over the last six months on this project. You are pleased with your performance because, despite adversity, the project was completed at the projected cost and on time. Near the project's end, it seemed likely that you were going to need additional time and money. But, through hard work on your part, and by pushing some of your people very hard, you met both time deadlines and cost projections.

In a meeting, your supervisor (having been in his position for six months), brings up the topic of your performance on the project. Expecting lavish praise, and perhaps even discussion of a possible increase in responsibility, you are stunned by his evaluation of your performance, which is entirely negative. He states that some of your subordinates have complained to him directly about their treatment at your hands in the last phase of project completion. He questions your ability to manage others, and wonders aloud about your ability to lead others. He says nothing positive about the fact that you completed the project on time and at cost under adverse circumstances, nor about how hard you worked on the project.

Rate the quality of the following things you might do in this situation on a 1- to 7- point scale						
1	**2**	**3**	**4**	**5**	**6**	**7**
Extremely bad			**Neither good nor bad**			**Extremely good**
21. Admit that you perhaps were too hard on your workers, but state that in your judgment, the importance of meeting the deadline and budget projection made your actions necessary						
22. Expresures disappointment with your performance appraisal, and state that you think it is one-sided						
23. Accept the criticism and explain how you will behave differently in the future						

(continued)

(continued)

24. Try to find out if anything else is behind this overly negative evaluation
25. Begin looking for a new position
26. Discuss with your supervisor specific examples of where he thinks you went wrong in dealing with the project, and how he would have handled it more effectively
27. Ask your supervisor to give you a second chance, resolving to yourself to keep him better informed about your activities in the future
28. Ask your supervisor to help you develop your skills at managing others
29. Seek the advice of others you trust in the department about what you should do
30. Admit you might have made some mistakes, but be sure your supervisor is aware of all that you accomplished and the adverse circumstances that you faced

Situation 4

Rate the quality of the following strategies for handling the day-to-day work of a manager on a 1- to 7-point scale.

1	2	3	4	5	6	7
Extremely bad			**Neither good nor bad**			**Extremely good**
31. Think in terms of tasks accomplished rather than hours spent working						
32. Use a daily list of goals arranged according to your priorities						
33. Reward yourself upon completion of important tasks for the day						
34. Be in charge of all phase of every task or project you are involved in						
35. Take frequent but short breaks (i.e., a quick walk to the mail room) throughout the day						
36. Only delegate inconsequential tasks, since you cannot guarantee that the tasks will be done properly and on time unless you do them yourself						
37. Do only what you are in the mood to do to maximize the quality of your work						
38. Take every opportunity to get feedback on early drafts of your work						
39. Set your own deadlines in addition to externally imposed ones						
40. Do not spend much time planning the best way to do something because the best way to do something may not be apparent until after you have begun doing it						

Situation 5
You are looking for a new project to tackle in the coming year. You have considered a number of possible projects and desire to pick the project that would be best for you.

Rate the importance of the following considerations when selecting new projects on a 1- to 7-point scale						
1	**2**	**3**	**4**	**5**	**6**	**7**
Extremely bad			**Neither good nor bad**			**Extremely good**
71. The project is the one my immediate superior most desires to be completed						
72. Doing the project would require my developing skills that may enhance my future career success						
73. The project should attract the attention of the local media						
74. Doing the project should prove to be fun						
75. The risk of making a mistake is virtually nonexistent						
76. The project will require my interacting with senior executives whom I would like to get to know better						
77. The project is valued by my superior even though it is not valued by me						
78. The project will enable me to demonstrate my talents that others may not be aware of						
79. The project is in an area with which I have a lot of experience						
80. The project is the one I most want to do						

Situation 6
You and a co-worker jointly are responsible for completing a report on a new project by the end of the week. You are uneasy about this assignment because he has a reputation for not meeting deadlines. The problem does not appear to be lack of effort. Rather, he seems to lack certain organizational skills necessary to meet a deadline and also is quite a perfectionist. As a result, too much time is wasted coming up with the "perfect" idea, project, or report.

Your goal is to produce the best possible report by the deadline at the end of the week. Rate the quality of the following strategies for meeting your goal on a 1- to 7-point scale						
1	**2**	**3**	**4**	**5**	**6**	**7**
Extremely bad			**Neither good nor bad**			**Extremely good**
81. Divide the work to be done in half and tell him that if he does not complete his part, you obviously will have to let your immediate superior know it was not your fault						
82. Politely tell him to be less of a perfectionist						
83. Set deadlines for completing each part of the report, and accept what you have accomplished at each deadline as the final version of that part of the report						
84. Ask your superior to check up on your progress on a daily basis (after explaining why)						
85. Praise your co-worker verbally for completion of parts of the assignment						
86. Get angry with him at the first sign of getting behind schedule						
87. As soon as he begins to fall behind, take responsibility for doing the report yourself, if need be, to meet the deadline						
88. Point out firmly, but politely, how he is holding up the report						
89. Avoid putting any pressure on him because it will just make him fall even more behind						
90. Offer to buy him dinner at the end of the week if you both meet the deadline						
91. Ignore his organizational problem so you don't give attention to maladaptive behavior						

Appendix E: Adaptive Style Inventory

Instructions

This inventory is designed to assess the ways you adapt to different situations. The inventory consists of eight items, or general situations, and asks you to indicate how you respond to each. Six choices are listed below each item. In each pair make the choice which is most like what you actually do in this situation. You will note that some of the choices repeat themselves, but with different alternatives. You need not always choose the same answer when it is repeated. Basing your choice on which of the two alternatives most frequently characterizes your behaviour in this situation.

Item 1. When I start something new

Choose A or B:

A. I rely on my feelings to guide me.
B. I set priorities.

Choose C or D:

C. I try out different ways of doing it.
D. I observe the situation.

Choose E or F:

E. I rely on my feelings to guide me.
F. I observe the situation.

Choose G or H:

G. I rely on my feelings to guide me.
H. I try out different ways of doing it.

Choose I or J:

I. I set priorities.
J. I observe the situation.

Choose K or L:

K. I set priorities.
L. I try out different ways of doing it.

Item 2. When deciding between two alternatives

Choose A or B:

A. I rely on what feels right to me.
B. I establish criteria for evaluating them.

Choose C or D:

C. I try out the one I like best.
D. I carefully consider the outcomes of each.

Choose E or F:

E. I rely on what feels right to me.
F. I carefully consider the outcomes of each.

Choose G or H:

G. I rely on what feels right to me.
H. I try out the one I like best.

Choose I or J:

I. I establish criteria for evaluating them.
J. I carefully consider the outcomes of each.

Choose K or L:

K. I establish criteria for evaluating them.
L. I try out the one I like best.

Item 3. When developing an idea

Choose A or B:

A. I need concrete examples.
B. I clarify the underlying concepts.

Choose C or D:

C. I consider its practical applications.
D. I review the relevant information.

Choose E or F:

E. I need concrete examples.
F. I review the relevant information.

Choose G or H:

G. I need concrete examples.
H. I consider its practical applications.

Choose I or J:

I. I clarify the underlying concepts.
J. I review the relevant information.

Choose K or L:

K. I clarify the underlying concepts.
L. I consider its practical applications.

Item 4. When I consider my feelings

Choose A or B:

A. I trust my instincts about them.
B. I analyze why I feel the way I do.

Choose C or D:

C. I decide what to do about them.
D. I listen for what they are telling me.

Choose E or F:

E. I trust my instincts about them.
F. I listen for what they are telling me.

Choose G or H:

G. I trust my instincts about them.
H. I decide what to do about them.

Choose I or J:

I. I analyze why I feel the way I do.
J. I listen for what they are telling me.

Choose K or L:

K. I analyze why I feel the way I do.
L. I decide what to do about them.

Item 5. When I try to complete a task on time

Choose A or B:

A. I take things as they come.
B. I plan systematically.

Choose C or D:

C. I work hard and get it done.
D. I reflect on each step.

Choose E or F:

E. I take things as they come.
F. I reflect on each step.

Choose G or H:

G. I take things as they come.
H. I work hard and get it done.

Choose I or J:

I. I plan systematically.
J. I reflect on each step.

Choose K or L:

K. I plan systematically.
L. I work hard and get it done.

Item 6. When evaluating an opportunity

Choose A or B:

A. I trust my sense of what is best.
B. I weigh the costs against the benefits.

Choose C or D:

C. I take risks.
D. I am careful to consider the alternatives.

Choose E or F:

E. I trust my sense of what is best.
F. I am careful to consider the alternatives.

Choose G or H:

G. I trust my sense of what is best.
H. I take risks.

Choose I or J:

I. I weigh the costs against the benefits.
J. I am careful to consider the alternatives.

Choose K or L:

K. I weigh the costs against the benefits.
L. I take risks.

Item 7. When systematically analyzing something

Choose A or B:

A. Intuition is often my best guide.
B. I think about how the basic principles relate to each other.

Choose C or D:

C. I plan for the results I need to achieve.
D. I take time to consider different perspectives.

Choose E or F:

E. Intuition is often my best guide.
F. I take time to consider different perspectives.

Choose G or H:

G. Intuition is often my best guide.
H. I plan for the results I need to achieve.

Choose I or J:

I. I think about how the basic principles relate to each other.
J. I take time to consider different perspectives.

Choose K or L:

K. I think about how the basic principles relate to each other.
L. I plan for the results I need to achieve.

Item 8. When I try to see the world as another person sees it

Choose A or B:

A. I am influenced by their feelings.
B. I consider how they are similar to other people.

Choose C or D:

C. I do things with them.
D. I observe them.

Choose E or F:

E. I am influenced by their feelings.
F. I observe them.

Choose G or H:

G. I am influenced by their feelings.
H. I do things with them.

Choose I or J:

I. I consider how they are similar to other people.
J. I observe them.

Choose K or L:

K. I consider how they are similar to other people.
L. I do things with them.

Appendix F: Cross-Cultural Adjustment Scale

Instructions

This scale consists of fourteen items. You need to rate your own degree of adjustment to each item. Rating anchors ranged from "not adjusted very well" (1) to "very well adjusted" (5).

1. Living conditions in general	1	2	3	4	5
2. Housing conditions	1	2	3	4	5
3. Food	1	2	3	4	5
4. Shopping	1	2	3	4	5
5. Cost of living	1	2	3	4	5
6. Entertainment/recreation facilities and opportunities	1	2	3	4	5
7. Health care facilities	1	2	3	4	5
8. Socializing with host nationals	1	2	3	4	5
9. Interacting with host nationals on a day-to-day basis	1	2	3	4	5
10. Interacting with host nationals outside of work	1	2	3	4	5
11. Speaking with host nationals	1	2	3	4	5
12. Specific job responsibilities	1	2	3	4	5
13. Performance standards and expectations	1	2	3	4	5
14. Supervisory responsibilities	1	2	3	4	5

References

Armstrong, S. J., & Mahmud, A. (2008). Experiential learning and the acquisition of managerial tacit knowledge. *Academy of Management Learning and Education*, *7*(2): 189–208.

Auyeung, P., & Sands, J. (1996). A cross-cultural study of the learning style of accounting students. *Accounting and Finance*, *36*, 261–274.

Babbie, E. (1973). *Survey research methods*. Belmont, CA: Wadsworth.

Black, J. S., & Mendenhall, M. (1989). A practical but theory-based framework for selecting cross-cultural training methods. *Human Resource Management*, *28*(4): 511–539.

Black, J. S., & Stephens, G. K. (1989). The influence of the spouse on American expatriate adjustment in overseas assignments. *Journal of Management*, *15*, 529–544.

Boyatzis, R. E., & Kolb, D. A. (1993). Adaptive style inventory: Self scored inventory and interpretation booklet. Boston, MA: TRG Hay/McBer, Training Resources Group, 116 Huntington Avenue, Boston, MA 02116.

Brislin, R. W. (1973). Translation and content analysis of oral and written materials. In: H. C. Triandis., & J. W. Berry. (Eds.), *Handbook of cross-cultural psychology: Methodology* (pp. 339–444). Boston: Allyn Bacon.

Bryman, A., & Bell, E. (2007). *Business research methods* (2nd ed.). Oxford: Oxford University Press.

Fisher, C., & Downes, B. (2008). Performance measurement and manipulation, Financial Management.

Forsythe, G., Hedlund, J., Snook, S., Horvath, J., Williams, W., Bullis, R., Dennis, M., & Sternberg, R. 1998. Construct validation of tacit knowledge for military leadership. Paper presented at the Annual Meeting of the American Educational Research Association, San Diego, California, April 13–17, 1998.

Fridland, G. H. (2002). *Adult learning styles and cultural background: A comparison of the learning style preferences of American teachers of English as a second language and Chinese teachers of English as a foreign language*. Unpublished doctoral dissertation, TN: University of Memphis.

Geiger, M. A., Boyle, E., & Pinto, J. (1992). A factor analysis of Kolb's revised learning style inventory. *Educational and Psychological Measurement, 52*, 753–759.

Geiger, M., Boyle, E., & Pinto, J. (1993). An examination of ipsative and normative versions of Kolb's revised learning style inventory. *Educational and Psychological Measurement, 53*, 717–726.

Greer, T., & Dunlap, W. P. (1997). Analysis of variance with Ipsative measures. *Psychological Methods, 2*, 200–207.

Hoppe, M. H. (1990). *A comparative study of country elites: International differences in work related values and learning and their implications for management training and development*. Unpublished doctoral dissertation, Chapel Hill, NC: University of North Carolina.

Katz, N. (1988). Individual learning style: Israeli norms and cross-cultural equivalence of Kolb's learning style inventory. *Journal of Cross-Cultural Psychology, 19*(3), 361–379.

Kerr, M. R. (1991). *An analysis and application of tacit knowledge to managerial selection*. Unpublished doctoral dissertation, Waterloo, Ontario: University of Waterloo.

Kolb, D. A. (1984). *Experiential learning: Experience as the source of learning and development*. Englewood Cliffs: Prentice-Hall.

Kolb, D. A. (1999). Learning Style Inventory, version 3: Technical specifications. TRG Hay/McBer, Training Resources Group. 116 Huntington Avenue, Boston, MA02116, trg_mcber@haygroup.com.

Loo, R. (1999). Confirmatory factor analyses of Kolb's learning style inventory (LSI-1985). *British Journal of Educational Psychology, 69*, 213–219.

Mainemelis, C., Boyatzis, R. E., & Kolb, D. A. (2002). Learning styles and adaptive flexibility: Testing experiential learning theory. *Management Learning, 33*(1), 5–33.

Selmer, J. (2002). Practice makes perfect? International experience and expatriate adjustment. *Management International Review, 42*(1), 71–87.

Selmer, J. (2006). Cultural novelty and adjustment: Western business expatriates in China. *International Journal of Human Resource Management, 17*(7), 1209–1222.

Saunders, J., Morson, S., & Aycan, Z. (2009). *New approaches to employee management*. Greenwich, CT: JAI Presures, *4*, 63–92.

Smith, D. M., & Kolb, D. A. (1985). *Learning style inventory: User's guide*. Boston, MA: Hay/Mcber.

Sternberg, R. J., Forsythe, G. B., Hedlund, J., Horvath, J. A., Wagner, R. K., Williams, W. M., et al. (2000). *Practical intelligence in everyday life*. New York: Cambridge University Presures.

Sternberg, R., J., & Grigorenko, E. (2001). Practical Intelligence and the Principal. Publication Series No. 2, Yale University. Retrieved 18 December, 2002 from http://www.temple.edu/Iss/pdf/publications.

Truluck, J. E., & Courtenay, B. C. (1999). Learning style preferences among older adults. *Educational Gerontology, 25*(3), 221–236.

Wagner, R. K. (1987). Tacit knowledge in everyday intelligence behaviour. *Journal of Personality and Social Psychology, 52*(6), 301–312.

Wagner, R. K., & Sternberg, R. J. (1991). *Tacit knowledge inventory for managers user manual*. San Antonio: Psychological Corporation.

Wagner, R. K., & Sternberg, R. J. (1985). Practical intelligence in real-world pursuits: The role of tacit knowledge. *Journal of Personality and Social Psychology, 49*(2), 436–458.

Yamazaki, Y. (2005). Learning styles and typologies of cultural differences: A theoretical and2829 empirical comparison. *International Journal of Intercultural Relations, 29*, 521–548.

Yamazaki, Y., & Kayes, D. C. (2007). Expatriate learning: exploring how Japanese managers adapt in the United States. *International Journal of Human Resource Management, 18*(8), 1373–1395.

Yuen, C., & Lee, S. N. (1994). Applicability of the learning style inventory in an Asian context and its predictive value. *Educational and Psychological Measurement, 54*(2), 541–549.

Chapter 4
Data Analysis: Structure Equation Modeling (SEM)

This chapter is reported in three parts. This chapter first provides a brief introduction about Structure Equation Modeling (SEM) and its definition and types. The purpose of this introduction is to illustrate the reasons for using SEM and the procedures used in the analysis. This chapter then reports data analysis of the measurement models for Learning Style, Managerial Tacit Knowledge, Adaptive Flexibility, and Expatriate Adjustment. In this part, this study will test the data reliability and validity and subsequently introduce the measurement models for the variables and identify the final factors that will be brought in the structure model. Finally, this chapter reports data analysis of the structure model for the research framework that was established in Chap. 2.

4.1 An Introduction to SEM

Structure equation modeling (SEM) is 'a multivariate statistical technique for testing structural theory that has gained popularity in many business disciplines'. SEM can be seen as a family of statistical models that look for explaining the relationships among multiple variables (Hair et al. 2006: 735). Simply, SEM estimates a series of separate but interdependent multiple regression equations at the same time by identifying the structure model (Hair et al. 2006). This structure model can be illustrated pictorially to enable a clearer conceptualization of the theory under study (Byrne 2010).

The methodology in SEM takes a confirmatory (i.e. hypothesis—testing) rather than an exploratory approach to data analysis (Byrne 2010). Therefore, testing SEM is viewed as a method of testing specified theory about relationships between theoretical constructs. First, the researcher should draw upon theory and the research objectives to identify the independent and dependent variables and to build the structure relations between these variables. Then the proposed relationships are translated into a series of structure equations for each dependent variable (Hair et al. 2006). The primary task in SEM is to determine the goodness of fit between the

Y. Li, *Expatriate Manager's Adaption and Knowledge Acquisition*,
DOI 10.1007/978-981-10-0053-9_4

hypothesized model and the sample data. Typically, the researcher imposes the structure of the hypothesized model on the sample data and tests how well the observed data fit into this restricted structure (Byrne 2010). SEM has many advantages compared to multiple regressions.

1. SEM include more flexible assumptions (particularly allowing interpretation even in the face of multicollinearity);
2. Use of confirmatory factor analysis to reduce measurement error by having multiple indicators per latent variable;
3. The desirability of testing models overall rather than coefficients individually;
4. The ability to test models with multiple dependents;
5. The ability to test coefficients across multiple between-subjects groups and ability to handle difficult data;
6. The ability to model error terms.

Furthermore, while regression is highly susceptible to error of interpretation by mis-specification, the SEM strategy of comparing alternative models to assess relative model fit makes the analysis more robust.

4.1.1 Three Modeling Approaches in SEM

There are three modeling approaches in SEM: strictly confirmatory approach, alternative models approach, and model developing approach.

1. Strictly confirmatory approach. In this approach, the researcher has formulated one single model and test this model using the empirical data. The model should be accepted or rejected according to the model goodness of fit. This approach is infrequently used in the literature because 'few researchers can just reject the model without suggesting an alternative one'.
2. Alternative models approach. In this approach, the researcher may test several alternative causal models to determine which has the best fit. One of the models should be selected. However, this approach faces a real-world problem that in most specific research topic areas, the literature does not support two well-developed alternative models to be tested.
3. Model developing (generating) approach. In this approach, the researcher develops a 'tentative initial model'. This model can then be modified based on the changes suggested by the SEM modification indices and retested if it does not fit the empirical data. This approach allows the researcher to modify the model several times and retest them to find a revised model that fits the data best and at the same time can be interpreted through the theory. In practice, the model developing approach is the most common approach found in the literature.

This research adopts the model developing approach. The main reason for this is that it gives the researcher the opportunity to benefit from the SEM technique to modify the model and retest it again. It is also more applicable compared to the other two approaches.

4.1.2 Two Steps in SEM

The process of SEM centers around two steps: validating the measurement model and fitting the structure model (Anderson and Gemberg 1988). The measurement model validation is accomplished through Confirmatory Factor Analysis (CFA) and provides the assessment of convergent validity and discriminant validity. The structure model fitting is accomplished primarily through path analyses with latent variables and provides the assessment of predictive validity (Anderson and Gemberg 1988).

This research follows these two steps. Before testing the structure model, which is reported in the Sect. 4.3, the measurement model for each construct (Learning style, Managerial tacit knowledge, Adaptive flexibility, and expatriate adjustment) is tested and reported in Sect. 4.2. The convergent and discriminant validity of each measurement construct are established before moving on to the analysis of the structure model.

4.1.3 Types of Variables in SEM

It is meaningful to distinguish terminologies of different types of variables used in SEM: latent variables versus observed variables, and exogenous versus endogenous variables (Byrne 2010).

Latent variables are those variables that cannot be observed and measured directly. The researcher must operationally define the latent variable in terms of behavior believed to represent it. By doing this, a latent variable is linked to one that is observable and thereby making its measurement possible. Assessment of the behavior constitutes the direct measurement of an *observed variable.* These measured scores are termed observed variables and serve as indicators of the underlying construct (latent variable) that they are presumed to represent in SEM.

Exogenous variables are synonymous with independent variables. They cause fluctuations in the values of other variables in the model. *Endogenous latent variables* are synonymous with dependent variables and they thus are influenced by the exogenous variables in the model. In SEM, changes in the values of exogenous variables are not explained by the model, whilst fluctuation in the values of endogenous variables is explained by the model. This is because all variables that influence them are included in the model specification.

4.1.4 Model Fit Indicators

This research adopts Analysis of Moment Structures (AMOS) software for SEM estimation. The AMOS outputs provide four groups of model fit indicators: Chi-square (CMIN), the absolute fit indices, the incremental fit indices, and the parsimony fit indices. The four types of model fit indices are further discussed below.

1. Chi square (CMIN). The Chi square value relative to the associated degrees of freedom (Chi square/Degrees of freedom) indicates the extent to which the observed matrix (S) differs from the estimated matrix (Z). It tests the extent to which the residuals in the matrix (Z − S) are zero. Researchers are interested in obtaining a non-significant value that is less than the tabled value with associated degrees of freedom. Due to the calculation process of Chi square, it becomes very sensitive to large sample sizes. The Chi square value increases with the sample size. For a sample size from 100 to 300, the value of (Chi square/Degrees of freedom) should be less than 3 (Byrne 2010).
2. Absolute fit indices. The absolute fit indices include Goodness of fit index (GFI), Adjusted goodness of fit index (AGFI), and Parsimony goodness of fit index (PGFI), Root mean square residual (RMR). This group of measure indices provides the most basic assessment of how a restricted model fits the sample data. They do not compare goodness of fit to any other model (Hair et al. 2006; Byrne 2010). Both GFI and AGFI range from 0 to 1, with values close to 1 being indicative of good fit. PGFI takes into account the complexity (i.e., number of estimated parameters) of the hypothesized model in the assessment of overall model fit and it has lower values than GFI and AGFI (Byrne 2010). The last indicator in this group is RMR. RMR is the average residual value obtained by calculating the square root of the mean squared differences between the individual observed and estimated covariance and variance terms (Hair et al. 2006: 771). Byrne (2010) recommends using the standardized RMR value that is based on standardized residuals. The value of RMR ranges from 0 to 1 and for a well-fitting model, the less the value the better the model fits.
3. Incremental fit indices. The incremental fit indices assess how well a model fits the data relative to some alternative baseline model (Hair et al. 2006). Incremental fit indices include two important indices: Normed fit index (NFI) and Relative fit index (RFI). Both NFI and RFI range from 0 to 1 with a value close to 1 indicating a better fit (Hair et al. 2006; Byrne 2010).
4. Parsimony fit indices. This group of indicators is designed to provide information about which model among a set of competing models is best. They are not useful in examining the fit of a single model. However, they are quite useful in comparing the fit of several models with different degrees of complexity (Hair et al. 2006). The criterions for all these model fit indices are summarized in Table 4.1.

Table 4.1 Criterions for model fit indices

Index	Criterion (critical value)
Absolute fit indices	
RMR	<0.05
RMSEA	<0.08 (<0.05, fit very well; <0.08 fit well)
GFI	>0.90
AGFI	>0.90
Incremental fit indices	
NFI	>0.80
RFI	>0.80
IFI	>0.90
CFI	>0.90
Parsimony fit indices	
PGFI	>0.50
PNFI	>0.50
PCFI	>0.50
CN	>200

4.2 Data Analysis: The Measurement Models

This section reports data analysis of the measurement models for Learning style, Managerial tacit knowledge, Adaptive flexibility, and Expatriate adjustment. In this part, this study will test the data reliability and validity and then introduce the measurement models for the variables and identify the final factors that will be brought in the structure model for the research framework. Being aware of the importance of validity and reliability, this study uses Cronbach's Coefficient Alpha and Confirmatory factor analysis to validate the measurement scales. Before these analyses are applied, a detailed assessment of the suitability of the data for factor analysis is conducted.

4.2.1 Assessment of the Suitability of Sample Data for Factor Analysis

In this research, the Kaiser-Meyer-Olkin (KMO) measure of sample for adequacy for factor analysis was applied. The KMO can be calculated for individual and multiple variables and represents the ratio of the squared correlation between variables to the squared partial correlation between variables. The KMO values range from 0 to 1. The high values near to 1 indicate that the items will form specific factors and the data set is appropriate for the application of factor analysis (KMO >0.50, acceptable; KMO >0.80, very well). In this study, the KMO values of each research scale are

Table 4.2 KMO values for all research scales

Scale	KMO value	
	Expatriate managers (N = 121)	Chinese managers (N = 133)
Learning style inventory	0.821	0.738
Tacit knowledge inventory for managers	0.735	0.677
Adaptive style inventory	0.671	0.614
Cross-cultural adjustment scale	0.810	None

calculated in two parts for two different research samples: expatriate managers and local Chinese managers. The KMO values of all research scales are summarized in Table 4.2. All KMO values in Table 4.2 are greater than 0.60, which indicate that they are acceptable for factor analysis.

4.2.2 *Assessing the Measurement Model Validity*

The primary objective in this section is to identify to what extent the hypothesized model fit the sample data. In case of an inadequate fit, the next step is to detect the sources of misfit in the model and adjust it for better fit. The main advantage of Confirmatory factor analysis (CFA) is its ability to identify the construct validity of a proposed measurement theory. Construct validity refers to the extent to which a set of measured items actually reflects the theoretical latent construct that those items are designed to measure (Hair et al. 2006).

4.2.2.1 Confirmatory Factor Analysis (CFA) for Learning Style

In this research, the researcher examines the confirmatory factor analysis (CFA) for the learning style construct using two different models to determine which one is more suitable for the data collected in this study: CFA for learning style as four factors [Concrete experience (CE), Reflective observation (RO), Abstract conceptualization (AC), and Active experimentation (AE)] and CFA for learning style as two factors (dimension AC-CE and dimension AE-RO).

4.2.2.1.1 Confirmatory Factor Analysis for Learning Style as Four Factors

In this section, the researcher examines three different types of models for CFA of learning style as four factors:

- Model A—no correlation between CE, RO, AC, and AE;
- Model B—only correlation between CE and AC, and between RO and AE;
- Model C—correlation between all four factors.

First, all 48 observed variables (Learning style inventory consists of 12 items and each item has four sub-items) of the learning style construct are initially incorporated in the model. Second, the researcher establishes four unobserved variables (CE, RO, AC, and AE) in the model. Third, the researcher sets different parameter constraints in different models as follows:

- Model A: C (Covariance) 1 = C2 = C3 = C4 = C5 = C6 = 0;
- Model B: C1 = C3 = C4 = C5 = 0;
- Model C: None.

Details of the model are shown in Fig. 4.1.

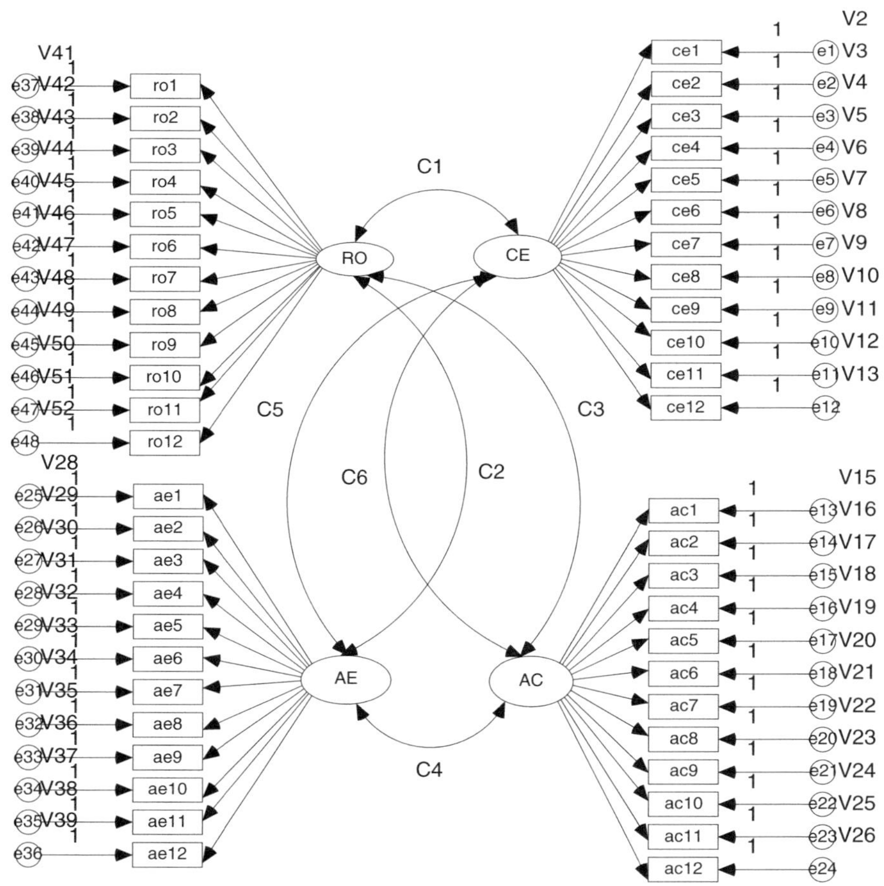

Fig. 4.1 Learning style measurement model as four factors

Table 4.3 Model fit summary for learning style

Model	CMIN	AIC	BCC	BIC	ECVI
Model [A]	1321.670	369.670	373.024	448.829	1.858
Model [B]	151.020	105.020	108.794	194.074	0.528
Model [C]	143.414	99.414	103.328	191.767	0.500
Saturated model	0.000	156.000	166.903	413.269	0.784
Independence model	1417.461	1441.461	1443.138	1481.040	7.244

In order to compare the three models, the model fit summary is shown in Table 4.3. In particular, the lower values of Index CMIN, AIC, and ECVI indicate a better fit of the model. As we can see in Table 4.3, the values of CMIN, AIC, ECVI of Model C are all less than that of Model A and Model B. In conclusion, Model C fits the data best. The model fit indices of Model C are GFI = 0.874; AGFI = 0.789; RMR = 0.234; NFI = 0.826; RFI = 0.817.

4.2.2.1.2 Confirmatory Factor Analysis for Learning Style as Two Factors

In this section, the researcher conducts CFA for learning style as two factors (dimension AC-CE and dimension AE-RO). First, all 48 observed variables of the learning style construct are initially incorporated in the model. Second, the researcher establishes two unobserved variables (AC-CE and AE-RO) in the model. Third, the researcher establishes correlation between the two factors. As the results of CFA of learning style as two factors, the model fit indices are CMIN = 138.879; GFI = 0.942; AGFI = 0.927; RMR = 0.083; NFI = 0.915; RFI = 0.908.

4.2.2.1.3 Conclusion

In conclusion, the CFA results for the two alternative models of learning style (four factors model that correlations between all four factors and two factors model) are summarized in Table 4.4. In respect of all the six fit indices, the two factors model fit the data better than the four factors models. The GFI value of the two factors model is 0.942 > 0.90, which indicates high degree of model fit. The AGFI value of

Table 4.4 CFA results for different models of learning style

Model	Absolute fit indices			Incremental fit indices	
	GFI	AGFI	RMR	NFI	RFI
Four factors model	0.774	0.789	0.234	0.826	0.817
Two factors model	0.942	0.927	0.083	0.915	0.908

the two factors model is 0.927 > 0.90, which indicates high degree of model fit too. The incremental fit indices of the two factors model are also higher than the four factors model. According to the results of the comparison, the two factors model will be used for the learning style construct in the following analysis of this study.

The second-order confirmatory factor analysis for the learning style construct is then conducted. The entire first-order two factors load very well onto the second-order learning style construct. The regression weights are 0.453 and 0.678 respectively. The model fit indices show similar result as the first-order CFA: CMIN = 137.070; GFI = 0.942; AGFI = 0.927; RMR = 0.083; NFI = 0.915; RFI = 0.908.

4.2.2.2 Confirmatory Factor Analysis for Managerial Tacit Knowledge

In this study, the researcher conducts confirmatory factor analysis (CFA) for the managerial tacit knowledge construct using a two factors model: managing-self and managing-other. First, all 6 observed variables (situation 1, 2, 3, 4, 5, 6 in the Tacit knowledge inventory for managers) of managerial tacit knowledge construct are initially incorporated in the model. Second, the researcher establishes two unobserved variables (managing-self and managing—other) in the model. Third, the researcher establishes correlations between the two factors. The initial model fit indices without any modification are CMIN = 14.498; GFI = 0.966; AGFI = 0.909; RMR = 0.001; NFI = 0.866; RFI = 0.886 and accordingly, the model fits the sample data well without any modification. Details of standardized estimates (variance, covariance, regression weight, and squared multiple correlation) are shown in Fig. 4.2.

The second-order confirmatory factor analysis for the managerial tacit knowledge construct is then conducted. The entire first-order two factors load very well onto the second-order managerial tacit knowledge construct. The regression weights are 0.676 and 0.532 respectively. The model fit indices reveals a similar result to the first-order CFA: CMIN = 14.008; GFI = 0.966; AGFI = 0.919; RMR = 0.001; NFI = 0.866; RFI = 0.886. The above statistics confirm that all the 6 items converge

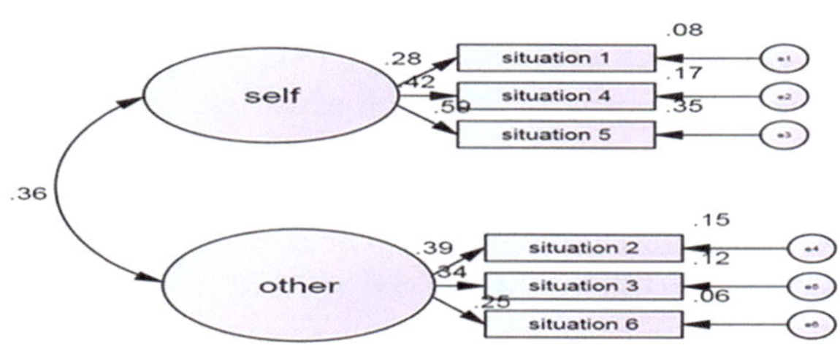

Fig. 4.2 CFA result of managerial tacit knowledge

into a single managerial tacit knowledge construct with two factors. The 6 items are partitioned into two factors: managing self and managing others.

4.2.2.3 Confirmatory Factor Analysis for Adaptive Flexibility

In this research, the researcher conducts confirmatory factor analysis (CFA) for the adaptive flexibility construct using a four factors model: Concrete experience adaptive flexibility (CEAF), Reflective observation adaptive flexibility (ROAF), Abstract conceptualization adaptive flexibility (ACAF), and Active experimentation adaptive flexibility (AEAF). First, all 16 observed variables [CEAF, ROAF, ACAF, and AEAF in four situations (acting, deciding, thinking, and valuing situations) respectively] of adaptive flexibility construct are initially incorporated in the model. Second, the researcher establishes four unobserved variables (CEAF, ROAF, ACAF, and AEAF) in the model. Third, the researcher establishes correlations between all four factors. The initial model fit indices without any modification are CMIN = 32.199; GFI = 0.972; AGFI = 0.959; RMR = 0.010; NFI = 0.943; RFI = 0.829 and accordingly, the model fits the sample data well without any modification.

The second-order confirmatory factor analysis for the adaptive flexibility construct is then conducted. The entire first-order four factors load well onto the second-order adaptive flexibility construct. The regression weights range from 0.336 to 0.587. The model fit indices show similar result to the first-order CFA: CMIN = 30.171; GFI = 0.972; AGFI = 0.940; RMR = 0.010; NFI = 0.943; RFI = 0.829. The slight difference in estimations of first-order and second-order confirmatory factor analyses for adaptive flexibility occurs due to the emergence of slightly different degrees of freedom between executing the first-order and second-order measurement models. The above statistics show that all the 16 items converge into a single adaptive flexibility construct with four factors. The 16 items are partitioned into four factors: CEAF, ROAF, ACAF, and AEAF.

4.2.2.4 Confirmatory Factor Analysis for Expatriate Adjustment

In this study, the researcher conducts confirmatory factor analysis (CFA) for the expatriate adjustment construct using a three factors model: general adjustment, socialization adjustment, and work adjustment. First, all 14 observed variables (the 14 items in expatriate adjustment scale) of expatriate adjustment construct are initially incorporated in the model. Second, the researcher establishes three unobserved variables in the model. Third, the researcher establishes correlations between the three factors. The initial model fit indices without any modification are CMIN = 55.633; GFI = 0.806; AGFI = 0.834; RMR = 0.120; NFI = 0.799; RFI = 0.829. According to these model fit indices and model modification indices, the initial model needs to be improved to fit the sample data better. Two criteria are employed to identify the items with imperfect behaviour in the model. The details of the criteria are as follows:

Table 4.5 CFA results for expatriate adjustment

Model	Absolute fit indices			Incremental fit indices	
	GFI	AGFI	RMR	NFI	RFI
Initial model	0.806	0.834	0.120	0.799	0.829
Adjusted model	0.931	0.886	0.080	0.901	0.856

- By examining the error variances and regression weights of all items, item 2 (housing conditions) is considered to be eliminated because it has a large error variance: 1.143. After the removal of item 2, the researcher tests the effects on remaining items. As a result, the model fit indices increased.
- For the remaining items, item 5 (cost of living) is considered to be eliminated because it has a very small least squared multiple correlation (0.056) with the factor general adjustment. After the removal of item 5, the researcher tests the effects on remaining items. As a result, the model fit indices increased.

Finally, a total of two items are removed from the model and this results in 12 items comprising the expatriate adjustment construct. The adjusted model's fit indices are: CMIN = 34. 122; GFI = 0.931; AGFI = 0.886; RMR = 0.080; NFI = 0.901; RFI = 0.856 and the adjusted model fits the sample data well. Comparisons between the initial model and adjusted model for the expatriate adjustment construct are summarized in Table 4.5.

The second-order confirmatory factor analysis for the expatriate adjustment construct is then conducted. The entire first-order three factors load well onto the second-order expatriate adjustment construct. The regression weights are 0.409, 0.468, and 0.511 respectively. The model fit indices show similar result to the first-order CFA: CMIN = 34. 100; GFI = 0.931; AGFI = 0.886; RMR = 0.080; NFI = 0.901; RFI = 0.856. The above statistics reveal that all the 12 items converge into a single expatriate adjustment construct with three factors. The 12 items are partitioned into three factors: general adjustment, socialization adjustment, and work adjustment.

4.3 Data Analysis: The Structure Model

This section reports data analysis of the structure model for the research framework that was established in Chap. 2 (see in Fig. 4.3). This provides an overall image of this research. The overall structural model incorporates 1 observed variable (expatriation time: months) and 4 latent variables consisting of 10 observed variables. The 4 latent variables are Learning style (with 2 observed variables), Managerial tacit knowledge (with 2 observed variables), Adaptive flexibility (with 2 observed variables), and Expatriate adjustment (with 3 observed variables).

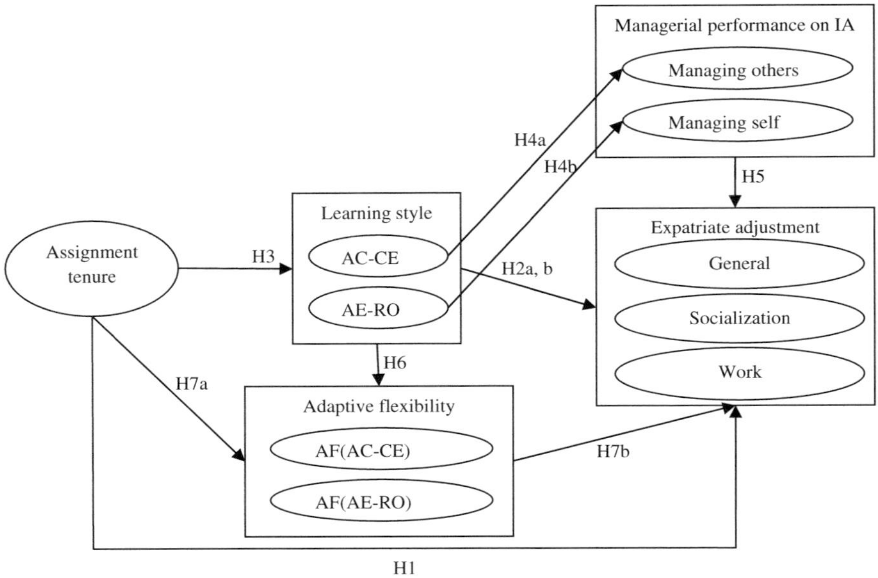

Fig. 4.3 Hypothesized model

4.3.1 The Structure Model for the Research Framework

The table shown in Appendix G presents the means, standard deviations, alphas, and correlations of the measured variables. In addition, a structural equation model was used to test the proposed hypotheses, which allowed for the simultaneous evaluation of all hypothesized correlations and also provided an assessment of the model's overall fit with the observed data. We evaluated our results by employing AMOS 16.0 analytical software and applying a two-step procedure recommended by Anderson and Gerbing (1988): first, validating the measurement model and second, fitting the structure model. Using the covariance matrix as input, parameters were estimated using maximum likelihood estimation. Before testing the hypothesized model, the measurement model for each construct was tested. The KMO values of all constructs in the study are greater than 0.60, which indicate that they are acceptable for factor analysis. Confirmatory factor analyses for each construct were then tested. The convergent and discriminant validity of each measurement construct were established and the final factors for each construct that will be brought in the structure model were identified. In the structure model of this study, there are 4 latent variables consisting of 10 observed variables (see in Fig. 4.3). Following Hair's (2006) rule of thumb, a sample size of between 100 and 150 would be required for SEM analysis. The sample size of this research is 121, which could be considered to be reasonable for running the structural model in this study.

Model fit was assessed using the following indices suggested by Hu and Bentler (1999): (a) chi-square goodness-of-fit to degrees of freedom ratio (x^2/df), (b) Tucker-Lewis Index (TLI), (c) root-mean-square error of approximation (RMSEA), (d) goodness of fit index (GFI) (Byrne 2010), (e) adjusted goodness of fit index (AGFI) (Byrne 2010), and (f) comparative fit index (CFI) (Browne and Cudeck 1993). Satisfactory model fit is indicated by TLI, GFI, and CFI values close to 0.95, AGFI value close to 0.90, RMSEA value no higher than 0.08, and x^2/df value no greater than 2 (Hu and Bentler 1999). Given the acceptable fit of our measurement model, we next assessed the hypothesized structural model (Fig. 4.3). As seen in Table 4.6, the hypothesized 10-factor structural model provides a relatively good fit to the data. Moreover, in order to test the Hypotheses 2a, 2b, 4a, and 4b, we constructed a direct path from the AC-CE learning dimension to the managing-others performance and expatriate adjustment, and from the AE-RO learning dimension to the managing-self performance and expatriate adjustment. As a result, this model, labeled 'Modified model' in Table 4.6, fits the data better. Although the modified model approached all fit indices (see Table 4.6), the modification indices indicated that a direct path from managing-self performance to work adjustment was warranted. Given this path is consistent with past research (Sternberg et al. 2000), we included it and re-ran our model. This model, labeled 'Final structural model' in Table 4.6, fits significantly better than other models, and was thus retained for hypothesis testing. Subsequently, the standardized regression path coefficients and the covariance for each of the model's 7 hypothesized relationships were examined. Testing results along with the significance levels are presented in Fig. 4.4.

In order to examine our framework of expatriate learning for success, we first examined the antecedent to expatriates' learning styles during their international assignments. Results from the standardized regression coefficients showed that the assignment tenure significantly influenced western expatriate managers' adjustment in China via their learning styles. Thus Hypothesis 3 was confirmed. In particular, the present research divided the sample of 121 western expatriates into four groups based on how long they have been in China: 1 year or less: N = 22; over 1 to 3 years: N = 42; over 3 to 5 years: N = 36; over 5 years: N = 21. Figure 4.5 presents how western expatriate managers' learning styles shift over the four groups. We then examined the antecedents to the development of adaptive flexibility. Results from the standardized regression coefficients showed that support was found for the relationship with the assignment tenure, learning style and adaptive flexibility.

Table 4.6 Model fit statistics

	x^2/df	TLI	RMSEA	CFI	GFI	AGFI
Hypothesized 10-factor model	1.914	0.877	0.087	0.925	0.899	0.803
Independence model	3.137	0.712	0.133	0.799	0.823	0.701
Modified model	1.706	0.905	0.077	0.941	0.904	0.818
Final structural model	1.519	0.930	0.066	0.959	0.919	0.838

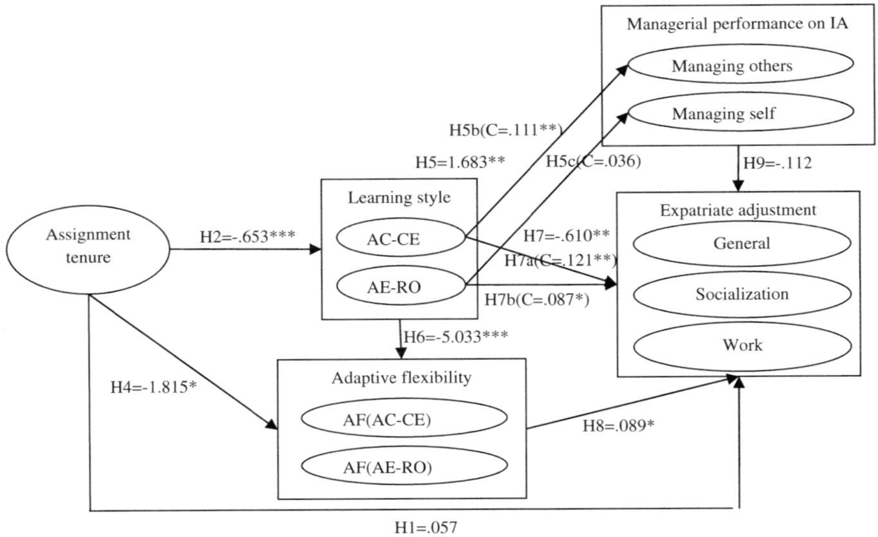

Fig. 4.4 Hypothesized model with testing results. *Note* N = 121; C = Covariance; *: $p < 0.05$; **: $p < 0.01$; ***: $p < 0.001$

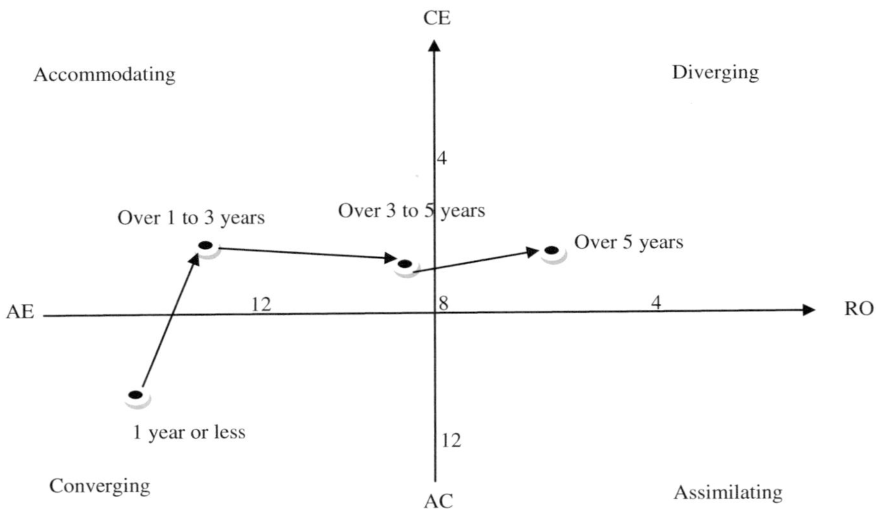

Fig. 4.5 Western expatriate managers' learning style transitional movements over four groups

Thus Hypothesis 7a was confirmed. Previous research suggests replacing the original learning dimension scores with their absolute values to represent the balancing level of learning style (Kolb and Kolb 2005). The absolute values of learning dimension scores are expected to decrease with the advancing level of learning styles. The result illustrated that there is a significant positive correlation between balanced learning styles and levels of adaptive flexibility. Thus Hypothesis 6 was confirmed.

Third, we examined how expatriate learning impacted the dependent variable of managerial performance on international assignment. Results from the standardized regression coefficients showed that western expatriate managers' learning styles significantly influenced their accumulation of managerial tacit knowledge during their international assignments. Results from the covariance illustrated that the relationship between the AC-CE learning dimension and managing-others performance was significant. Thus Hypothesis 4b was confirmed. However, the relationship between the AE-RO learning dimension and managing-self performance was not supported, and we therefore conclude that Hypothesis 4c was refuted. We further compared western expatriate managers' managerial performance by the four learning styles using one-way ANOVA. The result illustrated that Divergers had significantly higher levels of accumulated managerial tacit knowledge than participants with the other three learning styles (F = 8.644, df = 3, $p < 0.001$). Thus Hypothesis 4a was confirmed. Finally, we examined how expatriate learning and managerial performance helped model the variance in the dependent variable of expatriate adaptation. Results for the standardized regression coefficients showed that support was found for the relationship with learning style, adaptive flexibility and expatriate adjustment. Results from the covariance and the implied correlations illustrated that both the two learning dimensions have a significant negative correlation with adaptation. Thus Hypotheses 2a, 2b, and 7b were confirmed. However, the relationships between the assignment tenure, managerial performance and expatriate adaptation were not supported, and we therefore conclude that Hypotheses 1 and 5 were refuted. It should be noted that, based on the results from the covariance, the correlation between managing-self and expatriate work adjustment was significant (Covariance = 0.022, $p < 0.001$).

In addition, according to the results of the correlation analysis of all metric variables, we further examine all hypothesized correlations with the effects of related demographic characteristics on each correlation. We treat the related demographic characteristics as mediating variables in the regression analysis of each hypothesis. The results indicate that female expatriate managers show more learning preferences for concrete experience over abstract conceptualization when they work in China (F = 5.018, t = 4.07, $p < 0.01$). Western expatriate managers that have Chinese family members become more reflective and less active when they work in China (F = 5.988, t = 3.52, $p < 0.01$). Moreover, western expatriate managers become more concrete and less abstract, more reflective and less active if they experienced more previous international assignments (AC-CE: F = 9.517, t = 8.39, $p < 0.01$; AE-RO: F = 0.202, t = 3.53, $p < 0.05$). In other words, western expatriate managers with previous overseas work experience are easier to develop concrete and reflective learning modes in a cross-cultural context. With regard to managerial performance, the results indicate that western expatriate managers with higher hierarchical job positions achieve greater levels of accumulated managerial tacit knowledge (F = 16.839, t = 2, $p < 0.01$). With regard to expatriate adjustment, the results illustrate that managers' previous experiences of international assignments positively influenced their adjustment to international assignments in the host culture, especially the work adjustment (F = 4.028, t = 6.52, $p < 0.01$). Western expatriate managers that have Chinese family members adapt significantly better to socialization in China (F = 4.497, t = 5.10, $p < 0.01$).

4.3.2 *The Correlations in the Structure Model*

The correlations in the structure model are summarized in Table 4.7. Table 4.7 includes Parameter, regression weight (un-standardized), standard error (S.E.), C.R., and significance levels (*P**).

Table 4.8 summarizes the significant correlations (***) between four latent variables in Table 4.7 and their corresponding standardized regression weights. As illustrated in Tables 4.7 and 4.8, the following relations can be summarized:

- There is a significant relationship between expatriation time (Months) and learning style, adaptive flexibility; while there is no significant relationship between expatriation time and expatriate adjustment, level of accumulated.

Table 4.7 The regression weights in the structure model

	Parameter		Regression weight	S.E.	C.R.	*P**
LS	<—	MONTHS	−0.089	0.018	−4.935	***
Flexibility	<—	MONTHS	−0.005	0.003	−1.644	***
Flexibility	<—	LS	−0.148	0.033	−4.439	***
Adjustment	<—	LS	−0.059	0.013	−4.569	***
MTK	<—	MONTHS	0.000	0.000	−1.030	0.303
Adjustment	<—	MONTHS	0.083	0.001	2.459	0.100
Adjustment	<—	Flexibility	0.055	0.034	1.592	***
MTK	<—	LS	0.012	0.002	5.734	***
Managing self	<—	MTK	1.000			
Managing other	<—	MTK	1.023	0.209	4.891	***
General	<—	Adjustment	1.000			
Socialization	<—	Adjustment	2.215	0.426	5.202	***
Work	<—	Adjustment	1.368	0.275	4.970	***
ACCE	<—	LS	1.000			
AERO	<—	LS	0.772	0.126	6.136	***
AFAE-RO	<—	Flexibility	1.000			
AFAC-CE	<—	Flexibility	0.970	0.299	3.245	***

Note In column '*P**', '***' indicates that it's at significant level

Table 4.8 The significant correlations in the structure model

Parameter			Standardized regression weight	Hypothesis
LS	<—	MONTHS	−0.534	H2 receives support
Flexibility	<—	MONTHS	0.255	H4 receives support
MTK	<—	LS	0.702	H5 receives support
Flexibility	<—	LS	−0.327	H6 receives support
Adjustment	<—	LS	−0.790	H7 receives support
Adjustment	<—	Flexibility	0.304	H8 receives support

- There is a significant relationship between learning style and level of accumulated managerial tacit knowledge, adaptive flexibility, and expatriate adjustment.
- There is a significant relationship between adaptive flexibility and expatriate adjustment.

References

Anderson, J. C., & Gerbing, D. W. (1988). Structural equation modeling in practice. A review and recommended two-step approach. *Psychological Bulletin, 103*, 411–423.

Browne, M. W., & Cudeck, R. (1993). Alternative ways of assessing model fit. In K. A. Bollenm & J. S. Long (Eds.), *Testing structural equation models* (pp. 136–162). Newbury Park, CA: Sage Publications.

Byrne, B. M. (2010). *Structural equation modeling with AMOS*. Mahwah, NJ: Lawrence Erlbaum.

Hair, J. F., Black, W. C., Babin, B. J., Anderson, R. E., & Tatham, R. L. (2006). *Multivariate data analysis* (6th ed.). New Jersey: Pearson Prentice Hall.

Hu, L., & Bentler, P. M. (1999). Cutoff criteria for fit indexes in covariance structure analysis: Conventional criteria versus new alternatives. *Structural Equation Modeling, 6*, 1–55.

Kolb, A. Y., & Kolb, D. A. (2005). Learning styles and learning spaces: Enhancing experiential learning in higher education. *Academy of Management Learning and Education, 4*(2), 193–212.

Sternberg, R. J., Forsythe, G. B., Hedlund, J., Horvath, J. A., Wagner, R. K., Williams, W. M., et al. (2000). *Practical Intelligence in Everyday Life*. New York: Cambridge University Presures.

Chapter 5
Results: Western Expatriate Managers

This chapter presents the results of tests of 9 research hypotheses regarding western expatriate managers. First, this chapter provides the descriptive statistics and the results of the correlation analysis of all metric variables (including demographic characteristics) in this study. Then, the presentation concentrates on hypothesis-test results as follows:

1. The relationship between expatriate adjustment and expatriation time in China (hypothesis 1);
2. The relationship between learning style and expatriation time in China (hypotheses 2a, 2b, and 2c);
3. The relationship between level of accumulated managerial tacit knowledge and expatriation time in China (hypotheses 3a and 3b);
4. The relationship between adaptive flexibility and expatriation time in China (hypothesis 4);
5. The relationship between learning style and level of accumulated managerial tacit knowledge (hypotheses 5a, 5b, and 5c);
6. The relationship between learning style and adaptive flexibility (hypotheses 6a, 6b, and 6c);
7. The relationship between learning style and expatriate adjustment (hypotheses 7a, 7b);
8. The relationship between adaptive flexibility and expatriate adjustment (hypothesis 8);
9. The relationship between level of accumulated managerial tacit knowledge and expatriate adjustment (hypothesis 9).

5.1 Descriptive Statistics

Descriptive statistics for all metric variables are summarized in Table 5.1. The correlation matrix for all metric variables is included in table of Appendix G. Each correlation will be discussed in a following section in accordance with it pertains to a particular hypothesis. In Table 5.1, regarding the transformation of the variable

Y. Li, *Expatriate Manager's Adaption and Knowledge Acquisition*,
DOI 10.1007/978-981-10-0053-9_5

Table 5.1 Descriptive statistics for all metric variables (N = 121)

Variable	Mean	Std. deviation	Variable	Mean	Std. deviation
Nationality	2.17	1.135	Work adjustment	4.47	0.646
Gender	1.13	0.340	Situation 1	0.555	0.189
Age	2.31	0.646	Situation 2	0.434	0.164
International family	1.23	0.574	Situation 3	0.601	0.152
MONTHS	36.50	26.337	Situation 4	0.554	0.139
No. of previous IA	0.50	0.765	Situation 5	0.490	0.121
Overseas study experience	1.26	0.443	Situation 6	0.586	0.138
Educational achievement	2.59	0.511	Managing self	0.533	0.091
Job function	2.83	0.691	Managing others	0.540	0.085
Functional area	3.01	1.440	Total MTC	1.073	0.1313
CE	24.58	4.215	TOTAL CE	5.08	2.815
AC	31.83	3.974	TOTAL AC	16.46	3.096
RO	26.31	4.241	TOTAL AE	12.79	2.370
AE	37.12	3.920	TOTAL RO	13.66	2.920
AC-CE	7.26	5.969	CEAF	2.698	1.2458
AE-RO	10.89	5.861	ACAF	3.855	1.4895
LEARNING STYLE	3.00	0.548	AEAF	5.736	1.3526
General adjustment	4.08	0.690	ROAF	3.736	1.3277
Socialization	3.50	0.941	AF	16.025	2.5819

'*nationality*' in the questionnaire, '1' refers to UK/Ireland, '2' refers to USA, '3' refers to Canada, '4' refers to Australia, '5' refers to other; regarding the transformation of the variable '*gender*' in the questionnaire, '1' refers to male, '2' refers to female; regarding the transformation of the variable '*international family*' in the questionnaire, '1' refers to parents and spouse who come from the same country, '2' refers to parents and/or spouse who come from different countries but not from Greater China, '3' refers to parents and/or spouse who come from Greater China; regarding the transformation of the variable '*age*' in the questionnaire, '1' refers to age 20–29, '2' refers to age 30–39, '3' refers to age 40–49, '4' refers to 50–60, '5' refers to age over 60; regarding the transformation of the variable '*overseas study experience*' in the questionnaire, '1' refers to No experience, '2' refers to Yes; regarding the transformation of the variable '*educational achievement*' in the questionnaire, '1' refers to Ph. D., '2' refers to master, '3' refers to bachelor, '4' refers to other; regarding the transformation of the variable '*job function*' in the questionnaire, '1' refers to CEO/president, '2' refers to senior manager, '3' refers to middle manager, '4' refers to junior manager, '5' refers to other; regarding the transformation of the variable '*functional area*' in the questionnaire, '1' refers to Human resource management/general administration, '2' refers to Operations/production, '3' refers to Sales/marketing, '4' refers to Engineering/design, '5' refers to Finance/accounting, '6' refers to other.

5.2 Expatriate Adjustment and Expatriation Time

Research hypothesis 1 is associated with western expatriate managers' cross-cultural adjustment in China and their expatriation time. This section first presents an overview of western expatriate managers' adaptation and subsequently provides the results of test of hypothesis 1.

5.2.1 *An Overview of Western Expatriate Managers' Adjustment*

Table 5.2 summarizes the mean scores and standard deviations (s. d.) of four variables (general adjustment, socialization adjustment (socialize with host nationals), work adjustment, and expatriate adjustment) measured by the Expatriate adjustment scale. Expatriate adjustment measured in the scale is the average of general adjustment, socialization, and work adjustment. The mean scores of four expatriate adjustment variables range from 3.50 (socialization adjustment) to 4.47 (work adjustment). This suggests that western expatriate managers adjust better to the work environment but experience most difficulty with socializing with host nationals.

5.2.2 *Results of Hypothesis 1 Test*

As shown in the results of correlation analysis of all metric variables (Appendix G), the correlation between expatriate adjustment and expatriation time in China is statistically significant at the 0.05 level (*). However, according to the SEM analysis of the research framework, the correlation between expatriate adjustment and expatriation time is not significant. In this section, the researcher further examines the relationship between expatriate adjustment and expatriation time and the effects of related mediating variables on each correlation. Hypothesis 1 is described below:

- Hypothesis 1: Duration of expatriate managers' international experiences in the host culture will positively influence their adjustment to the current international assignment.

Table 5.2 A summary of the four expatriate adjustment variables (N = 121)

	General	Socialization	Work	Overall adjustment
Mean	4.08	3.50	4.47	4.02
s. d.	0.690	0.941	0.646	0.592

Hypothesis 1 relates to examining how western expatriate managers' adjustment rests on the expatriation time in China. According to the results of the correlation analysis of all metric variables, seven personal characteristics in demographic characteristics, two learning style dimensions, and adaptive flexibility have a significant relationship with expatriate adjustment. The seven personal characteristics are: age, international family, number of previous international assignments, overseas educational degree, educational achievement, job function, and functional area. This research then treats these ten variables as mediating variables in the regression analysis of Hypothesis 1. Table 5.3 presents the results of regression analysis testing hypothesis 1. According to the extant literature, the sample size required by regression analysis is calculated by the following formulas: $N >= 50 + 8 * m$ (m is the number of predictors) for testing the multiple correlation and $N >= 104 + m$ (m is the number of predictors) for testing individual predictors. These formulas assume a medium effect size ($\alpha = 0.05$) and power of 80 % ($\beta = 0.20$). In the examination of expatriate adjustment including control variables, the regression analysis with 10 predictor variables needs at least 114 cases for testing individual predictors under this assumption. The sample size of the present research is 121 and thus, it is reasonable to conduct the regression analysis.

As illustrated in Table 5.3, Model 1 tests the relationship between expatriate adjustment and expatriation time in China. The result indicates that they have a

Table 5.3 Results of regression analysis of Hypothesis 1

	Expatriate adjustment				
	Model 1		Model 2		
	Beta (standardized)	t	Beta (standardized)	t	Zero order
Independent variable					
Expatriation time	0.590	7.962**	0.373	3.819	0.590**
Mediating variables					
AC-CE			−0.429	−5.639**	−0.630**
AE-RO			−0.020	−0.267*	−0.544
Adaptive flexibility			0.138	1.944*	0.587*
Age			0.112	1.577	0.456
International family			0.208	3.602**	0.363**
No. of previous IAs			0.081	1.050	0.463
Overseas degree			0.051	0.835	0.288
Educational achievement			−0.060	−1.035	−0.185
Job function			−0.008	−0.091	−0.535
Functional area			−0.105	−1.834	−0.300
F	63.392**		26.236**		
R2	0.348		0.705		
Adjusted R2	0.342		0.678		

Note $*p < 0.05$; $**p < 0.01$

significant positive correlation ($p < 0.01$). This indicates that the longer western expatriate managers have continually worked in China, the better their adaptation. Model 2 examines the impact of ten mediating variables upon the relationship between expatriation time and western expatriate managers' adjustment. After the effects of the ten moderators were eliminated, the duration of expatriation time in China no longer impacted expatriate adjustment. This result suggests that the effect of the expatriation time on expatriate adjustment depends on that of the mediators. Therefore, hypothesis 1 is refuted.

The result of Model 2 in Table 5.3 shows that both the two learning dimensions: AC-CE and AE-RO has a significant negative relationship with expatriate adjustment (AC-CE: $p < 0.01$; AE-RO: $p < 0.05$). This indicates that concrete and reflective western expatriate managers adapt better than abstract and active western expatriate managers in cross-cultural context in China. Moreover, adaptive flexibility also has a significant positive impact upon expatriate adjustment ($p < 0.05$). It suggests that western expatriate managers with greater adaptive flexibility adapt better in cross-cultural context in China. The results also reveal that one personal characteristic (international family) has a significant positive influence on expatriate adjustment ($p < 0.01$). This suggests that western expatriate managers that have an international family, especially when the family member is from Greater China, adapt better in Chinese business environment. This research now further discusses the three parts of expatriate adjustment: general adjustment, socialization, and work adjustment respectively.

5.2.2.1 General Adjustment

General adjustment is regarding western expatriate managers' general adaptation in China. It includes 5 items in the expatriate adjustment scale. These five items are: item 1: living conditions in general; item 3: food; item 4: shopping; item 6: entertainment/recreation facilities and opportunities; item 7: health care facilities. It should be noted that item 2 and item 5 are removed base on the results of SEM analysis in Chap. 4. The score of general adjustment is the average of the scores of these five items. According to the results of correlation analysis, seven personal characteristics in demographic characteristics, two learning style dimensions, and adaptive flexibility have a significant relationship with general adjustment. Seven personal characteristics are: age, international family, number of previous international assignments, overseas educational degree, educational achievement, job function, and functional area. This research then treats these ten variables as mediating variables in the regression analysis of expatriation time on general adjustment. Table 5.4 presents the results of the regression analysis.

As illustrated in Table 5.4, Model 1 tests the relationship between general adjustment and expatriation time in China. The result indicates that they have a significant positive correlation ($p < 0.01$). This indicates that the longer western expatriate managers have continually worked in China, the better their general adaptation. Model 2 examines the impact of the ten mediating variables upon the

Table 5.4 Results of regression analysis of general adjustment

	General adjustment				
	Model 1		Model 2		
	Beta (standardized)	t	Beta (standardized)	t	Zero order
Independent variable					
Expatriation time	0.290	3.307**	0.040	0.271	0.290
Mediating variables					
AC-CE			−0.083	−0.724	−0.317
AE-RO			−0.233	−1.926	−0.410
Adaptive flexibility			0.090	0.791	0.347
Age			0.058	0.516	0.253
International family			0.048	0.525	0.212
No. of previous IAs			0.079	0.687	0.291
Overseas degree			0.048	0.495	0.173
Educational achievement			−0.054	−0.577	−0.139
Job function			0.029	0.233	−0.253
Functional area			−0.096	−1.071	−0.193

Note $*p < 0.05$; $**p < 0.01$

relationship between expatriation time and western expatriate managers' general adjustment. After the effects of the ten moderators were eliminated, the expatriation time in China no longer affects western expatriate managers' general adjustment. This result suggests that the effect of the expatriation time on general adjustment depends on that of the moderators.

5.2.2.2 Socialization Adjustment

Socialization adjustment is regarding western expatriate managers' socialization with local Chinese in China. It includes 4 items in the expatriate adjustment scale. These four items are: item 8: socializing with host nationals; item 9: interacting with host nationals on a day-to-day basis; item 10: interacting with host nationals outside of work; item 11: speaking with host nationals. The score of socialization adjustment is the average of the scores of these four items. According to the results of correlation analysis of all metric variables, seven personal characteristics in demographic characteristics, two learning style dimensions, and adaptive flexibility have a significant relationship with socialization adjustment. Seven personal characteristics are: age, international family, number of previous international assignments, overseas educational degree, educational achievement, job function, and functional area. This research then treats these ten variables as mediating variables in the regression analysis of expatriation time on socialization adjustment. Table 5.5 presents the results of the regression analysis.

Table 5.5 Results of regression analysis of socialization adjustment

	Socialization adjustment				
	Model 1		Model 2		
	Beta (standardized)	t	Beta (standardized)	t	Zero order
Independent variable					
Expatriation time	0.509	6.448**	0.393	4.010**	0.509**
Mediating variables					
AC-CE			−0.437	−5.683**	−0.649**
AE-RO			0.190	2.337*	−0.419*
Adaptive flexibility			0.112	1.458**	0.545**
Age			0.011	0.152	0.394
International family			0.196	3.195**	0.350**
No. of previous IAs			0.099	1.289	0.497
Overseas degree			0.068	1.046	0.257
Educational achievement			−0.036	−0.574	−0.152
Job function			−0.053	−0.630	−0.482
Functional area			−0.081	−1.345	−0.274

Note $*p < 0.05$; $**p < 0.01$

As illustrated in Table 5.5, Model 1 tests the relationship between expatriate socialization adjustment and expatriation time in China. The result indicates that they have a significant positive correlation ($p < 0.01$). Model 2 examines the impact of the ten mediating variables upon the relationship between expatriation time and western expatriate managers' socialization adjustment. After the effects of the ten moderators were eliminated, the expatriation time in China still has a significant positive influence upon the expatriate socialization adjustment ($p < 0.01$). This result suggests that the expatriation time independently affects western expatriate managers' socialization adjustment. It indicates that the longer western expatriate managers have continually worked in China, the better they socialize with local Chinese.

The result of Model 2 in Table 5.5 shows that the AC-CE learning dimensions has a significant negative relationship with socialization adjustment ($p < 0.01$). This indicates that concrete western expatriate managers socialize/interact better with host nationals than abstract western expatriate managers in cross-cultural context in China. On the contrary, the AE-RO learning dimension has a significant positive relationship with socialization adjustment ($p < 0.05$). This suggests that active western expatriate managers socialize/interact better with host nationals than reflective western expatriate managers in cross-cultural context. Moreover, adaptive flexibility also has a significant positive impact upon expatriate socialization adjustment ($p < 0.01$). This suggests that western expatriate managers with greater adaptive flexibility socialize/interact better with local nationals in a cross-cultural context. The results also reveal that one personal characteristic (international family) has a significant positive influence on socialization adjustment ($p < 0.01$). This suggests that western expatriate managers that have an international family, especially a family member from China, socialize/interact better with local Chinese.

5.2.2.3 Work Adjustment

Work adjustment is regarding western expatriate managers' adjustment to the work environment in China. It includes 3 items from the expatriate adjustment scale. These three items are: item 12: specific job responsibilities; item 13: performance standards and expectations; item 14: supervisory responsibilities. The score of work adjustment is the average of the scores of these three items. According to the results of the correlation analysis, seven personal characteristics in demographic characteristics, two learning style dimensions, and adaptive flexibility have a significant relationship with socialization adjustment. Seven personal characteristics are: age, international family, number of previous international assignments, overseas educational degree, educational achievement, job function, and functional area. This research then treats these ten variables as mediating variables in the regression analysis of expatriation time on work adjustment. Table 5.6 presents the results of the regression analysis.

As illustrated in Table 5.6, Model 1 tests the relationship between expatriate work adjustment and expatriation time in China. The result indicates that they have

Table 5.6 Results of regression analysis of work adjustment

	Work adjustment				
	Model 1		Model 2		
	Beta (standardized)	t	Beta (standardized)	t	Zero order
Independent variable					
Expatriation time	0.569	7.555**	0.427	3.554**	0.569**
Mediating variables					
AC-CE			−0.270	−2.868**	−0.448**
AE-RO			0.065	0.655	−0.446
Adaptive flexibility			0.120	1.275	0.447
Age			0.123	1.334	0.466
International family			0.102	1.356	0.249
No. of previous IAs			0.220	0.316**	0.302**
Overseas degree			0.034	0.435	0.231
Educational achievement			−0.040	−0.518	−0.137
Job function			0.022	0.218	−0.458
Functional area			−0.084	−1.132	−0.219

Note *$p < 0.05$; **$p < 0.01$

a significant positive correlation ($p < 0.01$). Model 2 examines the impact of the ten mediating variables upon the relationship between expatriation time and western expatriate managers' work adjustment. After the effects of the ten moderators were eliminated, the expatriation time in China still has a significant positive influence upon expatriate work adjustment ($p < 0.01$). This result suggests that the expatriation time independently affects western expatriate managers' work adjustment. This indicates that the longer western expatriate managers have continually worked in China, the better they adapt to a Chinese work environment.

The result of Model 2 shows that the AC-CE learning dimensions has a significant negative relationship with work adjustment ($p < 0.01$). This indicates that concrete western expatriate managers adapt better to work environments than abstract western expatriate managers working in a cross-cultural context. Moreover, the results reveal that one personal characteristic (number of previous international assignments) has a significant positive influence on work adjustment ($p < 0.01$). This suggests that western expatriate managers that have previous international assignment experiences are clearer about their job responsibilities and have more realistic performance expectations and therefore, adapt better in work environments in cross-cultural context. Managers' previous experiences of international assignments will positively influence their adjustment to international assignments in the work environment. In order to better understand the impact of previous international assignment experiences upon the expatriate work adjustment, Table 5.7 presents the results of independent sample t-tests of non-overseas experience (N = 79) versus overseas experience (N = 42) with regard to the work adjustment. As shown in Table 5.7, the mean score of the work adjustment of overseas experienced western expatriate managers is significantly higher than that of non overseas experienced western expatriate managers ($p < 0.01$).

5.2.3 *Expatriate Adjustment Improvements Over Time*

This section examines the improvement of western expatriate managers' cross-cultural adjustment as supplemental analysis through conducting the chi-square test of independence. In this study, the sample of 121 western expatriates is divided into four groups based on how long they have been in China. The first group has been in China for 1 year or less than 1 year; the second group for over 1–3 years; the third group for over 3–5 years; and the fourth group for over 5 years.

Table 5.7 Results of independent t-tests of overseas experience regarding work adjustment

	Work adjustment				
	N	Mean	s. d.	t	F
Overseas experience	42	4.74	0.497		
Non-overseas experience	79	4.33	0.674	3.793**	11.368

Note **$p < 0.01$ (two-tailed)

Tables 5.8a, 5.8b, and 5.8c presents a cross-tabulation of the four groups and the three facets of expatriate adjustment together with the results of chi-square test respectively.

The Pearson Chi-square value for general adjustment is 3.5, for socialization adjustment is 20.535 ($p < 0.01$), for work adjustment is 37.379 ($p < 0.01$). In addition, the Pearson Chi-square value for overall adjustment is 28.651 ($p < 0.01$), which led to a rejection of the null hypothesis that the four groups by years and socialization adjustment, work adjustment, and overall adjustment are independent. In socialization adjustment, the cross-tabulation illustrates that the first group of western expatriates has the largest positive Std. residuals for score '<2' and the largest negative Std. residuals for score '3–4' and '4–5'; on the contrary, the fourth

Table 5.8a A cross-tabulation of general adjustment and expatriation time by four groups

		General adjustment (score)				Total
		<2	2–3	3–4	4–5	
1 year or less	Count	0	4	13	6	23
	Std. residual	−0.4	0.0	0.1	−0.1	
Over 1–3 years	Count	1	14	22	8	45
	Std. residual	1.0	2.2	−0.5	−1.2	
Over 3–5 years	Count	0	1	19	13	33
	Std. residual	−0.5	−2.0	0.2	1.3	
Over 5 years	Count	0	2	12	6	20
	Std. residual	−0.4	−0.8	0.3	0.2	
Total	Count	1	21	66	33	121
Chi-square		3.5				

Note *$p < 0.05$; **$p < 0.01$; *Std. residual* Standardized residual

Table 5.8b A cross-tabulation of socialization adjustment and expatriation time by four groups

		Socialization adjustment (score)				Total
		<2	2–3	3–4	4–5	
1 year or less	Count	6	10	6	1	23
	Std. residual	1.4	0.6	−0.5	−1.4	
Over 1–3 years	Count	9	19	13	4	45
	Std. residual	0.9	0.7	−0.4	−1.3	
Over 3–5 years	Count	3	11	14	5	33
	Std. residual	−0.9	−0.3	1.0	−0.2	
Over 5 years	Count	0	4	6	10	20
	Std. residual	−1.7	−1.2	−0.2	3.7	
Total	Count	18	44	39	20	121
Chi-square		20.535**				

Note *$p < 0.05$; **$p < 0.01$; *Std. residual* Standardized residual

Table 5.8c A cross-tabulation of work adjustment and expatriation time by four groups

		Work adjustment (score)			
		2–3	3–4	4–5	Total
1 year or less	Count	8	10	5	23
	Std. residual	4.4	0.6	−2.2	
Over 1–3 years	Count	2	27	16	45
	Std. residual	−0.9	2.6	−1.8	
Over 3–5 years	Count	0	4	29	33
	Std. residual	−1.7	−2.3	2.5	
Over 5 years	Count	0	3	17	20
	Std. residual	−1.3	−1.6	1.8	
Total	Count	10	44	67	121
Chi-square		37.379**			

Note *$p < 0.05$; **$p < 0.01$; *Std. Residual* Standardized residual

group of western expatriates has the largest positive Std. residuals for score '4–5' and the largest negative Std. residuals for score '<2'. In work adjustment, similarly, the cross-tabulation illustrates that the first group of western expatriates has the largest positive Std. residuals for score '2–3' and the largest negative Std. residuals for score '4–5'. The results indicate that western expatriate managers' international adjustment is significantly increased along with their expatriation time in China. Additionally, Table 5.9 presents the mean scores of the three facets of, and overall expatriate adjustment by groups.

5.3 Learning Style and Expatriation Time

The first two research hypotheses concern the examination of the relationship between learning styles and the length of time that western expatriate managers have been interacting with Chinese business environments. This section first provides an overview of findings related to the learning styles of western expatriate managers in China, followed by the results of the tests of Hypotheses 2a and 2b.

Table 5.9 Expatriate adjustment and expatriation time by four groups

Western expatriate managers	N	General	Socialization	Work	Overall
		Mean	Mean	Mean	Mean
1 year or less	22	4.09	3.09	3.87	11.04
Over 1–3 years	42	3.82	3.27	4.31	11.40
Over 3–5 years	36	4.36	3.64	4.88	12.88
Over 5 years	21	4.20	4.30	4.85	13.35

5.3.1 *An Overview of Western Expatriate Managers' Learning Styles*

Table 5.10 summarizes the mean scores and standard deviations (s. d.) of six learning style variables (CE, RO, AC, AE, AC-CE, and AE-RO) of western expatriate managers and also of host Chinese managers for comparison. Table 5.10 also includes the results of paired sample t-test.

A comparison between the learning style inventory scores of western expatriate managers and of host Chinese managers would enable us to understand the learning characteristics of western expatriate managers overall. With regard to the active and reflective dimension, the AE-RO score of western expatriates is 10.89, which is significantly higher than Chinese managers' score (4.09). The RO score of western expatriates is 26.31, which is significantly lower than Chinese managers' score (30.59). The AE score of western expatriates displays 37.12, which is significantly higher than Chinese managers' score (34.68). These results suggest that western expatriate managers prefer to learn through active experimentation (AE) over reflective observation (RO) in comparison with local Chinese managers.

With regard to the abstract and concrete dimension, the AC-CE score of western expatriate managers is 7.26, which is significantly lower than the local Chinese managers' score (8.26). The AC score of western expatriates shows 31.83 that is not statistically different from the Chinese managers' score (31.50), while the CE score of western expatriates is 24.58, which is significantly higher than the Chinese managers' score (23.24). These results indicate that overall western expatriate managers prefer to learn using concrete experience (CE) rather than abstract conceptualization (AC) in comparison with host Chinese managers.

Based on the above research results, we can say that their learning orientation to the abstract and active modes should be remark upon as their learning style characteristics. The combination of their relative preference for abstract and active modes indicates that overall western expatriate managers prefer the Converging learning style. However, the high values of standard deviations (s. d.) of AE-RO

Table 5.10 A summary of the six learning style variables

	Western expatriate managers (N = 121)	Local Chinese managers (N = 133)		Paired sample	
	Mean	s. d.	Mean	s. d.	t-test (t score)
CE	24.58	4.215	23.24	4.479	2.619***
RO	26.31	4.241	30.59	6.770	−6.729***
AC	31.83	3.974	31.50	5.478	0.913
AE	37.12	3.920	34.68	6.897	3.938**
AC-CE	7.26	5.969	8.26	8.494	−0.910**
AE-RO	10.89	5.861	4.09	12.602	6.225***

Note ***$p < 0.001$; **$p < 0.01$ (two-tailed)

Accommodating 7.5%	Diverging 10.5%
Converging 28.6%	Assimilating 53.4%

Fig. 5.1 Learning styles distribution of 121 western expatriate managers

and AC-CE illustrate that western expatriate managers tend to have varied learning styles as individuals. Figure 5.1 depicts the distribution of the four learning styles of 121 western expatriate managers. The results indicate that western expatriate managers primarily tend to learn through converging or accommodating learning styles. The diverging learning style is the least preferred by western expatriate managers in China.

5.3.2 Four Learning Modes and Expatriation Time

The present research first examines the relationship between the four learning modes (CE, RO, AC, and AE) and expatriation time.

5.3.2.1 Concrete Experience Learning Mode and Expatriation Time

In this section, the present research first investigates the correlation between the Concrete Experience (CE) learning mode and the expatriate time. According to the results of correlation analysis of all metric variables, five personal characteristics in demographic characteristics have a significant relationship with the CE learning mode. They are: age, gender, Number of previous international assignments, job function, and function area. This research then treats these five personal characteristics as mediating variables in the regression analysis of the correlation between the Concrete Experience (CE) learning mode and the expatriate time. Table 5.11 presents the results of regression analysis testing CE.

As can be seen in Model 1 in Table 5.11, the expatriation time in China does not affect the CE learning mode. Model 2 in Table 5.11 examines the impact of the five mediating variables upon the relationship between the expatriation time and the CE learning mode. Results of Model 2 show that the expatriation time has no significant influence on the CE learning mode after the effects of the five mediating variables were eliminated. In addition, the results of Model 2 in Table 5.11 show that two demographic variables (gender and number of previous international assignments) significantly positively affect the CE learning mode ($p < 0.01$). This

Table 5.11 Results of regression analysis of CE

	CE			
	Model 1		Model 2	
	Beta (standardized)	t	Beta (standardized)	t
Independent variable				
Expatriation time	−0.039	−0.421	−0.158	1.392
Mediating variables				
Gender			0.238	3.169**
Age			−0.185	−1.844
No. of previous IA			0.544	6.709**
Job function			0.144	1.264
Functional area			0.035	0.448
F	0.177		11.763**	
R2	0.001		−0.007	
Adjusted R2	0.382		0.350	

Note $^*p < 0.05$; $^{**}p < 0.01$

indicates that female expatriate managers show more learning preferences for concrete experience than male expatriate managers when they work in China. In other words, female expatriate managers find it easier to develop concrete experience learning mode in cross-cultural context. Moreover, the results suggest that western expatriate managers become more concrete if they experienced more previous international assignments. On the contrary, western expatriate managers become more abstract and less concrete if they have no international assignment experience. In order to better understand the impact of these two demographic characteristics (gender and number of previous international assignments) upon the CE learning mode, Table 5.12 presents the results of independent t-tests of male (N = 105) versus female (N = 16) and non-overseas experience (N = 79) versus overseas experience (N = 42) with regard to the CE learning mode.

As shown in Table 5.12, the mean score of the CE learning mode of female western expatriate managers is significantly higher than that of male western expatriate manager ($p < 0.01$). Moreover, the mean score of the CE learning mode of overseas experienced western expatriate managers is significantly higher than that of non overseas experienced western expatriate managers ($p < 0.01$).

Table 5.12 Results of independent t-tests of gender and overseas experience regarding CE

	CE				
	N	Mean	s. d.	t	F
Male	105	24.02	3.685	−2.925**	3.511
Female	16	28.25	5.604		
Overseas experience	42	27.45	4.238	5.841**	1.100
Non-overseas experience	79	23.05	3.328		

Note $^{**}p < 0.01$ (two-tailed)

5.3.2.2 Reflective Observation Learning Mode and Expatriation Time

In this section, the present research investigates the correlation between the Reflective Observation (RO) learning mode and the expatriate time. According to the results of correlation analysis of all metric variables, six personal characteristics in demographic characteristics have a significant relationship with the RO learning mode. They are: nationality, age, international family, Number of previous international assignments, overseas educational degree, and job function. This research then treats these six personal characteristics as mediating variables in the regression analysis of the correlation between the Reflective observation learning mode and the expatriate time. Table 5.13 presents the results of regression analysis testing RO.

As can be seen in Model 1 in Table 5.13, the expatriation time in China has a significant positive relationship with the RO learning mode (Beta = 0.620, $p < 0.01$). The results indicate that the longer western expatriate managers have continually worked in China, the more they prefer to learn through reflective observation (RO) learning mode. Model 2 in Table 5.13 examines the impact of six mediating variables upon the relationship between the expatriation time and the RO learning mode. The results of Model 2 illustrate that the expatriation time in China still has a significant positive influence upon the RO learning mode after the effects of the six mediating variables were eliminated (Beta = 0.487, $p < 0.01$). This suggests that the expatriation time in China independently affects the RO learning mode.

Table 5.13 Results of regression analysis of RO

	RO			
	Model 1		Model 2	
	Beta (standardized)	t	Beta (standardized)	t
Independent variable				
Expatriation time	0.620	8.610**	0.487	4.341**
Mediating variables				
Nationality			0.090	1.250
Age			0.146	1.527
International family			0.120	1.604
No. of previous IA			0.055	0.727
Overseas degree			−0.105	−1.369
Job function			−0.056	−0.509
F	74.140**		12.483**	
R2	0.384		0.436	
Adjusted R2	0.379		0.401	

Note *$p < 0.05$; **$p < 0.01$

5.3.2.3 Abstract Conceptualization Learning Mode and Expatriation Time

In this section, the present research investigates the correlation between the Abstract Conceptualization (AC) learning mode and the expatriate time. According to the results of correlation analysis of all metric variables, four personal characteristics in demographic characteristics have a significant relationship with the AC learning mode. They are: gender, Number of previous international assignments, job function, and function area. This research then treats these four personal characteristics as mediating variables in the regression analysis of the correlation between the Abstract Conceptualization learning mode and the expatriate time. Table 5.14 presents the results of regression analysis testing AC.

As can be seen in Model 1 in Table 5.14, the expatriation time in China has a significant negative relationship with the AC learning mode (Beta = −0.360, $p < 0.01$). The results indicate that the longer western expatriate managers have continually worked in China, the less they prefer to learn through abstract conceptualization (AC) learning mode. Model 2 in Table 5.14 examines the impact of four mediating variables upon the relationship between the expatriation time and the AC learning mode. The results of Model 2 illustrate that the expatriation time in China still has a significant negative influence upon the AC learning mode after the effects of the four mediating variables were eliminated (Beta = −0.250, $p < 0.05$). This suggests that the expatriation time in China independently affects the AC learning mode.

In addition, the results of Model 2 in Table 5.14 show that one demographic variable (number of previous international assignments) significantly negatively affects the AC learning mode ($p < 0.01$). This indicates that western expatriate managers become less abstract if they experienced more previous international

Table 5.14 Results of regression analysis of AC

	AC			
	Model 1		Model 2	
	Beta (standardized)	t	Beta (standardized)	t
Independent variable				
Expatriation time	−0.360	−0.4.204**	−0.250	−2.347*
Mediating variables				
Gender			−0.102	−1.348
No. of previous IA			−0.397	−4.845**
Job function			0.124	1.110
Functional area			0.067	0.855
F	17.674**		13.089**	
R2	0.129		0.363	
Adjusted R2	0.122		0.335	

Note *$p < 0.05$; **$p < 0.01$

Table 5.15 Results of independent t-tests of overseas experience regarding AC

	AC				
	N	Mean	s. d.	t	F
Overseas experience	42	29.74	4.197		
Non-overseas experience	79	32.95	3.378	−4.277**	3.632

Note **$p < 0.01$ (two-tailed)

assignments. On the contrary, western expatriate managers become more concrete and less abstract if they have no international assignment experience. In order to better understand the impact of previous international assignments experience upon the AC learning mode, Table 5.15 presents the results of independent t-tests of non-overseas experience (N = 79) versus overseas experience (N = 42) with regard to the AC learning mode. As shown in Table 5.15, the mean score of the AC learning mode of overseas experienced western expatriate managers is significantly lower than that of non overseas experienced western expatriate managers ($p < 0.01$).

5.3.2.4 Active Experimentation Learning Mode and Expatriation Time

In this section, the present research investigates the correlation between the Active Experimentation (AE) learning mode and the expatriate time. According to the results of correlation analysis of all metric variables, six personal characteristics in demographic characteristics have a significant relationship with the AE learning mode. They are: nationality, age, international family, Number of previous international assignments, overseas educational degree, and job function. This research then treats these six personal characteristics as mediating variables in the regression analysis of the correlation between the Active experimentation learning mode and the expatriate time. Table 5.16 presents the results of regression analysis testing AE.

As can be seen in Model 1 in Table 5.16, the expatriation time in China has a significant negative relationship with the AE learning mode (Beta = −0.276, $p < 0.01$). The results indicate that the longer western expatriate managers have continually worked in China, the less they prefer to learn through active experimentation (AE) learning mode. Model 2 in Table 5.16 examines the impact of six mediating variables upon the relationship between the expatriation time and the AE learning mode. The results of Model 2 illustrate that the expatriation time in China still has a significant negative influence upon the AE learning mode after the effects of the six mediating variables were eliminated (Beta = −0.464, $p < 0.01$). This suggests that the expatriation time in China independently affects the AE learning mode.

In addition, the results of Model 2 show that two demographic variables (international family and number of previous international assignments) have a significant negative impact on the AE learning mode ($p < 0.05$). Regarding the

Table 5.16 Results of regression analysis of AE

	AE			
	Model 1		Model 2	
	Beta (standardized)	t	Beta (standardized)	t
Independent variable				
Expatriation time	−0.276	−3.136**	−0.464	−3.579**
Mediating variables				
Nationality			−0.163	−1.965
Age			0.176	1.588
International family			−0.207	−2.403*
No. of previous IA			−0.217	−2.503*
Overseas degree			−0.077	−0.875
Job function			−0.214	−1.673
F	9.833**		5.303**	
R2	0.076		0.247	
Adjusted R2	0.069		0.201	

Note *$p < 0.05$; **$p < 0.01$

transformation of the variable 'international family' in the questionnaire, '1' refers to parents and spouse come from same country, '2' refers to parents and/or spouse come from different country but not from Greater China, '3' refers to parents and/or spouse come from Greater China. It indicates that western expatriate managers that have an international family, especially the family member from Greater China, become less active when they work in China. This is consistent with the previous discussions in the literature review that Chinese prefer to learn through reflective observation rather than active experimentation in comparison with other nationalities. Moreover, the results suggest that western expatriate managers become less active in China if they have experienced more previous international assignments. On the contrary, western expatriate managers become more active and less reflective if they have no international assignment experience. In order to better understand the impact of these two demographic characteristics (international family and number of previous international assignments) upon the AE learning mode, Table 5.17 presents the results of independent t-tests of non-international

Table 5.17 Results of independent t-tests of international family and overseas experience regarding AE

	AE				
	N	Mean	s. d.	t	F
International family	19	34.42	4.776		
Non-international family	102	37.62	3.546	−2.778*	3.523
Overseas experience	42	35.62	4.455		
Non-overseas experience	79	37.91	3.371	−2.920**	2.976

Note *$p < 0.05$; **$p < 0.01$ (two-tailed)

family (N = 102) versus international family (N = 19) and non-overseas experience (N = 79) versus overseas experience (N = 42) with regard to the AE learning mode. As shown in Table 5.17, the mean score of the AE learning mode of western expatriate managers that have an international family is significantly lower than that of western expatriate managers that family members come from same country ($p < 0.05$). Moreover, the mean score of the AE learning mode of overseas experienced western expatriate managers is significantly lower than that of non-overseas experienced western expatriate managers ($p < 0.01$).

5.3.3 Results of Hypotheses Tests

As shown in the structure model for the research framework, the correlation between learning style and expatriation time in China is statistically significant. In particular, the relationship between the variable AC-CE and expatriation time is significant at the 0.05 level (*); while the relationship between the variable AE-RO and expatriation time is significant at the 0.01 level (**). Both are negative relations. This means that western expatriate managers become more concrete and reflective over time, while they become less abstract and active over time. Table 5.18 summarizes the standardized effects of expatriation time on learning style and two learning dimensions in the structure model.

In this section, the researcher further examines the relationship between the expatriation time and the two learning style variables (AC-CE and AE-RO) and the effects of related mediating variables on each correlation. Hypotheses 2a and 2b are hypothesized that the length of time that western expatriate managers have engaged in international assignments in China will positively influence their adjustment to the host culture via learning style, described below.

- Hypothesis 2a: The longer western expatriate managers have engaged in their International assignments in China, the more they will show their learning preferences for concrete experience over abstract conceptualization.
- Hypothesis 2b: The longer western expatriate managers have engaged in their International assignments in China, the more they will show their learning preferences for reflective observation over active experimentation.
- Hypothesis 2c: The longer western expatriate managers have engaged in their International assignments in China, the more balancing their learning styles will be.

Table 5.18 Standardized effects of expatriation time on learning style in the structure model

	Expatriation time		
	Total effect	Direct effect	Indirect effect
Learning style	−0.534**	−0.534**	0
AC-CE	−0.391*	0	−0.391*
AE-RO	−0.307**	0	−0.307**

Note *$p < 0.05$; **$p < 0.01$

5.3.3.1 Hypothesis 2a

Hypothesis 2a is related to examination of how the AC-CE learning dimension hinges upon the expatriation time spent in China. According to the results of correlation analysis of all metric variables, four personal characteristics in demographic characteristics have a significant relationship with the AC-CE learning dimension. They are: gender, Number of previous international assignments, job function, and function area. This research then treats these four personal characteristics as mediating variables in the regression analysis of hypothesis 2a. Table 5.19 presents the results of regression analysis testing hypothesis 2a.

As can be seen in Model 1 in Table 5.19, the expatriation time in China has a significant negative relationship with the AC-CE learning dimension (Beta = −0.212, $p < 0.05$). The results indicate that the longer western expatriate managers have continually worked in China, the more they prefer to learn through concrete experience (CE) rather than abstract conceptualization (AC). Model 2 in Table 5.19 examines the impact of four mediating variables upon the relationship between the expatriation time and the AC-CE learning dimension. Results of Model 2 show that the influence of expatriation time in China upon AC-CE become even stronger (Beta = −0.223, $p < 0.05$) after the effects of the four mediating variables were eliminated. This result suggests that the impact of expatriation time in China upon the AC-CE learning dimension is independent of the moderators. Therefore, Hypothesis 2a is supported.

Table 5.19 Results of regression analysis of Hypothesis 2a

	AC-CE				
	Model 1		Model 2		
	Beta (standardized)	t	Beta (standardized)	t	Zero order
Independent variable					
Expatriation time	−0.212	−2.369*	−0.223	−2.528*	−0.212*
Mediating variables					
Gender			−0.245	−3.910**	−0.349**
No. of previous IA			−0.647	−9.526**	−0.685**
Job function			−0.057	−0.614	0.263
Functional area			0.009	0.137	0.206
F	5.610*		29.612**		
R2	0.045		0.563		
Adjusted R2	0.037		0.544		

Note *$p < 0.05$; **$p < 0.01$

Two demographic variables (gender and number of previous international assignments) significantly negatively affect the AC-CE learning dimension ($p < 0.01$). This indicates that female expatriate managers show more learning preferences for concrete experience over abstract conceptualization when they work in China. In other words, female expatriate managers are easier to develop concrete experience learning mode in cross-cultural context. Moreover, the results suggest that western expatriate managers become more concrete and less abstract if they experienced more previous international assignments. Contrary to this, western expatriate managers become more abstract and less concrete if they have no international assignment experience. In order to better understand the impact of these two demographic characteristics (gender and number of previous international assignments) upon the AC-CE learning dimension, Table 5.20 presents the results of independent t-tests of male (N = 105) versus female (N = 16) and non-overseas experience (N = 79) versus overseas experience (N = 42) with regard to the AC-CE learning dimension. As shown in Table 5.20, the mean score of the AC-CE learning dimension of female western expatriate managers is significantly lower than that of male western expatriate managers ($p < 0.01$). Moreover, the mean score of the AC-CE learning dimension of overseas experienced western expatriate managers is significantly lower than that of non overseas experienced western expatriate managers ($p < 0.01$).

A story of western expatriates also seems to show the importance of the concrete learning mode in Chinese work environment. A western expatriate manager, working for administration in a western finance company in Beijing for seven years, told me her thoughts about working in China:

> In America, work is work, life is life. But in China, it seems like work is an outcome of life. Interpersonal relationship is so important in the Chinese business world. You have to develop relationships with your colleagues: have dinner sometime, talk about baba (father), mama (mother), and children. Then they will start to accept you.

This story of western expatriates seems to tell us that the concrete mode of learning is crucial for expatriate adjustment in China.

Table 5.20 Results of independent t-tests of gender and overseas experience regarding AC-CE

	AC-CE				
	N	Mean	s. d.	t	F
Male	105	8.07	5.407	4.066**	5.018
Female	16	1.94	6.894		
Non-overseas experience	79	9.90	4.410	8.392**	9.517
Overseas experience	42	2.29	5.339		

Note **$p < 0.01$ (two-tailed)

5.3.3.2 Hypothesis 2b

Hypothesis 2b is associated with investigation of how the AE-RO dimension rests on the expatriation time in China. According to the results of correlation analysis of all metric variables (Appendix G), six personal characteristics in demographic characteristics have a significant relationship with the AE-RO learning dimension. They are: nationality, age, international family, Number of previous international assignments, overseas educational degree, and job function. This research then treats these six personal characteristics as mediating variables in the regression analysis of hypothesis 1b. Table 5.21 presents the results of regression analysis testing hypothesis 2b.

As shown in Table 5.21, Model 1 indicates that the expatriation time in China has a significant negative association with the AE-RO learning dimension (Beta = −0.633, $p < 0.01$). The results suggest that the expatriation time in China makes a difference to the reflective or active modes of western expatriate managers' learning. In other words, reflective western expatriates stay longer in China than active western expatriates. The results are consistent with the prediction stated in hypothesis 1b. It predicts that the longer western expatriate managers have worked in China, the more they prefer to learn through reflective observation (RO) rather than active experimentation (AE). The results of Model 2 illustrate that the expatriation time in China still has a significant negative influence upon the AE-RO learning dimension after the effects of the six mediating variables were eliminated. This suggests that the expatriation time in China independently affects the active-reflective learning dimension. Therefore, hypothesis 2b receives support.

Table 5.21 Results of regression analysis of Hypothesis 2b

	AE-RO				
	Model 1		Model 2		
	Beta (standardized)	t	Beta (standardized)	t	Zero order
Independent variable					
Expatriation time	−0.633	−8.927**	−0.652	−6.306**	−0.633*
Mediating variables					
Nationality			−0.163	−2.462*	−0.215*
Age			0.002	0.019	−0.387
International family			−0.228	−3.316**	−0.337**
No. of previous IA			−0.193	−2.795**	−0.230**
Overseas degree			0.013	0.179	−0.214
Job function			−0.100	−0.985	0.454
F	79.697**		17.510**		
R2	0.401		0.396		
Adjusted R2	0.520		0.491		

Note *$p < 0.05$; **$p < 0.01$

Results of Model 2 show that two demographic variables (international family and number of previous international assignments) have a significant negative impact on the AE-RO learning dimension ($p < 0.01$). Regarding the transformation of the variable 'international family' in the questionnaire, '1' refers to parents and spouse come from same country, '2' refers to parents and/or spouse come from different country but not from Greater China, '3' refers to parents and/or spouse come from Greater China. It indicates that western expatriate managers that have an international family, especially the family member from Greater China, become more reflective and less active when they work in China. This is consistent with the discussions in the literature review before that Chinese are prefer to learn through reflective observation rather than active experimentation in comparison with other nationalities. Moreover, the results suggest that western expatriate managers become more reflective and less active in China if they experienced more previous international assignments. On the contrary, western expatriate managers become more active and less reflective if they have no international assignment experience.

In order to better understand the impact of these two demographic characteristics (international family and number of previous international assignments) upon the AE-RO learning dimension, Table 5.22 presents the results of independent t-tests of non-international family (N = 102) versus international family (N = 19) and non-overseas experience (N = 79) versus overseas experience (N = 42) with regard to the AE-RO learning dimension. As shown in Table 5.22, the mean score of the AE-RO learning dimension of western expatriate managers that have an international family is significantly lower than that of western expatriate managers that family members come from same country ($p < 0.01$). Moreover, the mean score of the AE-RO learning dimension of overseas experienced western expatriate managers is significantly lower than that of non-overseas experienced western expatriate managers ($p < 0.01$).

5.3.3.3 Hypothesis 2c

Hypothesis 2c is associated with the investigation of whether western expatriate managers' learning styles become balance along with their expatriation time in

Table 5.22 Results of independent t-tests of international family and overseas experience regarding AE-RO

	AE-RO				
	N	Mean	s. d.	t	F
Non-international family	102	11.67	5.158	3.523**	5.988
International family	19	6.74	7.622		
Non-overseas experience	79	12.20	5.569	3.529**	0.202
Overseas experience	42	8.43	5.657		

Note **$p < 0.01$ (two-tailed)

China. The present research adopt the summation of the two absolute values of the two dimensional scores [ABS (AC-CE) and ABS (AE-RO)] to represent the balancing level of learning styles. The lower the summated score, the more balancing the learning style is. According to the results of correlation analysis of all metric variables, four personal characteristics in demographic characteristics have a significant relationship with the balancing learning style. They are: gender, age, international family, and Number of previous international assignments. This research then treats these four personal characteristics as mediating variables in the regression analysis of hypothesis 2c. Table 5.23 presents the results of regression analysis testing hypothesis 2c.

As shown in Table 5.23, Model 1 indicates that the longer western expatriate managers have engaged in their International assignments in China, the more balancing their learning styles (Beta = −0.603, $p < 0.01$). The results suggest that the expatriation time in China makes a difference to the balancing or specializing modes of western expatriate managers' learning. The results of Model 2 illustrate that the expatriation time in China still has a significant positive influence upon the balancing level of learning styles after the effects of the four mediating variables were eliminated (Beta = −0.622, $p < 0.01$). This suggests that the length of the expatriation time independently affects the balancing level of western expatriate managers' learning styles. Therefore, hypothesis 2c receives support.

Results of Model 2 show that two demographic variables (international family and number of previous international assignments) have a significant negative impact on the balancing learning style. It indicates that western expatriate managers that have an international family, especially the family member from Greater China, become more balancing in their learning styles when they work in China. Moreover, the results suggest that western expatriate managers become more balancing in their learning styles if they experienced more previous international

Table 5.23 Results of regression analysis of hypothesis 2c

	Balancing learning style			
	Model 1		Model 2	
	Beta (standardized)	t	Beta (standardized)	t
Independent variable				
Expatriation time	−0.603	−8.245**	−0.622	−7.802**
Mediating variables				
Gender			−0.114	−1.805
Age			0.090	1.121
International family			−0.133	−2.113*
No. of previous IA			−0.388	−6.104**
F	67.987**		30.248**	
R2	0.364		0.358	
Adjusted R2	0.568		0.549	

Note *$p < 0.05$; **$p < 0.01$

Table 5.24 Results of independent t-tests of international family and overseas experience regarding balancing learning style

	Balancing learning style				
	N	Mean	s. d.	t	F
International family	19	14.84	7.726		
Non-international family	102	20.47	7.936	−2.903**	0.0233
Overseas experience	42	14.00	5.725		
Non-overseas experience	79	22.56	7.672	−6.928**	2.366

Note *$p < 0.05$; **$p < 0.01$ (two-tailed)

assignments. On the contrary, western expatriate managers are more specialized in their learning modes if they have no international assignment experience.

In order to better understand the impact of these two demographic characteristics (international family and number of previous international assignments) upon the balancing learning style, Table 5.24 presents the results of independent t-tests of non-international family (N = 102) versus international family (N = 19) and non-overseas experience (N = 79) versus overseas experience (N = 42) with regard to the balancing learning style. As shown in Table 5.24, the mean score of the balancing learning style of western expatriate managers that have an international family is significantly lower than that of western expatriate managers that family members come from same country ($p < 0.01$). Moreover, the mean score of the balancing learning style of overseas experienced western expatriate managers is significantly lower than that of non-overseas experienced western expatriate managers ($p < 0.01$).

5.3.4 *Learning Style Transitions Over Time*

This section examines transitional movement of western expatriate managers' learning styles as supplemental analysis through conducting the chi-square test of independence. In this study, the sample of 121 western expatriates is divided into four groups based on how long they have been in China. The first group has been in China for 1 year or less than 1 year; the second group for over 1–3 years; the third group for over 3–5 years; and the fourth group for over 5 years. Table 5.25 presents a cross-tabulation of the four groups and four learning styles together with the results of chi-square test.

The Pearson Chi-square value is 8.573 ($p < 0.05$), which led to a rejection of the null hypothesis that the four groups by years and four learning styles are independent. The cross-tabulation illustrates that the first group of western expatriates has the largest positive Std. residuals for Converging learning style and the largest negative Std. residuals for other three learning styles. The results indicate that the learning styles of western expatriate managers tend to have transited from Converging to Accommodating and Assimilating learning styles. The learning

Table 5.25 A cross-tabulation of four learning styles and expatriation time by four groups

		Learning styles				Total
		Diverging	Assimilating	Converging	Accommodating	
1 year or less	Count	0	0	18	4	22
	Percent	0.0 %	0.0 %	81.8 %	18.2 %	
	Std. residual	−0.7	−1.3	0.8	−0.4	
Over 1–years	Count	1	2	27	12	42
	Percent	2.4 %	4.8 %	64.3 %	28.6 %	
	Std. residual	0.0	−0.6	−0.3	0.9	
Over 3–5 years	Count	1	4	22	9	36
	Percent	2.8 %	11.1 %	61.1 %	25.0 %	
	Std. residual	0.1	0.8	−0.5	0.3	
Over 5 years	Count	1	3	15	2	21
	Percent	4.8 %	14.3 %	71.4 %	9.5 %	
	Std. residual	0.7	1.2	0.2	−1.2	
Total	Count	3	9	82	27	121
	Percent	2.5 %	7.4 %	67.8 %	22.3 %	100.0 %
Chi-square		8.573*				

Note *$p < 0.05$; *Std. residual* Standardized residual

Table 5.26 Two learning dimensions and expatriation time by four groups

Western expatriate managers	N	AC-CE	AE-RO
		Mean	Mean
1 year or less	22	10.18	15.27
Over 1–3 years	42	6.76	13.10
Over 3–5 years	36	6.44	8.06
Over 5 years	21	6.57	6.76

modes of western expatriate managers are directed from the abstract to the concrete mode as well as from the active to the reflective mode.

Additionally, Table 5.26 presents the mean scores of two learning style dimensions (AC-CE and AE-RO) by groups. Figure 5.2 shows how these two learning dimensions move according to the four different groups. In Fig. 5.2, each of the four groups is placed based on their two learning dimensions' scores. As the three arrows point out, the orientation of western expatriate managers' learning styles is shifted toward the reflective and concrete modes. Movement toward the reflective mode is drastic in particular. Moreover, there is a significant decrease from the first group to the second group in the abstract and concrete dimension ($p < 0.05$). These results are congruent with the results of examination of hypotheses 1a and 1b.

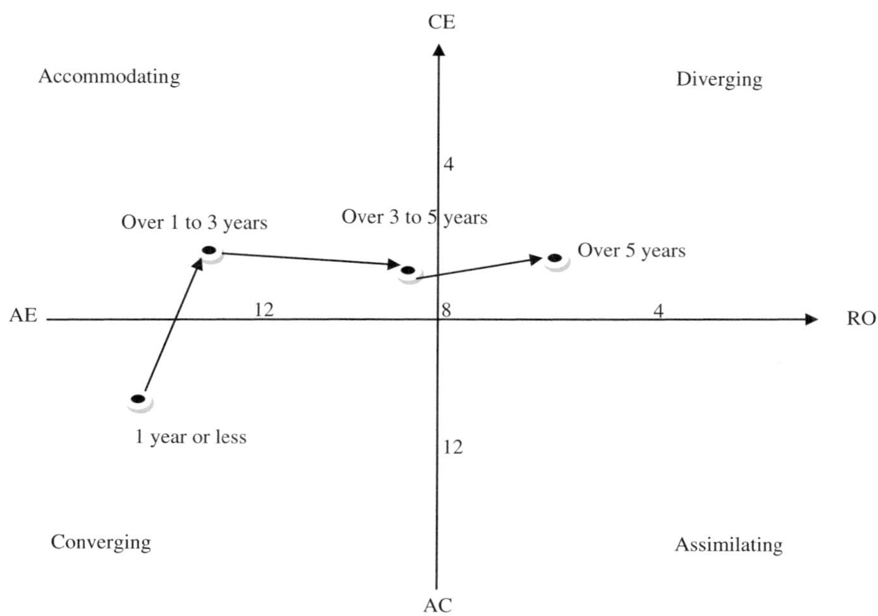

Fig. 5.2 Transitional movements of two learning dimensions over four groups

5.4 Managerial Tacit Knowledge and Expatriation Time

Research hypotheses 3a and 3b are associated with western expatriate managers' levels of accumulated managerial tacit knowledge and their expatriation time in China. This section first presents an overview of western expatriate managers' levels of accumulated managerial tacit knowledge and subsequently provides the results of tests of hypotheses 3a and 3b.

5.4.1 An Overview of Western Expatriate Managers' Managerial Tacit Knowledge

Table 5.27 summarizes the mean scores and standard deviations (s. d.) of nine variables (situation 1, situation 2, situation 3, situation 4, situation 5, situation 6, managing self, managing others, and total managerial tacit knowledge) measured by Tacit knowledge inventory for managers. The mean scores of six situations range from 0.434 (situation 2) to 0.601 (situation 3). The mean score of managing others is a little higher than of managing self. It indicates that western expatriate managers own relatively higher levels of accumulated managerial tacit knowledge in managing self.

Furthermore, the present research discusses western expatriate managers' responses to each situation in tacit knowledge inventory in detail. The study first discusses the situations related to managerial tacit knowledge in managing self: situation 1, situation 4, and situation 5. The content of situation 1 is 'You are an executive vice-president in the marketing division of Sherman Electronics, a company that sells audio and video supplies. You have been with Sherman Electronics since finishing college, having spent 13 years in a managerial role in human resources and two years in your present position. Sherman Electronics has been losing market share for its products steadily over the past five years. Sherman's strength in the past has been introducing new products before its competition, but now its product line seems to be three steps behind the leaders in a rapidly changing market. A strategy of focusing on more stable segments of the market has been aborted because of fierce competition from large overseas companies. You believe that your lack of knowledge about the latest audio and video products and technology limits your effectiveness. Your schedule is very busy, but you think it is important to catch up on, and keep up with, innovation that affects your industry.' This situation asks managers to rate the quality of the following

Table 5.27 A summary of the nine managerial tacit knowledge variables (N = 121)

	s 1	s 4	s 5	Self	s 2	s 3	s 6	Others	Total
Mean	0.555	0.554	0.490	0.533	0.434	0.601	0.586	0.540	1.073
s. d.	0.189	0.139	0.121	0.091	0.164	0.152	0.138	0.085	0.13

Table 5.28 Western expatriate managers' responses to situation 1 in TKIM (N = 121)

	Mean	s. d.
1. Ask for a leave of absence to pursue an advanced technical degree	2.03	1.189
2. Order a news clipping service (news clipping services provide news from a large number of sources on a given topic)	4.57	1.633
3. Subscribe to several technical journals relevant to your manufacturing operations	4.13	1.814
4. Subscribes to several consumer-oriented magazines that cover your products	4.70	1.622
5. Begin attending trade shows of products in your industry	5.73	1.112
6. Ask to sit in on weekly discussions of new product ideas held by the Research and Development division	6.43	0.858
7. Attend a series of technical presentations by research scientists from outside the company who are brought in by the Manufacturing Operations division	5.63	1.189
8. Hire a staff member whose primary responsibility is to keep you abreast of current trends in your industry	4.63	1.790
9. Ask the Engineering division to prepare monthly summary reports of innovative products	5.23	1.305
10. Ask for weekly presentations for you and your staff on technical issues by staff in the Research and Development and Manufacturing Operations divisions	5.63	1.402

strategies for becoming more knowledgeable about new products and technology on a 1 (extremely bad) to 7 (extremely good) point scale. Table 5.28 presents the 10 available strategies for situation 1 with western expatriate managers' mean rate for each strategy and according standard deviation. The mean rates for the 10 strategies of situation 1 range from 2.03 (strategy 1) to 6.43 (strategy 6). The top four good strategies for situation 1 are strategy 6 (Ask to sit in on weekly discussions of new product ideas held by the Research and Development division), strategy 5 (Begin attending trade shows of products in your industry), strategy 7 (Attend a series of technical presentations by research scientists from outside the company who are brought in by the Manufacturing Operations division), and strategy 10 (Ask for weekly presentations for you and your staff on technical issues by staff in the Research and Development and Manufacturing Operations divisions). Overall western expatriate managers think strategy 1 (Ask for a leave of absence to pursue an advanced technical degree) is a quite inappropriate response to situation 1.

Situation 4 asks managers to rate the quality of the following 10 strategies for handling the day-to-day work of a manager on a 1 'extremely bad' to 7 'extremely good' point scale. Table 5.29 presents the 10 available strategies for situation 4 with western expatriate managers' mean rate for each strategy and according standard deviation. The mean rates for the 10 strategies of situation 4 range from 2.63 (strategy 7) to 6.37 (strategy 2). The top three good strategies for situation 4 are strategy 2 (Use a daily list of goals arranged according to your priorities), strategy 9 (Set your own deadlines in addition to externally imposed ones), and strategy 1

Table 5.29 Western expatriate managers' responses to situation 4 in TKIM (N = 121)

	Mean	s. d.
1. Think in terms of tasks accomplished rather than hours spent working	5.50	1.592
2. Use a daily list of goals arranged according to your priorities	6.37	1.066
3. Reward yourself upon completion of important tasks for the day	4.57	1.501
4. Be in charge of all phase of every task or project you are involved in	2.90	1.689
5. Take frequent but short breaks (i.e., a quick walk to the mail room) throughout the day	4.67	1.241
6. Only delegate inconsequential tasks, since you cannot guarantee that the tasks will be done properly and on time unless you do them yourself	2.77	1.006
7. Do only what you are in the mood to do to maximize the quality of your work	2.63	1.326
8. Take every opportunity to get feedback on early drafts of your work	5.03	1.450
9. Set your own deadlines in addition to externally imposed ones	5.83	1.147
10. Do not spend much time planning the best way to do something because the best way to do something may not be apparent until after you have begun doing it	3.97	1.608

(Think in terms of tasks accomplished rather than hours spent working). Overall western expatriate managers think strategy 7 (Do only what you are in the mood to do to maximize the quality of your work) is an inappropriate response to situation 4.

The content of situation 5 is 'You are looking for a new project to tackle in the coming year. You have considered a number of possible projects and desire to pick the project that would be best for you.' This situation asks managers to rate the importance of the following considerations when selecting new projects on a 1 (extremely bad) to 7 (extremely good) point scale. Table 5.30 presents the 10 considerations for situation 5 with western expatriate managers' mean rate for each

Table 5.30 Western expatriate managers' responses to situation 5 in TKIM (N = 121)

	Mean	s. d.
1. The project is the one my immediate superior most desires to be completed	4.40	1.133
2. Doing the project would require my developing skills that may enhance my future career success	5.83	1.117
3. The project should attract the attention of the local media	3.10	1.296
4. Doing the project should prove to be fun	5.03	1.497
5. The risk of making a mistake is virtually nonexistent	2.47	1.137
6. The project will require my interacting with senior executives whom I would like to get to know better	5.10	1.494
7. The project is valued by my superior even though it is not valued by me	4.33	1.647
8. The project will enable me to demonstrate my talents that others may not be aware of	5.40	1.037
9. The project is in an area with which I have a lot of experience	5.47	1.358
10. The project is the one I most want to do	5.07	1.721

consideration and according standard deviation. The mean rates for the 10 considerations of situation 5 range from 2.47 (consideration 5) to 5.83 (consideration 2). The top three important considerations for situation 5 are consideration 2 (Doing the project would require my developing skills that may enhance my future career success), consideration 9 (The project is in an area with which I have a lot of experience), and consideration 8 (The project will enable me to demonstrate my talents that others may not be aware of). Overall western expatriate managers think consideration 5 (The risk of making a mistake is virtually nonexistent) is the least important consideration to situation 5.

The present research then discusses the situations related to managerial tacit knowledge in managing others: situation 2, situation 3, and situation 6. The content of situation 2 is 'An employee who reports to one of your subordinates has asked to talk with you about waste, poor management practices, and possible violations of both departmental policy and the law on the part of your subordinate. You have been in your present position only a year, but in that time you have had no indications of trouble about the subordinate in question. Neither you nor your department has an "open door" policy, so it is expected that employees should take their concerns to their immediate supervisors before bringing a matter to the attention of anyone else. The employee who wishes to meet with you has not discussed this matter with her supervisor because of its delicate nature.' This situation asks managers to rate the quality of the following strategies they are considering doing in this situation on a 1 'extremely bad' to 7 'extremely good' point scale. Table 5.31 presents the 10 strategies for situation 2 with western expatriate managers' mean rate for each strategy and according standard deviation. The mean

Table 5.31 Western expatriate managers' responses to situation 2 in TKIM (N = 121)

	Mean	s. d.
1. Refuse to meet with the employee unless the individual first discusses the matter with your subordinate	1.90	0.923
2. Meet with the employee but only with your subordinate present	2.63	1.159
3. Schedule a meeting with the employee and then with your subordinate to get both sides of the story	5.47	1.306
4. Meet with the employee and then investigate the allegations if an investigation appears warranted before talking with your subordinate	4.33	2.023
5. Find out more information about the employee, if you can, before making any decisions	5.40	1.354
6. Refuse to meet with the employee and inform your subordinate that the employee has attempted to sidestep the chain of command	1.93	1.143
7. Meet with your subordinate first before deciding whether to meet with the employee	3.70	1.860
8. Reprimand the employee for ignoring the chain of command	1.50	0.682
9. Ask a senior colleague whom you respect for advice about what to do in this situation	4.40	2.358
10. Turn the matter over to an assistant	1.47	0.973

rates for the 10 strategies of situation 2 range from 1.47 (strategy 10) to 5.47 (strategy 3). The top two good strategies for situation 2 are strategy 3 (Schedule a meeting with the employee and then with your subordinate to get both sides of the story) and strategy 5 (Find out more information about the employee, if you can, before making any decisions). Overall western expatriate managers think strategy 10 (Turn the matter over to an assistant), strategy 8 (Reprimand the employee for ignoring the chain of command) and strategy 1 (Refuse to meet with the employee unless the individual first discusses the matter with your subordinate) are inappropriate responses to situation 2.

The content of situation 3 is 'You have just completed your most important project ever, which involved automating the department's warehouses. You have worked many evenings and weekend days over the last six months on this project. You are pleased with your performance because, despite adversity, the project was completed at the projected cost and on time. Near the project's end, it seemed likely that you were going to need additional time and money. But, through hard work on your part, and by pushing some of your people very hard, you met both time deadlines and cost projections. In a meeting, your supervisor (having been in his position for six months), brings up the topic of your performance on the project. Expecting lavish praise and perhaps even discussion of a possible increase in responsibility, you are stunned by his evaluation of your performance, which is entirely negative. He states that some of your subordinates have complained to him directly about their treatment at your hands in the last phase of project completion. He questions your ability to manage others, and wonders aloud about your ability to lead others. He says nothing positive about the fact that you completed the project on time and at cost under adverse circumstances, nor about how hard you worked on the project.' This situation asks managers to rate the quality of the following things they might do in this situation on a 1 'extremely bad' to 7 'extremely good' point scale. Table 5.32 presents the 10 strategies for situation 3 with western expatriate managers' mean rate for each strategy and according standard deviation. The mean rates for the 10 strategies of situation 3 range from 2.03 (strategy 5) to 6.10 (strategy 6). The top three good strategies for situation 3 are strategy 6 (Discuss with your supervisor specific examples of where he thinks you went wrong in dealing with the project, and how he would have handled it more effectively), strategy 1 (Admit that you perhaps were too hard on your workers, but state that in your judgment, the importance of meeting the deadline and budget projection made your actions necessary), and strategy 4 (Try to find out if anything else is behind this overly negative evaluation). Overall western expatriate managers think strategy 5 (Begin looking for a new position) is an inappropriate responses to situation 3.

The content of situation 6 is 'You and a co-worker jointly are responsible for completing a report on a new project by the end of the week. You are uneasy about this assignment because he has a reputation for not meeting deadlines. The problem does not appear to be lack of effort. Rather, he seems to lack certain organizational skills necessary to meet a deadline and also is quite a perfectionist. As a result, too much time is wasted coming up with the "perfect" idea, project, or report.' In this

Table 5.32 Western expatriate managers' responses to situation 3 in TKIM (N = 121)

	Mean	s. d.
1. Admit that you perhaps were too hard on your workers, but state that in your judgment, the importance of meeting the deadline and budget projection made your actions necessary	5.30	1.055
2. Expressers disappointment with your performance appraisal, and state that you think it is one-sided	3.87	1.871
3. Accept the criticism and explain how you will behave differently in the future	3.10	1.845
4. Try to find out if anything else is behind this overly negative evaluation	5.23	1.331
5. Begin looking for a new position	2.03	1.520
6. Discuss with your supervisor specific examples of where he thinks you went wrong in dealing with the project, and how he would have handled it more effectively	6.10	0.995
7. Ask your supervisor to give you a second chance, resolving to yourself to keep him better informed about your activities in the future	3.40	1.850
8. Ask your supervisor to help you develop your skills at managing others	4.70	1.343
9. Seek the advice of others you trust in the department about what you should do	3.90	1.989
10. Admit you might have made some mistakes, but be sure your supervisor is aware of all that you accomplished and the adverse circumstances that you faced	5.20	1.669

situation, the manager's goal is to produce the best possible report by the deadline at the end of the week. The situation asks managers to rate the quality of the following strategies for meeting the goal on a 1 'extremely bad' to 7 'extremely good' point scale.

Table 5.33 presents the 10 available strategies for situation 6 with western expatriate managers' mean rate for each strategy and according standard deviation. The mean rates for the 10 strategies of situation 6 range from 1.63 (strategy 11) to 5.50 (strategy 5). The top three good strategies for situation 6 are strategy 5 (Praise your co-worker verbally for completion of parts of the assignment), strategy 8 (Point out firmly, but politely, how he is holding up the report), and strategy 3 (Set deadlines for completing each part of the report, and accept what you have accomplished at each deadline as the final version of that part of the report). Overall western expatriate managers think strategy 11 (Ignore his organizational problem so you don't give attention to maladaptive behaviour) is an inappropriate responses to situation 6.

5.4.2 *Results of Hypotheses Tests*

As shown in the results of correlation analysis of all metric variables (Appendix G), the correlation between the three managerial tacit knowledge variables (managing

Table 5.33 Western expatriate managers' responses to situation 6 in TKIM (N = 121)

	Mean	s. d.
1. Divide the work to be done in half and tell him that if he does not complete his part, you obviously will have to let your immediate superior know it was not your fault	2.73	1.741
2. Politely tell him to be less of a perfectionist	3.93	1.701
3. Set deadlines for completing each part of the report, and accept what you have accomplished at each deadline as the final version of that part of the report	4.93	1.701
4. Ask your superior to check up on your progress on a daily basis (after explaining why)	4.37	1.829
5. Praise your co-worker verbally for completion of parts of the assignment	5.50	1.225
6. Get angry with him at the first sign of getting behind schedule	2.07	1.230
7. As soon as he begins to fall behind, take responsibility for doing the report yourself, if need be, to meet the deadline	2.93	1.999
8. Point out firmly, but politely, how he is holding up the report	5.37	1.520
9. Avoid putting any pressure on him because it will just make him fall even more behind	2.97	1.497
10. Offer to buy him dinner at the end of the week if you both meet the deadline	4.20	1.919
11. Ignore his organizational problem so you don't give attention to maladaptive behavior	1.63	0.765

self, managing others, and total managerial tacit knowledge) and expatriation time in China is statistically significant. Both are significant negative relations at 0.01 levels (**). However, according to the SEM analysis of the research framework, the correlation between managerial tacit knowledge and expatriation time is not significant. In this section, the researcher further examines the relationship between managerial tacit knowledge and expatriation time and the effects of related mediating variables on each correlation. Hypotheses 3a and 3b are described below:

- Hypothesis 3a: The longer western expatriate managers have engaged in their International assignments in China, the greater their levels of accumulated managerial tacit knowledge in managing self.
- Hypothesis 3b: The longer western expatriate managers have engaged in their International assignments in China, the greater their levels of accumulated managerial tacit knowledge in managing others.

5.4.2.1 Hypothesis 3a

Hypothesis 3a is related to examination of how the managerial tacit knowledge in managing self relates to the expatriation time in China. According to the results of correlation analysis, three personal characteristics in demographic characteristics and two learning style dimensions have a significant relationship with managerial tacit knowledge in managing self. Three personal characteristics are: age, international family, and job function. This research then treats these five variables as mediating variables in the regression analysis of hypothesis 3a. Table 5.34 presents the results of regression analysis testing hypothesis 3a.

As illustrated in Table 5.34, Model 1 tests the relationship between the expatriation time in China and levels of accumulated managerial tacit knowledge in managing self. The result indicates that they have a significant negative correlation ($p < 0.01$). It should be noted that scores measured by TKIM (Tacit knowledge inventory for managers) are expected to decrease rather than increase with advancing levels of tacit knowledge because these scores represent respondents' deviations from the expert/successful group. Model 2 examines how five mediating variables as well as the expatriation time in China affect western expatriate managers' levels of accumulated managerial tacit knowledge in managing self. After the effects of the five moderators were eliminated, the expatriation time spent in China does not affect the accumulation of managerial tacit knowledge. This result suggests that the effect of the expatriation time on accumulation of managerial tacit knowledge depends on that of the moderators. Consequently, hypothesis 3a is rejected.

The result of Model 2 shows that the AE-RO learning dimension have a significant positive relationship with managerial tacit knowledge in managing self ($p < 0.01$). This means that reflective western expatriate managers are better at acquiring managerial tacit knowledge in managing self than active western

Table 5.34 Results of regression analysis of hypothesis 3a

	Managing self				
	Model 1		Model 2		
	Beta (standardized)	t	Beta (standardized)	t	Zero order
Independent variable					
Expatriation time	−0.505	−6.377**	−0.194	−1.514	−0.505
Mediating variables					
AC-CE			0.116	1.427	0.314
AE-RO			0.273	2.580**	0.525**
Age			0.100	0.995	−0.293
International family			−0.046	−0.574	−0.217
Job function			0.242	2.172*	0.480*
F	40.668**		11.373**		
R2	0.255		0.374		
Adjusted R2	0.248		0.342		

Note *$p < 0.05$; **$p < 0.01$

Table 5.35 Results of one-way ANOVA of job function regarding managing self

	Managing self				
	N	Mean	s. d.	F	df
Job function				16.839**	2
Senior managers	31	0.469	0.071		
Middle managers	75	0.545	0.088		
Junior managers	15	0.606	0.053		

Note **$p < 0.01$ (two-tailed)

expatriate managers. Moreover, one personal characteristic (job function) has a significant positive impact on the accumulation of managerial tacit knowledge in managing self ($p < 0.05$). with regard to the transformation of the variable 'job function' in the questionnaire, '1' refers to CEO/president; '2' refers to senior manager; '3' refers to middle manager; and '4' refers to junior manager. The result indicates that western expatriate managers with higher hierarchical job positions own greater levels of accumulated managerial tacit knowledge in managing self. In order to better understand the impact of job function upon the accumulation of managerial tacit knowledge in managing self, Table 5.35 presents the results of one-way ANOVA (Analysis of variance) of senior manages (1, 2) (N = 31) versus middle managers (3) (N = 75) versus junior managers (4) (N = 15) with regard to managerial tacit knowledge in managing self. As shown in Table 5.35, the mean scores of managerial tacit knowledge in managing self significantly decrease with advancing levels of western expatriate managers' job position ($p < 0.01$). Post hoc comparisons using Duncan's multiple range tests revealed that: senior managers accumulated significantly higher levels of managerial tacit knowledge related to managing self than either the junior or the middle level managers; middle managers accumulated significantly higher levels of managerial tacit knowledge related to managing self than junior level managers.

5.4.2.2 Hypothesis 3b

Hypothesis 3b is related to examination of how the managerial tacit knowledge in managing others hinges upon the expatriation time in China. According to the results of correlation analysis, four personal characteristics in demographic characteristics and two learning style dimensions have a significant relationship with managerial tacit knowledge in managing others. Four personal characteristics are: gender, age, number of previous international assignments, and job function. This research then treats these six variables as mediating variables in the regression analysis of hypothesis 3b. Table 5.36 presents the results of regression analysis testing hypothesis 3b.

As illustrated in Table 5.36, Model 1 tests the relationship between the expatriation time in China and levels of accumulated managerial tacit knowledge in managing others. The result shows that they have a significant negative correlation

Table 5.36 Results of regression analysis of hypothesis 3b

	Managing others				
	Model 1		Model 2		
	Beta (standardized)	t	Beta (standardized)	t	Zero order
Independent variable					
Expatriation time	−0.273	−3.098**	−0.087	−0.700	−0.273
Mediating variables					
AC-CE			0.429	4.053**	0.599**
AE-RO			−0.165	−1.756	0.220
Gender			−0.064	−0.859	−0.212
Age			−0.206	−2.205*	−0.323*
No. of previous IAs			−0.205	−2.030*	−0.523*
Job function			0.087	0.818	0.362
F	9.601**		13.940**		
R2	0.075		0.463		
Adjusted R2	0.067		0.430		

Note $*p < 0.05$; $**p < 0.01$

($p < 0.01$). Model 2 in Table 5.36 examines the impacts of the six mediating variables upon the relationship between expatriation time in China and western expatriate managers' levels of accumulated managerial tacit knowledge in managing others. After the effects of the six moderators were eliminated, the expatriation time no longer affects the accumulation of managerial tacit knowledge in managing others. This result suggests that the effect of the expatriation time on accumulation of managerial tacit knowledge depends on that of the moderators. Therefore, hypothesis 3b is refuted.

The result of Model 2 shows that the AC-CE learning dimension have a significant positive relationship with managerial tacit knowledge in managing others ($p < 0.01$). This indicates that concrete western expatriate managers are better at acquiring managerial tacit knowledge in managing others than abstract western expatriate managers. Moreover, two personal characteristics (age and number of previous international assignments) both have a significant negative impact on the accumulation of managerial tacit knowledge in managing others ($p < 0.05$). This means that older western expatriate managers tend to accumulate higher levels of managerial tacit knowledge in managing others. The results also suggest that western expatriate managers that have previous international assignment experiences are better at acquiring managerial tacit knowledge in managing others. In order to better understand the impact of these two demographic characteristics (age and number of previous international assignments) upon managerial tacit knowledge in managing others, Table 5.37 presents the results of one-way ANOVA of age (20–29) (N = 8) versus age (30–39) (N = 71) versus age (over 40) (N = 42) and

Table 5.37 Results of one-way ANOVA of age and overseas experience regarding managing others

	Managing others				
	N	Mean	s. d.	F	df
Age				7.234**	2
20–29	8	0.591	0.105		
30–39	71	0.556	0.082		
Over 40	42	0.503	0.073		
Overseas experience				48.129**	1
Non-overseas experience	79	0.573	0.081		
Overseas experience	42	0.478	0.051		

Note $^{**}p < 0.01$ (two-tailed)

non-overseas experience (N = 79) versus overseas experience (N = 42) with regard to managing others. As shown in Table 5.37, the mean scores of managerial tacit knowledge in managing others significantly decrease with advancing levels of western expatriate managers' age ($p < 0.01$). Moreover, the mean score of managing others of overseas experienced western expatriate managers is significantly lower than that of non overseas experienced western expatriate managers ($p < 0.01$).

5.4.3 Accumulation of Managerial Tacit Knowledge Over Time

Expatriation time has a significant relationship with managerial tacit knowledge and the effect of expatriation time on the accumulation of managerial tacit knowledge depends on that of moderators. In this research, the sample of 121 western expatriate managers is divided into four groups based on how long they have been in China: 1 year or less, over 1–3 years, over 3–5 years, over 5 years. Table 5.38 presents the mean scores of the three managerial tacit knowledge variables (managing self, managing others, and total managerial tacit knowledge) by four groups.

Table 5.38 Managerial tacit knowledge and expatriation time (four groups)

Western expatriate managers	N	Managing self	Managing others	Total
		Mean	Mean	Mean
1 year or less	22	0.621	0.550	1.171
Over 1–3 years	42	0.539	0.554	1.093
Over 3–5 years	36	0.501	0.539	1.041
Over 5 years	21	0.483	0.505	0.988
F		13.782**	1.713	9.783**

Note $^{**}p < 0.01$ (two-tailed)

Table 5.38 also presents the results of one-way ANOVA of four groups of western expatriate managers with regard to managing self, managing others, total managerial tacit knowledge respectively. As shown in Table 5.38, the mean scores of managerial tacit knowledge in managing self are significantly different among the four groups ($p < 0.01$). It indicates that western expatriate managers' levels of accumulated managerial tacit knowledge in managing self significantly increase along with the expatriation time.

5.5 Adaptive Flexibility and Expatriation Time

Research hypothesis 4 is associated with western expatriate managers' adaptive flexibility and their expatriation time in China. This section first presents an overview of western expatriate managers' levels of adaptive flexibility and subsequently provides the results of test of hypothesis 4.

5.5.1 *An Overview of Western Expatriate Managers' Adaptive Flexibility*

Table 5.39 summarizes the mean scores and standard deviations (s. d.) of five variables [concrete experience adaptive flexibility (CEAF), reflective observation adaptive flexibility (ROAF), abstract conceptualization adaptive flexibility (ACAF), active experimentation adaptive flexibility (AEAF), and total adaptive flexibility (AF)] measured by Adaptive style inventory. AF is the summation of CEAF, ROAF, ACAF, and AEAF. As can be seen in Table 5.39, the mean score of total adaptive flexibility is 16.025. The mean scores of adaptive flexibility in four different learning modes range from 2.698 (CEAF) to 5.736 (ACAF). It suggests that western expatriate managers tend to have greater adaptive flexibility in abstract conceptualization learning modes than in the other three learning modes.

5.5.2 *Results of Hypothesis 4 Test*

As shown in the structure model for the research framework, the correlation between expatriation time and adaptive flexibility is statistically significant. In this

Table 5.39 A summary of the five adaptive flexibility variables (N = 121)

	CEAF	ROAF	ACAF	AEAF	AF
Mean	2.698	3.855	5.736	3.736	16.025
s. d.	1.25	1.49	1.35	1.33	2.58

section, the researcher further examines the relationship between adaptive flexibility and expatriation time and the effects of related mediating variables on their correlation. Hypothesis 4 is described below:

- Hypothesis 4: Duration of western expatriate managers' engagement in international assignments in China will positively influence their adjustment to the host culture via adaptive flexibility.

Hypothesis 4 is related to examination of how the development of adaptive flexibility rests on the expatriation time in China. According to the results of correlation analysis, five personal characteristics in demographic characteristics and two learning style dimensions have a significant relationship with adaptive flexibility. Five personal characteristics are: age, international family, number of previous international assignments, job function, and functional area. This research then treats these seven variables as mediating variables in the regression analysis of hypothesis 4. Table 5.40 presents the results of regression analysis testing hypothesis 4.

As illustrated in Table 5.40, Model 1 tests the relationship between the expatriation time in China and the development of adaptive flexibility. The result indicates that they have a significant positive correlation ($p < 0.01$). It indicates that the longer western expatriate managers have continually worked in China, the greater their levels of adaptive flexibility.

Table 5.40 Results of regression analysis of hypothesis 4

	Adaptive flexibility				
	Model 1		Model 2		
	Beta (standardized)	t	Beta (standardized)	t	Zero order
Independent variable					
Expatriation time	0.308	3.527**	0.162	0.477*	0.308
Mediating variables					
AC-CE			−0.312	−3.004**	−0.554**
AE-RO			−0.211	−2.065*	−0.448*
Age			0.113	1.163	0.293
International family			0.075	0.971	0.230
No. of previous IAs			0.182	1.733	0.496
Job function			−0.112	−1.006	−0.378
Functional area			−0.007	−0.097	−0.202
F	12.436**		10.655**		
R2	0.095		0.432		
Adjusted R2	0.087		0.392		

Note $*p < 0.05$; $**p < 0.01$

Model 2 examines the impact of the seven mediating variables upon the relationship between expatriation time and western expatriate managers' levels of adaptive flexibility. After the effects of the seven moderators were eliminated, the expatriation time spent in China still impact the development of adaptive flexibility. This result suggests that the expatriation time independently influences the development of adaptive flexibility. Therefore, hypothesis 4 is supported.

The result of Model 2 in Table 5.40 shows that the AC-CE and AE-RO two learning dimensions both have a significant negative relationship with adaptive flexibility ($p < 0.01$ for AC-CE; $p < 0.05$ for AE-RO). This result suggests that concrete western expatriate managers are better at developing adaptive flexibility than abstract western expatriate managers. On the other hand, reflective western expatriate managers are better at developing adaptive flexibility than active western expatriate managers.

5.5.2.1 Concrete Experience Adaptive Flexibility and Expatriation Time

In this section, the researcher further examines the relationship between the Concrete Experience Adaptive Flexibility (CEAF) and the expatriation time and the effects of related mediating variables on their correlation. According to the results of correlation analysis, five personal characteristics in demographic characteristics and two learning style dimensions have a significant relationship with CEAF. These five personal characteristics are: gender, age, international family, number of previous international assignments, and job function. This research then treats these seven variables as mediating variables in the regression analysis of the correlation between CEAF and the expatriation time. Table 5.41 presents the results of regression analysis testing CEAF.

As illustrated in Table 5.41, Model 1 tests the relationship between the expatriation time in China and the development of CEAF. The result indicates that they have a significant positive correlation ($p < 0.05$). It indicates that the longer western expatriate managers have continually worked in China, the greater their levels of CEAF. Model 2 examines the impact of the seven mediating variables upon the relationship between expatriation time and western expatriate managers' levels of CEAF. After the effects of the seven moderators were eliminated, the expatriation time spent in China no longer affect the development of CEAF. This result suggests that the effect of the expatriation time on development of CEAF depends on that of the moderators.

The result of Model 2 in Table 5.41 shows that three demographic characteristics (gender, international family, and number of previous international assignments) have a significant positive relationship with CEAF ($p < 0.01$ for gender; $p < 0.05$ for international family and number of previous international assignments). This result suggests that female western expatriate managers are better at developing CEAF than male western expatriate managers. The results also indicate that western expatriate managers that have an international family are better at developing CEAF.

Table 5.41 Results of regression analysis of CEAF

	CEAF			
	Model 1		Model 2	
	Beta (standardized)	t	Beta (standardized)	t
Independent variable				
Expatriation time	0.167	0.729*	0.058	0.409
Mediating variables				
AC-CE			−0.158	−1.312
AE-RO			0.168	1.494
Gender			0.326	3.787**
Age			0.053	0.496
International family			0.193	2.258*
No. of previous IAs			0.254	2.212*
Job function			0.009	0.074
F	0.532		6.446**	
R2	0.004		0.315	
Adjusted R2	−0.004		0.266	

Note $^{*}p < 0.05$; $^{**}p < 0.01$

Moreover, the results suggest that western expatriate managers are better at developing CEAF if they experienced more previous international assignments. In order to better understand the impact of these three demographic characteristics (gender, international family, and number of previous international assignments) upon the development of CEAF over time, Table 5.42 presents the results of independent t-tests of male (N = 105) versus Female (N = 16), non-international family (N = 102) versus international family (N = 19), and non-overseas experience (N = 79) versus overseas experience (N = 42) with regard to the CEAF. As shown in Table 5.42, the mean score of CEAF of female western expatriate managers is significantly higher than that of male western expatriate managers ($p < 0.01$). The mean score of CEAF of western expatriate managers that have an international family is significantly higher than that of western expatriate managers that family members come from

Table 5.42 Results of independent t-tests of gender, international family, and overseas experience regarding CEAF

	CEAF				
	N	Mean	s. d.	t	F
Female	16	3.906	1.0680		
Male	105	2.514	1.1694	4.794**	0.268
International family	19	3.342	1.0145		
Non-international family	102	2.578	1.2522	2.896**	1.193
Overseas experience	42	3.310	1.2044		
Non-overseas experience	79	2.373	1.1477	4.137**	0.243

Note $^{*}p < 0.05$; $^{**}p < 0.01$ (two-tailed)

same country ($p < 0.05$). Moreover, the mean score of CEAF of overseas experienced western expatriate managers is significantly higher than that of non-overseas experienced western expatriate managers ($p < 0.05$).

5.5.2.2 Reflective Observation Adaptive Flexibility and Expatriation Time

In this section, the researcher examines the relationship between the Reflective Observation Adaptive Flexibility (ROAF) and the expatriation time and the effects of related mediating variables on their correlation. According to the results of correlation analysis, five personal characteristics in demographic characteristics and two learning style dimensions have a significant relationship with ROAF. These five personal characteristics are: gender, age, international family, number of previous international assignments, and job function. This research then treats these seven variables as mediating variables in the regression analysis of the correlation between ROAF and the expatriation time. Table 5.43 presents the results of regression analysis testing ROAF.

As illustrated in Table 5.43, Model 1 tests the relationship between the expatriation time in China and the development of ROAF. Model 2 examines the impact of the seven mediating variables upon the relationship between expatriation time and western expatriate managers' levels of ROAF. The result indicates that there is no significant relationship between the expatriation time and the development of ROAF.

Table 5.43 Results of regression analysis of ROAF

	ROAF			
	Model 1		Model 2	
	Beta (standardized)	t	Beta (standardized)	t
Independent variable				
Expatriation time	0.174	1.929	−0.030	−0.185
Mediating variables				
AC-CE			0.157	1.136
AE-RO			−0.187	−1.453
Gender			0.024	0.239
Age			0.066	0.537
International family			−0.053	−0.544
No. of previous IAs			0.229	1.742
Job function			−0.107	−0.770
F	3.721		1.539	
R2	0.030		0.099	
Adjusted R2	0.022		0.035	

Note $^{*}p < 0.05$; $^{**}p < 0.01$

5.5.2.3 Abstract Conceptualization Adaptive Flexibility and Expatriation Time

In this section, the researcher examines the relationship between the Abstract Conceptualization Adaptive Flexibility (ACAF) and the expatriation time and the effects of related mediating variables on their correlation. According to the results of correlation analysis, five personal characteristics in demographic characteristics and two learning style dimensions have a significant relationship with ACAF. These five personal characteristics are: gender, age, international family, number of previous international assignments, and job function. This research then treats these seven variables as mediating variables in the regression analysis of the correlation between ACAF and the expatriation time. Table 5.44 presents the results of regression analysis testing ACAF.

As illustrated in Table 5.44, Model 1 tests the relationship between the expatriation time in China and the development of ACAF. Model 2 examines the impact of the seven mediating variables upon the relationship between expatriation time and western expatriate managers' levels of ACAF. The result indicates that there is no significant relationship between the expatriation time and the development of ACAF. Furthermore, the result of Model 2 in Table 5.44 shows that the AE-RO learning dimension has a significant negative influence on the development of ACAF.

Table 5.44 Results of regression analysis of ACAF

	ACAF			
	Model 1		Model 2	
	Beta (standardized)	t	Beta (standardized)	t
Independent variable				
Expatriation time	0.102	1.115	−0.215	−1.343
Mediating variables				
AC-CE			−0.263	−1.944
AE-RO			−0.270	−2.132*
Gender			−0.172	−1.772
Age			0.112	0.931
International family			0.030	0.312
No. of previous IAs			−0.084	−0.651
Job function			−0.024	−0.174
F	1.244		2.095*	
R2	0.010		0.130	
Adjusted R2	0.002		0.068	

Note $*p < 0.05$; $**p < 0.01$

5.5.2.4 Active Experimentation Adaptive Flexibility and Expatriation Time

In this section, the researcher examines the relationship between the Active Experimentation Adaptive Flexibility (AEAF) and the expatriation time and the effects of related mediating variables on their correlation. According to the results of correlation analysis, five personal characteristics in demographic characteristics and two learning style dimensions have a significant relationship with AEAF. These five personal characteristics are: gender, age, international family, number of previous international assignments, and job function. This research then treats these seven variables as mediating variables in the regression analysis of the correlation between AEAF and the expatriation time. Table 5.45 presents the results of regression analysis testing AEAF.

As illustrated in Table 5.45, Model 1 tests the relationship between the expatriation time in China and the development of AEAF. The result indicates that they have a significant positive correlation ($p < 0.01$). It indicates that the longer western expatriate managers have engaged in their international assignments in China, the greater their levels of AEAF. Model 2 examines the impact of the seven mediating variables upon the relationship between expatriation time and western expatriate managers' levels of AEAF. After the effects of the seven moderators were eliminated, the expatriation time spent in China still has a significant positive influence upon the development of AEAF over time. This result suggests that the expatriation time independently affects the development of AEAF. Furthermore, the result of Model 2 in Table 5.45 shows that both the AE-RO and the AC-CE learning

Table 5.45 Results of regression analysis of AEAF

	AEAF			
	Model 1		Model 2	
	Beta (standardized)	t	Beta (standardized)	t
Independent variable				
Expatriation time	0.366	4.286**	0.198	1.321*
Mediating variables				
AC-CE			−0.319	−2.512*
AE-RO			−0.177	−0.645*
Gender			−0.147	−1.611
Age			−0.019	−0.166
International family			−0.016	−0.173
No. of previous IAs			−0.017	−0.144
Job function			−0.092	−0.719
F	18.368**		4.276**	
R2	0.134		0.234	
Adjusted R2	0.126		0.179	

Note *$p < 0.05$; **$p < 0.01$

dimensions have a significant negative influence upon the development of ACAF over time.

5.6 Learning Style and Managerial Tacit Knowledge

Research hypotheses 5a, 5b, and 5c are associated with western expatriate managers' levels of accumulated managerial tacit knowledge and their learning styles. This section first presents the comparison of western expatriate managers' levels of managerial tacit knowledge in four different learning styles and subsequently provides the results of tests of hypotheses 5a, 5b, and 5c.

5.6.1 *Levels of Managerial Tacit Knowledge in Different Learning Styles*

Table 5.46 summarizes the mean scores of managerial tacit knowledge in managing self and in managing others for four different learning styles. The mean scores of managing self in four learning styles range from 0.457 (Diverging) to 0.549 (Converging); on the other hand, the mean scores of managing others in four learning styles range from 0.453 (Diverging) to 0.563 (Converging). It suggests that compare to Converging and Accommodating learning styles, western expatriate managers with Diverging or Assimilating learning styles own relatively higher levels of accumulated managerial tacit knowledge in managing self; compare to Assimilating and Converging learning styles, western expatriate managers with Diverging or Accommodating learning styles own relatively higher levels of accumulated managerial tacit knowledge in managing others.

5.6.2 *Results of Hypotheses Tests*

As shown in the structure model for the research framework, the correlation between managerial tacit knowledge and learning style is statistically significant (**). In this section, the researcher further examines the relationship between the

Table 5.46 Levels of managerial tacit knowledge in different learning styles (N = 121)

	Mean			
	Diverging	Assimilating	Converging	Accommodating
Managing self	0.457	0.455	0.549	0.520
Managing others	0.453	0.550	0.563	0.477

two managerial tacit knowledge variables (managing self and managing others) and the two learning style variables (AC-CE and AE-RO) and the effects of related mediating variables on each correlation. Hypotheses 5a, 5b, and 5c are described below:

- Hypothesis 5a: Western expatriate managers' learning styles will differentiate between levels of managerial tacit knowledge accumulated during their international assignments in China.
- Hypothesis 5b: Western expatriate managers with learning preference for reflective observation over active experimentation accumulate greater levels of managerial tacit knowledge related to managing self during their International assignments in China.
- Hypothesis 5c: Western expatriate managers with learning preference for concrete experience over abstract conceptualization accumulate greater levels of managerial tacit knowledge related to managing others during their International assignments in China.

5.6.2.1 Hypotheses 5a

Hypothesis 5a is related to examination of how the accumulation of managerial tacit knowledge hinges on western expatriate managers' learning styles. As shown in the structure model for the research framework, the standardized regression coefficients revealed that western expatriate managers' learning styles significantly influenced their accumulation of managerial tacit knowledge during their international assignments. The present research then compared western expatriate managers' levels of accumulated managerial tacit knowledge according to their dominant learning styles using one-way analysis of variance. Results indicated that those with diverger learning styles had accumulated significantly higher levels of managerial tacit knowledge than those with assimilator, converger or accommodator learning styles ($F = 8.644$, $df = 3$, $p < 0.001$). Thus hypothesis 5a is supported.

5.6.2.2 Hypotheses 5b

Hypothesis 5b is related to examination of how the managerial tacit knowledge in managing self rests on western expatriate managers' learning styles. According to the results of correlation analysis of all metric variables, three personal characteristics in demographic characteristics and the expatriation time have a significant relationship with managerial tacit knowledge in managing self. Three personal characteristics are: age, international family, and job function. This research then treats these four variables as mediating variables in the regression analysis of hypothesis 5b. Table 5.47 presents the results of regression analysis testing hypothesis 5b.

Table 5.47 Results of regression analysis of hypothesis 5b

	Managing self				
	Model 1		Model 2		
	Beta (standardized)	t	Beta (standardized)	t	Zero order
Independent variable					
AE-RO	0.474	5.694**	0.273	2.580	0.474*
AC-CE	0.139	1.674*	0.116	1.427	0.314
Mediating variables					
Age			0.100	0.995	−0.293
International family			−0.046	−0.574	−0.217
Expatriation time			−0.194	−1.514	−0.505
Job function			0.242	2.172*	0.480*
F	45.330**		11.373**		
R2	0.276		0.374		
Adjusted R2	0.270		0.342		

Note $^{*}p < 0.05$; $^{**}p < 0.01$

As illustrated in Table 5.47, Model 1 tests the relationship between learning style and levels of accumulated managerial tacit knowledge in managing self. The result indicates that the two learning dimensions both have a significant positive correlation with managerial tacit knowledge. It should be noted that the scores for managerial tacit knowledge are expected to decrease rather than increase with advancing levels of tacit knowledge. The more western expatriate managers show their learning preferences for reflective observation over active experimentation, the greater their levels of accumulated managerial tacit knowledge in managing self. Model 2 examines the impact of the four mediating variables upon the relationship between managerial tacit knowledge in managing self and learning styles. After the effects of the four moderators were eliminated, the two learning dimensions no longer impact the accumulation of managerial tacit knowledge related to managing self. It indicates that the effect of the two learning dimensions on the accumulation of managerial tacit knowledge in managing self depends on that of the mediators. Consequently, hypothesis 5b is refuted.

The result of Model 2 in Table 5.47 shows that one personal characteristic (job function) has a significant positive impact on the accumulation of managerial tacit knowledge in managing self ($p < 0.05$). This result is similar as the result of hypothesis 2a tested in Sect. 5.4 (Managerial Tacit Knowledge and Expatriation Time). It indicates that western expatriate managers with higher management levels own greater levels of accumulated managerial tacit knowledge in managing self.

5.6.2.3 Hypotheses 5c

Hypothesis 5c is related to examination of how the managerial tacit knowledge in managing others hinges upon western expatriate managers' learning styles. According to the results of correlation analysis, four personal characteristics in demographic characteristics and expatriation time have a significant relationship with managerial tacit knowledge in managing others. Four personal characteristics are: gender, age, number of previous international assignments, and job function. This research then treats these five variables as mediating variables in the regression analysis of hypothesis 5c. Table 5.48 presents the results of regression analysis testing hypothesis 5c.

As illustrated in Table 5.48, Model 1 tests the relationship between learning style and levels of accumulated managerial tacit knowledge in managing others. The result indicates that only the AC-CE learning dimension has a significant positive correlation with managerial tacit knowledge in managing others ($p < 0.01$). The AE-RO learning dimension does not affect western expatriate managers' accumulation of managing others tacit knowledge. Model 2 examines the impact of the five mediating variables upon the relationship between managerial tacit knowledge in managing others and learning styles. After the effects of the five moderators were eliminated, the AC-CE learning dimension still has significant positive influence on managing others ($p < 0.01$). It indicates that the AC-CE learning dimension independently affects the accumulation of managerial tacit knowledge in managing others. The more western expatriate managers show their learning preferences for

Table 5.48 Results of regression analysis of hypothesis 5c

	Managing others				
	Model 1		Model 2		
	Beta (standardized)	t	Beta (standardized)	t	Zero order
Independent variable					
AC-CE	0.598	7.547**	0.429	4.053**	0.598**
AE-RO	0.001	0.007	−0.165	−1.756	−0.220
Mediating variables					
Gender			−0.064	−0.859	−0.212
Age			−0.206	−2.205*	−0.323*
Expatriation time			−0.087	−0.700	−0.273
No. of previous IAs			−0.205	−2.030*	−0.523*
Job function			0.087	0.818	0.362
F	66.441**		13.940**		
R2	0.358		0.463		
Adjusted R2	0.353		0.430		

Note $^{*}p < 0.05$; $^{**}p < 0.01$

concrete experience over abstract conceptualization, the greater their levels of accumulated managerial tacit knowledge in managing others. Accordingly, hypothesis 5c is refuted and hypothesis 5d is supported.

The result of Model 2 in Table 5.48 shows that two personal characteristics (age and number of previous international assignments) both have a significant negative impact on the accumulation of managerial tacit knowledge in managing others ($p < 0.05$). This result is similar as the result of hypothesis 2b tested in Sect. 5.4 (Managerial Tacit Knowledge and Expatriation Time). This suggests that elder western expatriate managers tend to own higher levels of accumulated managerial tacit knowledge in managing others. The results also indicate that western expatriate managers that have previous international assignment experiences are better at acquiring managerial tacit knowledge in managing others.

5.7 Learning Style and Adaptive Flexibility

Research hypotheses 6a, 6b, and 6c are associated with western expatriate managers' adaptive flexibility and their learning styles. This section first presents the comparison of western expatriate managers' levels of adaptive flexibility in four different learning styles and subsequently provides the results of tests of hypotheses 6a, 6b, and 6c.

5.7.1 Levels of Adaptive Flexibility in Different Learning Styles

Table 5.49 summarizes the mean scores of concrete experience adaptive flexibility (CEAF), reflective observation adaptive flexibility (ROAF), abstract conceptualization adaptive flexibility (ACAF), active experimentation adaptive flexibility (AEAF), and total adaptive flexibility (AF) in four different learning styles. Table 5.49 also presents the results of one-way ANOVA of Diverging (N = 3)

Table 5.49 Levels of adaptive flexibility in different learning styles (N = 121)

	Mean				
	Diverging	Assimilating	Converging	Accommodating	F
CEAF	4.167	2.222	2.579	3.056	2.955*
ROAF	3.500	4.722	3.585	3.889	2.224
ACAF	5.833	4.611	3.591	4.185	4.136**
AEAF	7.000	6.278	5.451	6.278	4.346**
AF	20.500	17.833	15.207	17.407	12.651**

Note *$p < 0.05$; **$p < 0.01$ (two-tailed)

versus Assimilating (N = 9) versus Converging (N = 82) versus Accommodating (N = 27) learning styles with regard to adaptive flexibility. The mean scores of adaptive flexibility (AF) in four learning styles range from 15.207 (Converging) to 20.500 (Diverging). It suggests that compare to Converging learning style, western expatriate managers with Diverging or Assimilating or Accommodating learning styles own relatively higher levels of adaptive flexibility. The levels of CEAF, ACAF, AEAF, and AF are significantly different among the four learning styles, while the levels of ROAF tend to be homogeneous among the four learning styles.

5.7.2 *Results of Hypotheses 6a, 6b Tests*

As shown in the structure model for the research framework, the correlation between adaptive flexibility and learning style is statistically significant (**). In this section, the researcher further examines the relationship between western expatriate managers' development of adaptive flexibility and the two learning dimensions (AC-CE and AE-RO) and the effects of related mediating variables on each correlation. Hypotheses 6a and 6b are described below:

- Hypothesis 6a: Western expatriate managers with learning preference for concrete experience over abstract conceptualization develop higher levels of adaptive flexibility during their International assignments in China.
- Hypothesis 6b: Western expatriate managers with learning preference for reflective observation over active experimentation develop higher levels of adaptive flexibility during their International assignments in China.

Hypotheses 6a and 6b are related to examination of how the development of adaptive flexibility rests on western expatriate managers' learning styles. According to the results of correlation analysis, five personal characteristics in demographic characteristics and the expatriation time have a significant relationship with adaptive flexibility. Five personal characteristics are: age, international family, number of previous international assignments, job function, and functional area. This research then treats these six variables as mediating variables in the regression analysis of hypotheses 6a and 6b. Table 5.50 presents the results of regression analysis testing hypotheses 6a and 6b.

As illustrated in Table 5.50, Model 1 tests the relationship between learning style and levels of adaptive flexibility. The result indicates that the two learning dimensions both have a significant negative correlation with adaptive flexibility. Model 2 examines the impact of the six mediating variables upon the relationship between adaptive flexibility and learning styles. After the effects of the six moderators were eliminated, the AC-CE learning dimension still has significant negative influence on adaptive flexibility ($p < 0.01$). It indicates that the AC-CE learning dimension independently affects the development of adaptive flexibility. The more western expatriate managers prefer to learn by concrete experience rather than abstract conceptualization, the greater their levels of adaptive flexibility. Therefore,

Table 5.50 Results of regression analysis of hypotheses 6a and 6b

	Adaptive flexibility				
	Model 1		Model 2		
	Beta (standardized)	t	Beta (standardized)	t	Zero order
Independent variable					
AE-RO	−0.283	−3.621**	−0.185	−1.888	−0.448
AC-CE	−0.450	−5.754**	−0.291	−3.222**	−0.554**
Mediating variables					
Age			0.172	1.873	0.359
International family			0.080	1.081	0.261
Expatriation time			−0.080	−0.680	0.308
Previous IAs			0.228	2.496*	0.533*
Job function			−0.094	−0.918	−0.385
Functional area			−0.017	−0.234	−0.202
F	35.568**		12.101**		
R2	0.376		0.464		
Adjusted R2	0.366		0.425		

Note $^{*}p < 0.05$; $^{**}p < 0.01$

hypothesis 6a is supported. On the other hand, in Model 2 in Table 5.50, it shows that the AE-RO learning dimension no longer affects the development of adaptive flexibility. This result suggests that the effect of the AE-RO learning dimension on development of adaptive flexibility depends on that of the moderators and the AC-CE learning dimension. Consequently, hypothesis 6b is refuted.

The results of Model 2 in Table 5.50 show that one personal characteristic (number of previous international assignments) has a significant positive impact on the relationship between learning style and adaptive flexibility ($p < 0.05$). It suggests that western expatriate managers' previous international assignment experiences accelerate their development of adaptive flexibility.

5.7.3 *Results of Hypotheses 6c Tests*

In this section, the researcher further examines the relationship between western expatriate managers' development of adaptive flexibility and the balancing learning style and the effects of related mediating variables on the correlation. Hypothesis 6c is described below:

- Hypothesis 6c: Western expatriate managers with balanced learning styles demonstrate higher levels of adaptive flexibility during their International assignments in China.

Hypotheses 6c is related to examination of whether western expatriate managers with balancing learning styles demonstrate higher levels of adaptive flexibility during their international assignments in China. According to the results of correlation analysis, five personal characteristics in demographic characteristics, two learning dimensions, and the expatriation time have a significant relationship with adaptive flexibility. Five personal characteristics are: age, international family, number of previous international assignments, job function, and functional area. This research then treats these eight variables as mediating variables in the regression analysis of hypotheses 6c. Table 5.51 presents the results of regression analysis testing hypotheses 6c.

As illustrated in Table 5.51, Model 1 tests the relationship between the balancing learning style and levels of adaptive flexibility. The result indicates that the balancing learning style has a significant negative correlation with adaptive flexibility ($p < 0.01$). Model 2 examines the impact of the eight mediating variables upon the relationship between adaptive flexibility and the balancing learning style. After the effects of the eight moderators were eliminated, the balancing learning style still has significant negative influence on adaptive flexibility ($p < 0.05$). This indicates that the balancing learning style independently affects the development of adaptive flexibility. The more balancing western expatriate managers' learning styles are, the greater their levels of adaptive flexibility. Therefore, hypothesis 6c is supported.

Table 5.51 Results of regression analysis of hypotheses 6c

	Adaptive flexibility			
	Model 1		Model 2	
	Beta (standardized)	t	Beta (standardized)	t
Independent variable				
Balancing LS	−0.610	−8.407**	−0.526	−2.416*
Mediating variables				
Age			0.128	1.341
International family			0.076	1.006
Expatriation time			−0.122	−0.946
Previous IAs			0.203	1.970
Job function			−0.075	−0.680
Functional area			−0.036	−0.472
AE-RO			0.084	0.532
AC-CE			−0.042	−0.281
F	70.684**		10.529**	
R2	0.373		0.461	
Adjusted R2	0.367		0.417	

Note $*p < 0.05$; $**p < 0.01$

5.8 Learning Style and Expatriate Adjustment

Research hypotheses 7a and 7b are associated with western expatriate managers' cross-cultural adjustment and their learning styles. This section first presents the comparison of western expatriate managers' levels of adaptation in four different learning styles and subsequently provides the results of tests of hypotheses 7a and 7b.

5.8.1 Levels of Expatriate Adjustment in Different Learning Styles

Table 5.52 summarizes the mean scores of general adjustment, socialization adjustment, work adjustment, and overall expatriate adjustment in four different learning styles. Table 5.52 also presents the results of one-way ANOVA of Diverging (N = 3) versus Assimilating (N = 9) versus Converging (N = 82) versus Accommodating (N = 27) learning styles with regard to the four expatriate adjustment variables. The mean scores of overall expatriate adjustment in four learning styles range from 3.85 (Converging) to 4.78 (Diverging). It suggests that compare to Converging learning style, western expatriate managers with Diverging or Assimilating or Accommodating learning styles adapt relatively better in cross-cultural context in China. The levels of general adjustment, socialization adjustment, work adjustment, and overall expatriate adjustment are all significantly different among the four learning styles.

5.8.2 Results of Hypotheses 7a, 7b Tests

As shown in the structure model for the research framework, the correlation between expatriate adjustment and learning style is statistically significant (**). In this section, the researcher further examines the relationship between western expatriate managers' adaptation and the two learning dimensions (AC-CE and

Table 5.52 Expatriate adjustment in different learning styles (N = 121)

	Mean				
	Diverging	Assimilating	Converging	Accommodating	F
General	4.33	4.67	4.00	4.11	2.808*
Socialization	5.00	3.78	3.21	4.15	12.513**
Work	5.00	4.89	4.33	4.70	4.824**
Overall adjustment	4.78	4.44	3.85	4.32	9.567**

Note *$p < 0.05$; **$p < 0.01$ (two-tailed)

AE-RO) and the effects of related mediating variables on each correlation. Hypotheses 7a and 7b are described below:

- Hypothesis 7a: Western expatriate managers with strong learning preferences for concrete experience will adjust better to their international assignment in China than those with a strong learning preference for abstract conceptualization.
- Hypothesis 7b: Western expatriate managers with strong learning preferences for reflective observation will adjust better to their international assignment in China than those with a strong learning preference for active experimentation.

Hypotheses 7a and 7b are related to examination of how western expatriate managers' adaptation rests on their learning styles. According to the results of correlation analysis of all metric variables, seven personal characteristics in demographic characteristics and the expatriation time have a significant relationship with expatriate adjustment. Seven personal characteristics are: age, international family, number of previous international assignments, overseas educational degree, educational achievement, job function, and functional area. This research then treats these eight variables as mediating variables in the regression analysis of hypotheses 7a and 7b. Table 5.53 presents the results of regression analysis testing hypotheses 7a and 7b.

As illustrated in Table 5.53, Model 1 tests the relationship between the learning style and expatriate adjustment. The result indicates that the two learning

Table 5.53 Results of regression analysis of hypotheses 7a and 7b

	Expatriate adjustment				
	Model 1		Model 2		
	Beta (standardized)	t	Beta (standardized)	t	Zero order
Independent variable					
AC-CE	−0.498	−7.181**	−0.402	−5.856**	−0.630**
AE-RO	−0.361	−5.208**	−1.08	−1.104*	−0.544
Mediating variables					
Age			0.097	1.405	0.477
International family			0.170	2.988**	0.358**
Expatriation time			0.367	4.021**	0.590**
No. of previous IAs			0.107	1.543	0.487
Overseas degree			0.070	1.160	0.288
Educational achievement			−0.051	−0.880	−0.185
Job function			−0.022	−0.285	−0.520
Functional area			−0.112	−2.000*	−0.300*
F	61.378**		25.629**		
R2	0.510		0.700		
Adjusted R2	0.502		0.672		

Note $^{*}p < 0.05$; $^{**}p < 0.01$

dimensions both have a significant negative correlation with expatriate adjustment. Model 2 examines the impact of the eight mediating variables upon the relationship between expatriate adjustment and learning styles. After the effects of the eight moderators were eliminated, both the two learning dimension still have significant negative influence on expatriate adjustment (AC-CE: $p < 0.01$; AE-RO: $p < 0.05$). It indicates that the two learning dimensions AC-CE and AE-RO independently affect expatriate adjustment. The more western expatriate managers prefer to learn by concrete experience and reflective observation rather than abstract conceptualization and active experimentation, the better they adjust in cross-cultural context in China. Therefore, hypotheses 7a and 7b are supported.

The results of Model 2 in Table 5.53 also show that two personal characteristics (international family and functional area) have a significant impact on the relationship between learning style and expatriate adjustment. It suggests that western expatriate managers that have an international family, especially the family member from China, adapt better in Chinese business environment. This result is similar as the result of hypothesis 1 tested in Sect. 5.2 (Expatriate Adjustment and Expatriation Time). Moreover, the results indicates that western expatriate manages' cross-cultural adjustment are significantly different among different job functional areas.

5.9 Adaptive Flexibility and Expatriate Adjustment

Research hypothesis 8 is associated with western expatriate managers' adaptive flexibility and their cross-cultural adjustment in China. This section provides the results of test of hypothesis 8.

5.9.1 Results of Hypothesis 8 Test

As shown in the structure model for the research framework, the correlation between western expatriate managers' adaptive flexibility and their cross-cultural adjustment is statistically significant (**). In this section, the researcher further examines the relationship between adaptive flexibility and expatriate adjustment and the effects of related mediating variables on their correlation. Hypothesis 8 is described below:

- Hypothesis 8: Western expatriate managers' who arrive with higher levels of adaptive flexibility will adjust better to their international assignment in China.

Hypothesis 8 is related to examination of how western expatriate managers' cross-cultural adaptation rests on their adaptive flexibility. According to the results of correlation analysis of all metric variables, seven personal characteristics in demographic characteristics and the expatriation time have a significant relationship with expatriate adjustment. Seven personal characteristics are: age, international family, number of previous international assignments, overseas educational degree, educational achievement, job function, and functional area. This research then treats these eight variables as mediating variables in the regression analysis of hypothesis 8. Table 5.54 presents the results of regression analysis.

As illustrated in Table 5.54, Model 1 tests the relationship between adaptive flexibility and expatriate adjustment. The result indicates that they have a significant positive correlation ($p < 0.01$). Model 2 examines the impact of the eight mediating variables upon the relationship between adaptive flexibility and western expatriate managers' adjustment. After the effects of the eight moderators were eliminated, adaptive flexibility still has significant positive influence on expatriate adjustment ($p < 0.01$). It indicates that the adaptive flexibility independently affects expatriate adaptation. The greater levels of western expatriate managers' adaptive flexibility, the better they adapt in a cross-cultural context in China. Therefore, hypothesis 8 is supported.

The results of Model 2 in Table 5.54 also show that three personal characteristics (international family, number of previous international assignments, and functional area) have a significant impact on the relationship between adaptive flexibility and expatriate adjustment. It suggests that western expatriate managers that have an international family, especially the family member from China, adapt better in Chinese business environment. This result is similar as the result of hypothesis 4 tested in Sect. 5.2 (Expatriate Adjustment and Expatriation Time). The results also indicates that western expatriate managers' cross-cultural adjustment are significantly different among different job functional areas. Moreover, the results suggest

Table 5.54 Results of regression analysis of hypothesis 8

	Expatriate adjustment				
	Model 1		Model 2		
	Beta (standardized)	t	Beta (standardized)	t	Zero order
Independent variable					
Adaptive flexibility	0.587	7.902**	0.243	3.345**	0.587**
Mediating variables					
Age			0.045	0.584	0.477
International family			0.140	2.302*	0.358*
Expatriation time			0.395	4.600**	0.590**
No. of previous IAs			0.233	3.345**	0.487**
Overseas degree			0.091	1.389	0.288
Educational achievement			−0.061	−0.969	−0.185
Job function			−0.006	−0.065	−0.520
Functional area			−0.132	−2.163*	−0.300*
F	62.436**		21.947**		
R2	0.344		0.640		
Adjusted R2	0.339		0.611		

Note *$p < 0.05$; **$p < 0.01$

that western expatriate managers that have previous international assignment experiences are better at developing adaptive flexibility and therefore benefit in terms of their cross-cultural adjustment.

5.10 Managerial Tacit Knowledge and Expatriate Adjustment

Research hypothesis 9 is associated with western expatriate managers' levels of managerial tacit knowledge and their cross-cultural adjustment in China. This section provides the results of test of hypothesis 9.

5.10.1 Results of Hypothesis 9 Test

As shown in the structure model for the research framework, the correlation between western expatriate managers' levels of managerial tacit knowledge and their cross-cultural adjustment is insignificant. In this section, the researcher further examines the relationship between managerial tacit knowledge and expatriate adjustment and the effects of related mediating variables on their correlation. Hypothesis 9 is described below:

- Hypothesis 9: Learning styles will positively influence expatriate managers' adjustment to the host culture via levels of accumulated managerial tacit knowledge.

Hypothesis 9 is related to examination of how western expatriate managers' cross-cultural adjustment rests on their levels of managerial tacit knowledge. According to the results of correlation analysis of all metric variables, seven personal characteristics in demographic characteristics, two learning dimensions, and the expatriation time have a significant relationship with expatriate adjustment. Seven personal characteristics are: age, international family, number of previous international assignments, overseas educational degree, educational achievement, job function, and functional area. This research then treats these ten variables as mediating variables in the regression analysis of hypothesis 9. Table 5.55 presents the results of regression analysis testing hypothesis 9.

As illustrated in Table 5.55, Model 1 tests the relationship between managerial tacit knowledge and expatriate adjustment. The result indicates that they have a significant negative correlation ($p < 0.01$). Model 2 examines the impact of the ten mediating variables upon the relationship between managerial tacit knowledge and western expatriate managers' adjustment. After the effects of the ten mediators were eliminated, managerial tacit knowledge no longer impact expatriate adjustment. It indicates that the effect of levels of managerial tacit knowledge on expatriate adjustment depends on that of the mediators. Therefore, hypothesis 9 is refuted.

Table 5.55 Results of regression analysis of hypothesis 9

	Expatriate adjustment			
	Model 1		Model 2	
	Beta (standardized)	t	Beta (standardized)	t
Independent variable				
Managerial tacit knowledge	−0.715	−11.171**	−0.275	−3.450
Mediating variables				
Age			−0.275	−3.450
International family			0.144	2.122**
Expatriation time			0.163	2.827**
No. of previous IAs			0.183	2.238**
Overseas degree			0.080	1.005
Educational achievement			0.070	1.141
Job function			−0.041	−0.722
Functional area			0.001	0.013
AC-CE			−0.108	−1.897**
AE-RO			−0.291	−3.405
F	124.789**		24.474	
R2	0.512		0.712	
Adjusted R2	0.508		0.683	

Note *$p < 0.05$; **$p < 0.01$

The results of Model 2 in Table 5.55 also show that two personal characteristics (international family and number of previous international assignments) and the AC-CE learning dimension have a significant impact on the relationship between managerial tacit knowledge and expatriate adjustment. It suggests that western expatriate managers that have an international family, especially the family member from China, adapt better in Chinese business environment. This result is similar as the result of hypothesis 1 tested in Sect. 5.2 (Expatriate Adjustment and Expatriation Time). Moreover, the results suggest that western expatriate managers that have previous international assignment experiences are better at acquiring managerial tacit knowledge and therefore are benefited for their cross-cultural adjustment.

5.11 Conclusion

Table 5.56 summarizes the results of tests of all hypotheses regarding western expatriate managers in this research. This table illustrates all hypotheses, the dependent and independent variables in each hypothesis, test result, and significant mediating variables in each hypothesis.

Table 5.56 A summary of the research hypotheses and results

Independent variable	Dependent variable	Result	Significant mediating variables
Hypothesis 1: Duration of expatriate managers' international experiences in the host culture will positively influence their adjustment to the current international assignment			
Expatriation time	Adjustment	Rejected	AC-CE; AE-RO; adaptive flexibility; international family
Expatriation time	General adjustment	Rejected	None
Expatriation time	Socialization	Accepted	AC-CE; AE-RO; adaptive flexibility; international family
Expatriation time	Work adjustment	Accepted	AC-CE; previous international assignment experience
Hypothesis 2a: The longer western expatriate managers have engaged in their International assignments in China, the more they show their learning preferences for concrete experience over abstract conceptualization			
Expatriation time	AC-CE	Accepted	Gender; previous international assignment experience
Hypothesis 2b: The longer western expatriate managers have engaged in their International assignments in China, the more they show their learning preferences for reflective observation over active experimentation			
Expatriation time	AE-RO	Accepted	Nationality; international family; previous international assignment experience
Hypothesis 2c: The longer western expatriate managers have engaged in their International assignments in China, the more balancing their learning styles			
Expatriation time	Balancing learning style	Accepted	International family; previous international assignment experience
Hypothesis 3a: The longer western expatriate managers have engaged in their International assignments in China, the greater their levels of accumulated managerial tacit knowledge in managing self			
Expatriation time	Managing self	Rejected	AE-RO; job function
Hypothesis 3b: The longer western expatriate managers have engaged in their International assignments in China, the greater their levels of accumulated managerial tacit knowledge in managing others			
Expatriation time	Managing others	Rejected	AC-CE; age; previous international assignment experience
Hypothesis 4: Duration of western expatriate managers' engagement in international assignments in China will positively influence their adjustment to the host culture via adaptive flexibility			
Expatriation time	Adaptive flexibility	Accepted	AC-CE; AE-RO

(continued)

Table 5.56 (continued)

Independent variable	Dependent variable	Result	Significant mediating variables
Hypothesis 5a: Western expatriate managers' learning styles will differentiate between levels of managerial tacit knowledge accumulated (LAMTK) during their international assignments in China			
Learning style	LAMTK	Accepted	Job function
Hypothesis 5b: Western expatriate managers with learning preference for reflective observation over active experimentation accumulate greater levels of managerial tacit knowledge related to managing self during their International assignments in China			
AE-RO	Managing self	Rejected	Job function
Hypothesis 5c: Western expatriate managers with learning preference for concrete experience over abstract conceptualization accumulate greater levels of managerial tacit knowledge related to managing others during their International assignments in China			
AC-CE	Managing others	Accepted	Age; previous international assignment experience
Hypothesis 6a: Western expatriate managers with learning preference for concrete experience over abstract conceptualization develop higher levels of adaptive flexibility during their International assignments in China			
AC-CE	Adaptive flexibility	Accepted	Previous international assignment experience
Hypothesis 6b: Western expatriate managers with learning preference for reflective observation over active experimentation develop higher levels of adaptive flexibility during their International assignments in China			
AE-RO	Adaptive flexibility	Rejected	Previous international assignment experience
Hypothesis 6c: Western expatriate managers with balanced learning styles demonstrate higher levels of adaptive flexibility during their International assignments in China			
Balanced learning style	Adaptive flexibility	Accepted	None
Hypothesis 7a: Western expatriate managers with strong learning preferences for concrete experience will adjust better to their international assignment in China than those with a strong learning preference for abstract conceptualization			
AC-CE	Adjustment	Accepted	International family; functional area
Hypothesis 7b: Western expatriate managers with strong learning preferences for reflective observation will adjust better to their international assignment in China than those with a strong learning preference for active experimentation			
AE-RO	Adjustment	Accepted	International family; functional area
Hypothesis 8: Western expatriate managers' who arrive with higher levels of adaptive flexibility will adjust better to their international assignment in China			
Adaptive flexibility	Adjustment	Accepted	International family; functional area; previous international assignment experience
Hypothesis 9: Learning styles will positively influence expatriate managers' adjustment to the host culture via levels of accumulated managerial tacit knowledge			
LAMTK	Adjustment	Rejected	International family; AC-CE; previous international assignment experience

Appendix G: Correlation Matrix (Western Expatriates)

Means, standard deviations and inter-correlations for all research variables

	Mean	SD	1	2	3	4	5	6	7	8	9	10
1. Gender	1.13	0.340	–									
2. Age	2.31	0.646	−0.077	–								
3. Tenure	36.50	26.337	−0.012	0.629**	–							
4. Previous IA	0.50	0.765	0.162	0.121	0.048	–						
5. Job position	2.83	0.691	0.028	−0.60**	−0.199*	−0.261*	–					
6. AC-CE	7.26	5.969	−0.349**	−0.125	−0.212*	−0.485**	0.163	0.77				
7. AE-RO	10.89	5.861	−0.097	−0.187*	−0.433**	−0.230*	0.154	0.367**	0.74			
8. Expatriate adaptation	4.02	0.741	0.153	0.156	0.590**	0.263**	−0.135*	−0.430**	−0.344**	0.90		
9. Managerial tacit knowledge	1.07	0.13	−0.150	−0.111	−0.226**	−0.225**	0.266**	0.204**	0.206**	−0.115*	0.88	
10. Adaptive flexibility	16.025	2.5819	0.134	0.193	0.308**	0.496**	−0.078	−0.554**	−0.448**	0.387**	−0.159*	0.79

n = 121; $*p < 0.05$; $**p < 0.01$

Coefficient alpha reliabilities are reported in parentheses in the correlation diagonals

Gender 1 = male; 2 = female

Chapter 6
Results: Chinese Managers

The present research also sought to determine if there were significant empirical differences between western expatriate managers and host Chinese managers working in the same MNCs in terms of the ways they learn and adapt to managerial responsibilities within MNCs. To explore this question, the researcher returned to the western MNCs that participated in the study and asked 12 of the medium to large organizations that supported the previous research regarding western expatriate managers to participate in a further study. Eight western MNCs agreed to participate in the further study. The participating organization members were administered the Chinese version of the LSI, the Chinese version of the TKIM, and a revised demographic questionnaire in Chinese. One hundred and thirty-three host Chinese managers participated in the study. This chapter first provides the descriptive statistics and the results of the correlation analysis of all metric variables (including demographic characteristics) regarding host Chinese managers in this study. Then, the presentation concentrates on host Chinese managers' learning styles, their levels of accumulated managerial tacit knowledge, and the differences between them and western expatriate managers in terms of these two characteristics.

6.1 Descriptive Statistics

Descriptive statistics for all metric variables regarding host Chinese managers are summarized in Table 6.1. The correlation matrix for all metric variables is included in table of Appendix H.

In Table 6.1, regarding the transformation of the variable 'gender' in the questionnaire, '1' refers to male, '2' refers to female; regarding the transformation of the variable 'age' in the questionnaire, '1' refers to age 20–29, '2' refers to age 30–39, '3' refers to age 40–49, '4' refers to 50–60, '5' refers to age over 60; regarding the transformation of the variable 'overseas study experience' in the questionnaire, '1' refers to No experience, '2' refers to Yes; regarding the transformation of the variable 'educational achievement' in the questionnaire, '1' refers to Ph.D., '2' refers to master, '3' refers to bachelor, '4' refers to other; regarding the transformation of the variable 'job function' in the questionnaire, '1' refers to ordinary employee,

Y. Li, *Expatriate Manager's Adaption and Knowledge Acquisition*,
DOI 10.1007/978-981-10-0053-9_6

Table 6.1 Descriptive statistics for all metric variables (N = 133)

Variable	Mean	Std. deviation	Variable	Mean	Std. deviation
Gender	1.51	0.502	AC	31.50	5.478
Age	2.17	0.510	RO	30.59	6.770
No. of previous IA	1.00	0.252	AE	34.68	6.897
Overseas study experience	1.07	0.252	Situation 1	0.577817	0.1614336
Educational achievement	2.86	0.617	Situation 2	0.571172	0.1832458
Job function	2.41	0.565	Situation 3	0.562152	0.1459843
Functional area	3.83	2.772	Situation 4	0.538794	0.1339029
Time in managerial role	3.47	1.105	Situation 5	0.494770	0.1536242
Time in western MNCs	4.57	0.568	Situation 6	0.543080	0.1521386
AC-CE	8.26	8.494	Managing self	0.53712	0.1005513
AE-RO	4.09	12.602	Managing others	0.558801	0.1021897
LEARNING STYLE	2.67	0.766	Total managerial tacit knowledge	1.087785	0.1502338
CE	23.24	4.479			

‘2’ refers to junior manager, ‘3’ refers to middle manager, ‘4’ refers to senior manager, ‘5’ refers to other; regarding the transformation of the variable ‘functional area’ in the questionnaire, ‘1’ refers to Human resource management/general administration, ‘2’ refers to Operations/production, ‘3’ refers to Sales/marketing, ‘4’ refers to Engineering/design, ‘5’ refers to Finance/accounting, ‘6’ refers to other; regarding the transformation of the variable ‘overall time in managerial role’ in the questionnaire, ‘1’ refers to less than one year, ‘2’ refers to 1–3 years, ‘3’ refers to 3–5 years, ‘4’ refers to 5–10 years, and ‘5’ refers to above 10 years; regarding the transformation of the variable ‘overall time in western MNCs’ in the questionnaire, ‘1’ refers to less than three years, ‘2’ refers to 3–5 years, ‘3’ refers to 5–10 years, ‘4’ refers to 10–15 years, and ‘5’ refers to above 15 years

Table 6.1 describes demographic characteristics of the second sample of only local Chinese managers. Subjects have spent an average of 3.47 years in a managerial role, an average of 4.57 years in western MNCs, and 2.3 % of them are in senior management positions. In comparison to the sample of western expatriate managers in the previous research, the second sample held significantly less senior positions and was more diverse in terms of gender. Moreover, all of the host Chinese managers have no previous overseas work experience. Only 6.8 % of them have previous overseas study experience.

6.2 Learning Style

This section first provides an overview of findings related to the learning styles of host Chinese managers in western MNCs in China, followed by the differences between host Chinese managers and western expatriate managers in terms of learning style, and finally, the transition of local Chinese managers' learning styles over time working in western MNCs.

6.2.1 An Overview of Chinese Managers' Learning Styles

Table 6.2 summarizes the mean scores and standard deviations (s. d.) of the eight learning style variables (CE, RO, AC, AE, AC-CE, AE-RO, ABS (AC-CE), and ABS (AE-RO)) of host Chinese managers.

Figure 6.1 depicts the distribution of the four learning styles of the 133 host Chinese managers. The learning styles distribution as shown in Fig. 6.1 illustrate that 14 (10.5 %) of host Chinese managers prefer diverging learning style; 71 (53.4 %) of them prefer assimilating learning style; 38 (28.6 %) of them prefer converging learning style; and 10 (7.5 %) of them prefer accommodating learning style. These results indicate that host Chinese managers primarily tend to learn through assimilating or converging learning styles. The accommodating learning style is the least preferred by host Chinese managers.

6.2.2 Differences Between the Two Samples in Terms of Learning Styles

Table 6.3 summarizes the mean scores and standard deviations (s. d.) of the six learning style variables (CE, RO, AC, AE, AC-CE, and AE-RO) of host Chinese

Table 6.2 A summary of the eight learning style variables for Chinese managers

	Local Chinese managers (N = 133)	
	Mean	s. d.
CE	23.24	4.479
RO	30.59	6.770
AC	31.50	5.478
AE	34.68	6.897
AC-CE	8.26	8.494
AE-RO	4.09	12.602
ABS (AC-CE)	10.03	6.281
ABS (AE-RO)	11.31	6.843

Accommodating 7.5%	Diverging 10.5%
Converging 28.6%	Assimilating 53.4%

Fig. 6.1 Learning styles distribution of 133 host Chinese managers

Table 6.3 A summary of the six learning style variables for the two samples

	Western expatriate managers (N = 121)		Local Chinese managers (N = 133)		Independent sample t-test (t score)
	Mean	s. d.	Mean	s. d.	
CE	24.58	4.215	23.24	4.479	2.619***
RO	26.31	4.241	30.59	6.770	−6.729***
AC	31.83	3.974	31.50	5.478	0.913
AE	37.12	3.920	34.68	6.897	3.938**
AC-CE	7.26	5.969	8.26	8.494	−0.910**
AE-RO	10.89	5.861	4.09	12.602	6.225***
Primary LS		Converging		Assimilating	

Note *** $p < 0.001$; **$p < 0.01$ (two-tailed)

managers and also of western expatriate managers for comparison. Table 6.3 also includes the results of independent sample t-test and the main learning styles for the two samples.

With regard to the active and reflective dimension, the AE-RO score of western expatriates is 10.89, which is significantly higher than Chinese managers' score (4.09). The RO score of western expatriates is 26.31, which is significantly lower than Chinese managers' score (30.59). The AE score of western expatriates displays 37.12, which is significantly higher than Chinese managers' score (34.68). These results suggest that host Chinese managers prefer to learn through reflective observation (RO) over active experimentation (AE) in comparison with western expatriate managers.

With regard to the abstract and concrete dimension, the AC-CE score of western expatriate managers is 7.26, which is significantly lower than the local Chinese managers' score (8.26). The AC score of western expatriates shows 31.83 that is not statistically differ from the Chinese managers' score (31.50), while the CE score of western expatriates is 24.58, which is significantly higher than the Chinese managers' score (23.24). These results indicate that overall host Chinese managers prefer to learn using abstract conceptualization (AC) rather than concrete experience (CE) in comparison with western expatriate managers.

Table 6.4 Results of the independent t-test between the two samples by groups regarding learning preferences

	AC-CE	AE-RO
Chinese managers versus first group (less 1 year)	−1.38	−6.52**
Chinese managers versus second group (1 to less 3 years)	−2.16*	−3.70*
Chinese managers versus third group (3 to less 5 years)	−3.77**	−1.13
Chinese managers versus fourth group (above 5 years)	−0.95*	−0.78

Note $^*p < 0.05$; $^{**}p < 0.01$ (two-tailed)

Considering that host Chinese managers engage in business contexts, we can say that their learning orientation to the abstract and reflective modes should be remark upon as their learning style characteristics, while western expatriate managers' learning orientation to the active and abstract modes. The combination of host Chinese managers' relative preference for abstract and reflective modes indicates that they prefer the Assimilating learning style, while western expatriate managers prefer the Converging learning style. However, the high values of standard deviations (s. d.) of the AE-RO and AC-CE two learning dimensions illustrate that host Chinese managers tend to have varied learning styles as individuals. Furthermore, the present research compares host Chinese managers with each of the four groups of the western expatriate managers for comprehensive understanding: the first (N = 22), the second (N = 42), the third (N = 36), and the fourth (N = 21), see in Table 6.4.

As shown in Table 6.4, for the first group of western expatriate managers compared with host Chinese managers, there was no significant difference in AC-CE learning dimension and a significant difference in AE-RO learning dimension ($t = -6.52$, $p < 0.01$). The results imply that the first group of western expatriate managers have similar preferences for abstract learning mode on the AC-CE learning dimension as host Chinese managers, while they heavily rely on an active learning mode on the AE-RO learning dimension, unlike Chinese managers rely on a reflective learning mode. Results of the independent test revealed that the second group of western expatriates were different from host Chinese managers in both the learning dimensions of AC-CE and AE-RO (AC-CE: $t = -2.16$, $p < 0.05$; AE-RO: $t = -3.70$, $p < 0.01$). That is, the second group of expatriate managers is more concrete and more active than host Chinese managers. At last, the results show that the third and fourth groups were significantly different from local Chinese managers on the AC-CE learning dimension (third group: $t = -3.77$, $p < 0.01$; fourth group: $t = -0.95$, $p < 0.05$). However, there was significant difference between them in terms of the AE-RO learning dimension. The results suggest that western expatriate managers with three or more years of international experience in China demonstrate a different learning strategy using more concrete learning mode than do host Chinese managers, however, they become similar to host Chinese managers who prefer to learn through reflective learning mode.

6.2.3 Learning Style Transitions Over Time

In the present research, the second sample is host Chinese managers working in same western MNCs as western expatriates in China. These Chinese managers have different characteristics: they work in western organizations and experience western organizational culture. In this research, 25.6 % of the sample has been working in western MNCs for less than 5 years; 29.3 % of the sample for 5–10 years; 26.3 % of the sample for 10–15 years; and 18.8 % of the sample for over 15 years. As we have discussed in the literature review, western organizational culture is different from native Chinese organizational culture: more active and low-context communication pattern; and the environmental change has influence on individuals learning style. The change of environmental demands accrues the shift of learning style. The longer the exposure of the environmental demands, the greater the tendency for a person to specialize more in the learning style that is matched with such demands. Therefore, this section further examines transitional movement of host Chinese managers' learning styles along with they work in western MNCs over time. In this study, the sample of 133 host Chinese managers is divided into four groups based on overall how long they have been worked in western MNCs, including previous working experience in other western MNCs. The first group has been working in western MNCs for 5 years or less; the second group for over 5–10 years; the third group for over 10–15 years; and the fourth group for over 15 years. Table 6.5 presents the correlation between the overall working experience in western MNCs and the six learning style variables. As shown in Table 6.5, there is significant positive relationship between the overall working experience in western MNCs and the abstract learning mode, the AC-CE learning dimension, and the AE-RO learning dimension ($p < 0.01$); there is a significant negative relationship between the overall working experience in western MNCs and the reflective learning mode ($p < 0.05$). The results suggest that host Chinese managers become more abstract and less concrete, more active and less reflective along with they working in western MNCs in China over time. Tables 6.6 and 6.7 present the results of ANOVA of the six learning style variables by work length in western MNCs, along with the dominant learning style for each group.

As shown in Tables 6.6 and 6.7, there are significant differences in learning variables scores across groups on concrete experience learning mode ($F = 2.846$, $p < 0.05$), abstract conceptualization learning mode ($F = 6.273$, $p < 0.01$), the AC-CE learning dimension ($F = 4.715$, $p < 0.01$), and the AE-RO learning dimension ($F = 7.032$, $p < 0.01$). Specifically, it shows a movement towards more

Table 6.5 The correlation between the time in western MNCs and the six learning style variables

	CE	AC	RO	AE	AC-CE	AE-RO
Overall time in western MNCs	−0.093	0.354**	−0.197*	−0.128	0.277**	0.225**

Note *$p < 0.05$; **$p < 0.01$ (two-tailed)

Table 6.6 Results of ANOVA of the six learning style variables by work length in western MNCs

	CE		RO		AC		AE	
	Mean	s. d.	Mean	s. d.	Mean	s. d.	Mean	s. d.
First group	24.44	3.878	32.32	7.425	28.88	5.014	34.35	7.571
Second group	22.00	3.035	31.00	6.905	31.05	4.279	35.95	6.513
Third group	24.17	5.289	29.94	6.615	32.31	5.619	33.57	7.413
Fourth group	22.24	5.349	28.48	5.386	34.60	5.979	34.68	5.764
ALL	23.24	4.479	30.59	6.770	31.50	5.478	34.68	6.897
df	3		3		3		3	
F	2.846*		1.735		6.273**		0.763	

Note *$p < 0.05$; **$p < 0.01$ (two-tailed)

Table 6.7 Results of ANOVA of the six learning style variables by work length in western MNCs

	AC-CE		AE-RO		Primary LS
	Mean	s. d.	Mean	s. d.	
First group	4.44	7.382	−3.97	11.738	Assimilating
Second group	9.05	6.000	1.79	7.252	Assimilating
Third group	8.14	9.610	6.17	13.557	Converging
Fourth group	12.36	9.738	15.72	9.620	Converging
ALL	8.26	8.494	4.09	12.602	Assimilating
df	3		3		
F	4.715**		7.032**		

Note *$p < 0.05$; **$p < 0.01$ (two-tailed)

abstract on the AC-CE dimension and a movement towards more active on the AE-RO dimension, as host Chinese managers stay longer in western MNCs. The mean scores of the two learning dimensions AC-CE and AE-RO for the first group (less than 5 years) of host Chinese managers are 4.44 and −3.97, respectively, indicating that the first group has primarily an Assimilating learning style. The results suggest that the first group of Chinese managers demonstrated a strong tendency towards reflective observation rather than active experimentation as the norm mean of the AE-RO dimension is 5.9. On the other hand, the first group showed a weak orientation toward abstract conceptualization over concrete experience: the mean score of 4.44 on the AC-CE dimension is very close to the norm mean of 4.3. The mean scores of the two learning dimensions AC-CE and AE-RO for the second group (5–10 years) of host Chinese managers are 9.05 and 1.79, respectively, indicating that the second group also has primarily an Assimilating learning style. This result suggests that the second group of host Chinese managers demonstrated a strong tendency towards reflective observation over active experimentation and also a strong tendency towards abstract conceptualization rather than concrete experience.

The mean scores of the two learning dimensions AC-CE and AE-RO for the third group (10–15 years) of host Chinese managers are 8.14 and 6.17, respectively, indicating that the third group has primarily a Converging learning style. The second group and the third group of host Chinese managers have similar mean score on the AC-CE dimension, however, the third group of Chinese managers shifted dramatically on the AE-RO dimension and showed an orientation toward active experimentation rather than reflective observation. The mean scores of the two learning dimensions AC-CE and AE-RO for the fourth group (over 15 years) of host Chinese managers are 12.36 and 15.72, respectively, indicating that the fourth group has primarily a Converging learning style. The fourth group showed both a strong tendency towards abstract conceptualization over concrete experience and towards active experimentation over reflective observation. In addition, on the dimension of AC-CE, the first group has significantly lower mean score than the other three groups. This result suggests that if Chinese managers remain in western organizations for 5 years or more, they will tend to become more abstract learners. On the dimension of AE-RO, on the other hand, the first group and the second group have significantly lower scores than the third and the fourth group. The result illustrates that if Chinese managers remain in western MNCs for 10 years or more, they will tend to become more active learners. It is reasonable to conclude that, based on analyses of the results of the correlation and the ANOVA tests, the longer host Chinese managers work in western MNCs in China, the more they learn using abstract conceptualization and active experimentation rather than concrete experience and reflective observation. Figure 6.2 presents how these two learning

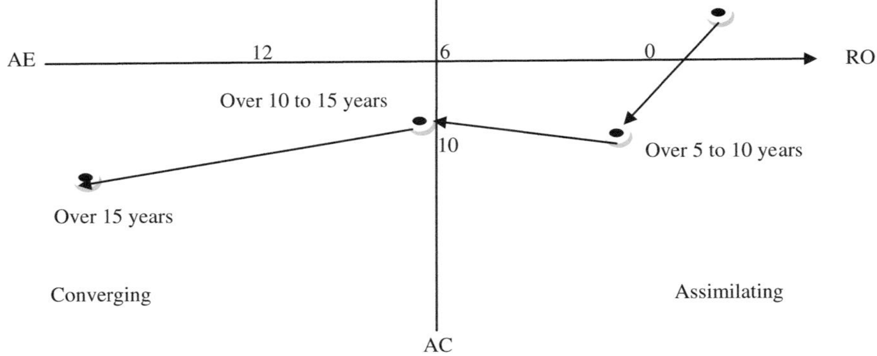

Fig. 6.2 Transitional movements of two learning dimensions over four groups of Chinese managers

dimensions move according to the four different groups. In Fig. 6.2, each of the four groups is placed based on their two learning dimensions' scores. As the three arrows point out, the orientation of host Chinese managers' learning styles is shifted toward the abstract and active learning modes. Movement toward the active learning mode over time is particularly noticeable.

6.3 Managerial Tacit Knowledge

This section fist provides an overview of findings related to levels of accumulated managerial tacit knowledge of host Chinese managers working in western MNCs in China, followed by the differences between host Chinese managers and western expatriate managers in terms of levels of accumulated managerial tacit knowledge, and finally, the acquisition of local Chinese managers' managerial tacit knowledge over time working in a predominantly managerial context.

6.3.1 *An Overview of Chinese Managers' Managerial Tacit Knowledge*

Table 6.8 summarizes the mean scores and standard deviations (s. d.) of nine variables (situation 1, situation 2, situation 3, situation 4, situation 5, situation 6, managerial tacit knowledge related to managing self, managerial tacit knowledge related to managing others, and total managerial tacit knowledge) measured by Tacit knowledge inventory for managers. The mean scores of six situations range from 0.495 (situation 5) to 0.578 (situation 1). The mean score of managerial tacit knowledge related to managing others is a little higher than that of managerial tacit knowledge related to managing self. It indicates that host Chinese managers own relatively higher levels of accumulated managerial tacit knowledge in managing self.

Furthermore, the present research discusses Chinese managers' responses to each situation in tacit knowledge inventory in detail. The study first discusses the situations related to managerial tacit knowledge in managing self: situation 1, situation 4, and situation 5. The content of situation 1 is 'You are an executive vice-president in the marketing division of Sherman Electronics, a company that sells audio and video supplies. You have been with Sherman Electronics since

Table 6.8 A summary of the nine managerial tacit knowledge variables (N = 133)

	s1	s4	s5	Self	s2	s3	s6	Others	Total
Mean	0.578	0.539	0.495	0.537	0.571	0.562	0.543	0.558	1.096
s. d.	0.161	0.134	0.154	0.101	0.183	0.146	0.152	0.102	0.150

finishing college, having spent 13 years in a managerial role in human resources and two years in your present position. Sherman Electronics has been losing market share for its products steadily over the past five years. Sherman's strength in the past has been introducing new products before its competition, but now its product line seems to be three steps behind the leaders in a rapidly changing market. A strategy of focusing on more stable segments of the market has been aborted because of fierce competition from large overseas companies. You believe that your lack of knowledge about the latest audio and video products and technology limits your effectiveness. Your schedule is very busy, but you think it is important to catch up on, and keep up with, innovation that affects your industry.' This situation asks managers to rate the quality of the following strategies for becoming more knowledgeable about new products and technology on a 1 (extremely bad) to 7 (extremely good) point scale. Table 6.9 presents the 10 available strategies for situation 1 with host Chinese managers' mean rate for each strategy and according standard deviation. The mean rates for the 10 strategies of situation 1 range from 2.50 (strategy 1) to 5.91 (strategy 6). The top three good strategies for situation 1 are strategy 6 (Ask to sit in on weekly discussions of new product ideas held by the Research and Development division), strategy 5 (Begin attending trade shows of products in your industry), and strategy 4 (Subscribes to several consumer-oriented magazines that cover your products). Overall Chinese managers think strategy 1 (Ask for a leave of absence to pursue an advanced technical degree) is a quite inappropriate response to situation 1.

Table 6.9 Chinese managers' responses to situation 1 in TKIM (N = 133)

	Mean	s. d.
1. Ask for a leave of absence to pursue an advanced technical degree	2.50	1.511
2. Order a news clipping service (news clipping services provide news from a large number of sources on a given topic)	5.04	1.389
3. Subscribe to several technical journals relevant to your manufacturing operations	4.69	1.404
4. Subscribes to several consumer-oriented magazines that cover your products	5.59	1.213
5. Begin attending trade shows of products in your industry	5.67	1.120
6. Ask to sit in on weekly discussions of new product ideas held by the Research and Development division	5.91	1.055
7. Attend a series of technical presentations by research scientists from outside the company who are brought in by the Manufacturing Operations division	5.41	1.256
8. Hire a staff member whose primary responsibility is to keep you abreast of current trends in your industry	4.14	1.850
9. Ask the Engineering division to prepare monthly summary reports of innovative products	5.24	1.462
10. Ask for weekly presentations for you and your staff on technical issues by staff in the Research and Development and Manufacturing Operations divisions	4.95	1.527

Table 6.10 Chinese managers' responses to situation 4 in TKIM (N = 133)

	Mean	s. d.
1. Think in terms of tasks accomplished rather than hours spent working	3.79	1.533
2. Use a daily list of goals arranged according to your priorities	6.55	0.763
3. Reward yourself upon completion of important tasks for the day	5.01	1.171
4. Be in charge of all phase of every task or project you are involved in	4.14	1.670
5. Take frequent but short breaks (i.e., a quick walk to the mail room) throughout the day	4.89	1.350
6. Only delegate inconsequential tasks, since you cannot guarantee that the tasks will be done properly and on time unless you do them yourself	2.98	1.351
7. Do only what you are in the mood to do to maximize the quality of your work	3.30	1.571
8. Take every opportunity to get feedback on early drafts of your work	5.43	1.082
9. Set your own deadlines in addition to externally imposed ones	6.17	1.001
10. Do not spend much time planning the best way to do something because the best way to do something may not be apparent until after you have begun doing it	4.49	1.659

Situation 4 asks managers to rate the quality of the following 10 strategies for handling the day-to-day work of a manager on a 1 'extremely bad' to 7 'extremely good' point scale. Table 6.10 presents the 10 available strategies for situation 4 with host Chinese managers' mean rate for each strategy and according standard deviation. The mean rates for the 10 strategies of situation 4 range from 2.98 (strategy 6) to 6.55 (strategy 2). The top three good strategies for situation 4 are strategy 2 (Use a daily list of goals arranged according to your priorities), strategy 9 (Set your own deadlines in addition to externally imposed ones), and strategy 8 (Take every opportunity to get feedback on early drafts of your work). Overall Chinese managers think strategy 6 (Only delegate inconsequential tasks, since you cannot guarantee that the tasks will be done properly and on time unless you do them yourself) is an inappropriate response to situation 4.

The content of situation 5 is 'You are looking for a new project to tackle in the coming year. You have considered a number of possible projects and desire to pick the project that would be best for you.' This situation asks managers to rate the importance of the following considerations when selecting new projects on a 1 (extremely bad) to 7 (extremely good) point scale. Table 6.11 presents the 10 considerations for situation 5 with host Chinese managers' mean rate for each consideration and according standard deviation. The mean rates for the 10 considerations of situation 5 range from 3.21 (consideration 5) to 5.98 (consideration 2). The top three important considerations for situation 5 are consideration 2 (Doing the project would require my developing skills that may enhance my future career success), consideration 10 (The project is the one I most want to do), and consideration 8 (The project will enable me to demonstrate my talents that others may not be aware of). Overall Chinese managers think consideration 5 (The risk of making a mistake is virtually nonexistent) is the least important consideration to situation 5.

Table 6.11 Chinese managers' responses to situation 5 in TKIM (N = 133)

	Mean	s. d.
1. The project is the one my immediate superior most desires to be completed	5.56	1.257
2. Doing the project would require my developing skills that may enhance my future career success	5.98	0.977
3. The project should attract the attention of the local media	4.02	1.433
4. Doing the project should prove to be fun	4.80	1.319
5. The risk of making a mistake is virtually nonexistent	3.21	1.420
6. The project will require my interacting with senior executives whom I would like to get to know better	5.12	1.285
7. The project is valued by my superior even though it is not valued by me	4.82	1.429
8. The project will enable me to demonstrate my talents that others may not be aware of	5.57	1.068
9. The project is in an area with which I have a lot of experience	5.38	1.248
10. The project is the one I most want to do	5.85	1.138

The present research then discusses the situations related to managerial tacit knowledge in managing others: situation 2, situation 3, and situation 6. The content of situation 2 is 'An employee who reports to one of your subordinates has asked to talk with you about waste, poor management practices, and possible violations of both departmental policy and the law on the part of your subordinate. You have been in your present position only a year, but in that time you have had no indications of trouble about the subordinate in question. Neither you nor your department has an "open door" policy, so it is expected that employees should take their concerns to their immediate supervisors before bringing a matter to the attention of anyone else. The employee who wishes to meet with you has not discussed this matter with her supervisor because of its delicate nature.' This situation asks managers to rate the quality of the following strategies they are considering doing in this situation on a 1 'extremely bad' to 7 'extremely good' point scale. Table 6.12 presents the 10 strategies for situation 2 with host Chinese managers' mean rate for each strategy and according standard deviation. The mean rates for the 10 strategies of situation 2 range from 1.37 (strategy 8) to 5.93 (strategy 5). The top three good strategies for situation 2 are strategy 5 (Find out more information about the employee, if you can, before making any decisions), strategy 4 (Meet with the employee and then investigate the allegations if an investigation appears warranted before talking with your subordinate), and strategy 3 (Schedule a meeting with the employee and then with your subordinate to get both sides of the story). Overall Chinese managers think strategy 8 (Reprimand the employee for ignoring the chain of command), strategy 6 (Refuse to meet with the employee and inform your subordinate that the employee has attempted to sidestep the chain of command), and strategy 10 (Turn the matter over to an assistant) are inappropriate responses to situation 2.

Table 6.12 Chinese managers' responses to situation 2 in TKIM (N = 133)

	Mean	s. d.
1. Refuse to meet with the employee unless the individual first discusses the matter with your subordinate	2.61	1.691
2. Meet with the employee but only with your subordinate present	2.77	1.507
3. Schedule a meeting with the employee and then with your subordinate to get both sides of the story	5.70	1.255
4. Meet with the employee and then investigate the allegations if an investigation appears warranted before talking with your subordinate	5.76	1.426
5. Find out more information about the employee, if you can, before making any decisions	5.93	1.001
6. Refuse to meet with the employee and inform your subordinate that the employee has attempted to sidestep the chain of command	1.71	0.991
7. Meet with your subordinate first before deciding whether to meet with the employee	4.21	1.697
8. Reprimand the employee for ignoring the chain of command	1.37	0.754
9. Ask a senior colleague whom you respect for advice about what to do in this situation	4.65	1.605
10. Turn the matter over to an assistant	1.74	1.186

The content of situation 3 is 'You have just completed your most important project ever, which involved automating the department's warehouses. You have worked many evenings and weekend days over the last six months on this project. You are pleased with your performance because, despite adversity, the project was completed at the projected cost and on time. Near the project's end, it seemed likely that you were going to need additional time and money. But, through hard work on your part, and by pushing some of your people very hard, you met both time deadlines and cost projections. In a meeting, your supervisor (having been in his position for six months), brings up the topic of your performance on the project. Expecting lavish praise and perhaps even discussion of a possible increase in responsibility, you are stunned by his evaluation of your performance, which is entirely negative. He states that some of your subordinates have complained to him directly about their treatment at your hands in the last phase of project completion. He questions your ability to manage others, and wonders aloud about your ability to lead others. He says nothing positive about the fact that you completed the project on time and at cost under adverse circumstances, nor about how hard you worked on the project.' This situation asks managers to rate the quality of the following things they might do in this situation on a 1 'extremely bad' to 7 'extremely good' point scale.

Table 6.13 presents the 10 strategies for situation 3 with host Chinese managers' mean rate for each strategy and according standard deviation. The mean rates for the 10 strategies of situation 3 range from 1.95 (strategy 5) to 6.30 (strategy 6). The top three good strategies for situation 3 are strategy 6 (Discuss with your supervisor specific examples of where he thinks you went wrong in dealing with the project,

Table 6.13 Chinese managers' responses to situation 3 in TKIM (N = 133)

	Mean	s. d.
1. Admit that you perhaps were too hard on your workers, but state that in your judgment, the importance of meeting the deadline and budget projection made your actions necessary	5.29	1.271
2. Expresures disappointment with your performance appraisal, and state that you think it is one-sided	3.17	1.638
3. Accept the criticism and explain how you will behave differently in the future	4.31	1.498
4. Try to find out if anything else is behind this overly negative evaluation	5.14	1.582
5. Begin looking for a new position	1.95	1.186
6. Discuss with your supervisor specific examples of where he thinks you went wrong in dealing with the project, and how he would have handled it more effectively	6.30	0.826
7. Ask your supervisor to give you a second chance, resolving to yourself to keep him better informed about your activities in the future	4.75	1.367
8. Ask your supervisor to help you develop your skills at managing others	4.74	1.376
9. Seek the advice of others you trust in the department about what you should do	4.74	1.385
10. Admit you might have made some mistakes, but be sure your supervisor is aware of all that you accomplished and the adverse circumstances that you faced	5.26	1.424

and how he would have handled it more effectively), strategy 1 (Admit that you perhaps were too hard on your workers, but state that in your judgment, the importance of meeting the deadline and budget projection made your actions necessary), and strategy 10 (Admit you might have made some mistakes, but be sure your supervisor is aware of all that you accomplished and the adverse circumstances that you faced). Overall Chinese managers think strategy 5 (Begin looking for a new position) is an inappropriate responses to situation 3.

The content of situation 6 is 'You and a co-worker jointly are responsible for completing a report on a new project by the end of the week. You are uneasy about this assignment because he has a reputation for not meeting deadlines. The problem does not appear to be lack of effort. Rather, he seems to lack certain organizational skills necessary to meet a deadline and also is quite a perfectionist. As a result, too much time is wasted coming up with the "perfect" idea, project, or report.' In this situation, the manager's goal is to produce the best possible report by the deadline at the end of the week. The situation asks managers to rate the quality of the following strategies for meeting the goal on a 1 'extremely bad' to 7 'extremely good' point scale. Table 6.14 presents the 10 available strategies for situation 6 with host Chinese managers' mean rate for each strategy and according standard deviation. The mean rates for the 10 strategies of situation 6 range from 2.03 (strategy 11) to 5.98 (strategy 5). The top three good strategies for situation 6 are strategy 5 (Praise your co-worker verbally for completion of parts of the assignment), strategy 3 (Set deadlines for completing each part of the report, and accept what you have

Table 6.14 Chinese managers' responses to situation 6 in TKIM (N = 133)

	Mean	s. d.
1. Divide the work to be done in half and tell him that if he does not complete his part, you obviously will have to let your immediate superior know it was not your fault	2.55	1.495
2. Politely tell him to be less of a perfectionist	4.32	1.293
3. Set deadlines for completing each part of the report, and accept what you have accomplished at each deadline as the final version of that part of the report	5.63	1.328
4. Ask your superior to check up on your progress on a daily basis (after explaining why)	3.95	1.468
5. Praise your co-worker verbally for completion of parts of the assignment	5.98	0.957
6. Get angry with him at the first sign of getting behind schedule	2.52	1.390
7. As soon as he begins to fall behind, take responsibility for doing the report yourself, if need be, to meet the deadline	3.53	1.505
8. Point out firmly, but politely, how he is holding up the report	5.34	1.249
9. Avoid putting any presuresure on him because it will just make him fall even more behind	2.75	1.464
10. Offer to buy him dinner at the end of the week if you both meet the deadline	5.50	1.165
11. Ignore his organizational problem so you don't give attention to maladaptive behavior	2.03	1.279

accomplished at each deadline as the final version of that part of the report), and strategy 10 (Offer to buy him dinner at the end of the week if you both meet the deadline). Overall Chinese managers think strategy 11 (Ignore his organizational problem so you don't give attention to maladaptive behavior) is an inappropriate responses to situation 6.

6.3.2 Differences Between the Two Samples in Terms of Managerial Tacit Knowledge

Table 6.15 summarizes the mean scores and standard deviations (s. d.) of the nine managerial tacit knowledge variables (situation 1, situation 2, situation 3, situation 4, situation 5, situation 6, managerial tacit knowledge related to managing self, managerial tacit knowledge related to managing others, and total managerial tacit knowledge) of host Chinese managers and also of western expatriate managers for comparison, along with the results of independent sample t-test.

With regard to managerial tacit knowledge related to managing self, there is no significant difference between the two samples. However, there is significant difference between the two samples regarding managerial tacit knowledge related to managing others ($p < 0.01$ for situation 2; $p < 0.05$ for situation 3 and situation 6).

Table 6.15 A summary of the nine managerial tacit knowledge variables for the two samples

	Western expatriate managers (N = 121)		Local Chinese managers (N = 133)		Independent sample t-test (t score)
	Mean	s. d.	Mean	s. d.	
S1	0.5548343604	0.18910311557	0.577817	0.1614336	1.044
S2	0.434421836	0.1637861323	0.571172	0.1832458	6.247**
S3	0.600838235	0.1515861694	0.562152	0.1459843	−2.071*
S4	0.55386481	0.138523768	0.538794	0.1339029	−0.881
S5	0.4902813	0.12054112	0.494770	0.1536242	0.257
S6	0.5855478501	0.13814978241	0.543080	0.1521386	−2.321*
Self	0.5329934950	0.09081225436	0.537127	0.1005513	0.343
Others	0.5402693050	0.08486549512	0.558801	0.1021897	1.564**
Total	1.0732628013	0.13133768263	1.095928	0.1500779	1.875**

Note ***$p < 0.001$; **$p < 0.01$ (two-tailed)

Overall, western expatriate managers own relatively higher levels of accumulated managerial tacit knowledge in both managing self and managing others than host Chinese managers. The present research further compares the two samples' different responses to each of the six situations in TKIM. Situation 1 asks managers to rate the quality of the following 10 strategies for becoming more knowledgeable about new products and technology on a 1 (extremely bad) to 7 (extremely good) point scale. Table 6.16 illustrates host Chinese managers' and western expatriate managers' mean rates for each strategy of situation 1 for comparison. As shown in Table 6.16, host Chinese managers and western expatriate managers have the same tendency on the 'bad-good' dimension to all the 10 available strategies of situation 1.

Situation 4 asks managers to rate the quality of the following 10 strategies for handling the day-to-day work of a manager on a 1 'extremely bad' to 7 'extremely good' point scale. Table 6.17 illustrates host Chinese managers' and western expatriate managers' mean rates for each strategy of situation 4 for comparison. As shown in Table 6.17, host Chinese managers and western expatriate managers have the same tendency on the 'bad-good' dimension to all the 10 available strategies of situation 4 except strategy 1 and strategy 4. With regard to strategy 1, overall Chinese managers suggest that 'think in terms of tasks accomplished rather than hours spent working' is a relatively bad strategy for handling the day-to-day work of a manager, while western expatriate managers think this is a quite good strategy. With regard to strategy 4, overall Chinese managers think 'be in charge of all phase of every task or project you are involved in' is a neither good nor bad strategy for handling the day-to-day work of a manager, western expatriate managers, on the other hand, regard it as a quite bad strategy.

Situation 5 asks managers to rate the importance of the following 10 considerations when selecting new projects on a 1 (extremely bad) to 7 (extremely good) point scale. Table 6.18 illustrates host Chinese managers' and western expatriate managers' mean rates for each strategy of situation 5 for comparison. As shown in

Table 6.16 The two samples' different responses to situation 1

	Chinese mean	Expatriate mean
1. Ask for a leave of absence to pursue an advanced technical degree	2.50	2.03
2. Order a news clipping service (news clipping services provide news from a large number of sources on a given topic)	5.04	4.57
3. Subscribe to several technical journals relevant to your manufacturing operations	4.69	4.13
4. Subscribes to several consumer-oriented magazines that cover your products	5.59	4.70
5. Begin attending trade shows of products in your industry	5.67	5.73
6. Ask to sit in on weekly discussions of new product ideas held by the Research and Development division	5.91	6.43
7. Attend a series of technical presentations by research scientists from outside the company who are brought in by the Manufacturing Operations division	5.41	5.63
8. Hire a staff member whose primary responsibility is to keep you abreast of current trends in your industry	4.14	4.63
9. Ask the Engineering division to prepare monthly summary reports of innovative products	5.24	5.23
10. Ask for weekly presentations for you and your staff on technical issues by staff in the Research and Development and Manufacturing Operations divisions	4.95	5.63

Table 6.17 The two samples' different responses to situation 4

	Chinese mean	Expatriate mean
1. Think in terms of tasks accomplished rather than hours spent working	3.79	5.50
2. Use a daily list of goals arranged according to your priorities	6.55	6.37
3. Reward yourself upon completion of important tasks for the day	5.01	4.57
4. Be in charge of all phase of every task or project you are involved in	4.14	2.90
5. Take frequent but short breaks (i.e., a quick walk to the mail room) throughout the day	4.89	4.67
6. Only delegate inconsequential tasks, since you cannot guarantee that the tasks will be done properly and on time unless you do them yourself	2.98	2.77
7. Do only what you are in the mood to do to maximize the quality of your work	3.30	2.63
8. Take every opportunity to get feedback on early drafts of your work	5.43	5.03
9. Set your own deadlines in addition to externally imposed ones	6.17	5.83
10. Do not spend much time planning the best way to do something because the best way to do something may not be apparent until after you have begun doing it	4.49	3.97

Table 6.18 The two samples' different responses to situation 5

	Chinese mean	Expatriate mean
1. The project is the one my immediate superior most desires to be completed	5.56	4.40
2. Doing the project would require my developing skills that may enhance my future career success	5.98	5.83
3. The project should attract the attention of the local media	4.02	3.10
4. Doing the project should prove to be fun	4.80	5.03
5. The risk of making a mistake is virtually nonexistent	3.21	2.47
6. The project will require my interacting with senior executives whom I would like to get to know better	5.12	5.10
7. The project is valued by my superior even though it is not valued by me	4.82	4.33
8. The project will enable me to demonstrate my talents that others may not be aware of	5.57	5.40
9. The project is in an area with which 1 have a lot of experience	5.38	5.47
10. The project is the one I most want to do	5.85	5.07

Table 6.18, host Chinese managers and western expatriate managers have the same tendency on the 'bad-good' dimension to all the 10 considerations of situation 5.

Situation 2, situation 3, and situation 6 are designed to examine managers' levels of accumulated managerial tacit knowledge related to managing others. Situation 2 asks managers to rate the quality of the following 10 strategies they are considering doing in this situation on a 1 'extremely bad' to 7 'extremely good' point scale. Table 6.19 illustrates host Chinese managers' and western expatriate managers' mean rates for each strategy of situation 2 for comparison. As shown in Table 6.19, host Chinese managers and western expatriate managers have same tendency on the 'bad-good' dimension to all the 10 available strategies of situation 2 except the strategy 7. Overall host Chinese managers regard the strategy 7 'meet with your subordinate first before deciding whether to meet with the employee' as a relatively good response to situation 2, while western expatriate managers think it is a relatively bad solution.

Situation 3 asks managers to rate the quality of the following things they might do in this situation on a 1 'extremely bad' to 7 'extremely good' point scale. Table 6.20 illustrates host Chinese managers' and western expatriate managers' mean rates for each strategy of situation 3 for comparison. As shown in Table 6.20, overall host Chinese managers and western expatriate managers have the same tendency on the 'bad-good' dimension to all the 10 available strategies of situation 3 except the strategy 3 and the strategy 7. With regard to strategy 3, overall Chinese managers think 'accept the criticism and explain how you will behave differently in the future' to situation 3 is a relatively good response, while western expatriate managers suggest it is a quite bad strategy. With regard to strategy 7, overall Chinese managers regard the strategy 'ask your supervisor to give you a second

Table 6.19 The two samples' different responses to situation 2

	Chinese mean	Expatriate mean
1. Refuse to meet with the employee unless the individual first discusses the matter with your subordinate	2.61	1.90
2. Meet with the employee but only with your subordinate present	2.77	2.63
3. Schedule a meeting with the employee and then with your subordinate to get both sides of the story	5.70	5.47
4. Meet with the employee and then investigate the allegations if an investigation appears warranted before talking with your subordinate	5.76	4.33
5. Find out more information about the employee, if you can, before making any decisions	5.93	5.40
6. Refuse to meet with the employee and inform your subordinate that the employee has attempted to sidestep the chain of command	1.71	1.93
7. Meet with your subordinate first before deciding whether to meet with the employee	4.21	3.70
8. Reprimand the employee for ignoring the chain of command	1.37	1.50
9. Ask a senior colleague whom you respect for advice about what to do in this situation	4.65	4.40
10. Turn the matter over to an assistant	1.74	1.47

Table 6.20 The two samples' different responses to situation 3

	Chinese mean	Expatriate mean
1. Admit that you perhaps were too hard on your workers, but state that in your judgment, the importance of meeting the deadline and budget projection made your actions necessary	5.29	5.30
2. Expresures disappointment with your performance appraisal, and state that you think it is one-sided	3.17	3.87
3. Accept the criticism and explain how you will behave differently in the future	4.31	3.10
4. Try to find out if anything else is behind this overly negative evaluation	5.14	5.23
5. Begin looking for a new position	1.95	2.03
6. Discuss with your supervisor specific examples of where he thinks you went wrong in dealing with the project, and how he would have handled it more effectively	6.30	6.10
7. Ask your supervisor to give you a second chance, resolving to yourself to keep him better informed about your activities in the future	4.75	3.40
8. Ask your supervisor to help you develop your skills at managing others	4.74	4.70
9. Seek the advice of others you trust in the department about what you should do	4.74	3.90
10. Admit you might have made some mistakes, but be sure your supervisor is aware of all that you accomplished and the adverse circumstances that you faced	5.26	5.20

Table 6.21 The two samples' different responses to situation 6

	Chinese mean	Expatriate mean
1. Divide the work to be done in half and tell him that if he does not complete his part, you obviously will have to let your immediate superior know it was not your fault	2.55	2.73
2. Politely tell him to be less of a perfectionist	4.32	3.93
3. Set deadlines for completing each part of the report, and accept what you have accomplished at each deadline as the final version of that part of the report	5.63	4.93
4. Ask your superior to check up on your progress on a daily basis (after explaining why)	3.95	4.37
5. Praise your co-worker verbally for completion of parts of the assignment	5.98	5.50
6. Get angry with him at the first sign of getting behind schedule	2.52	2.07
7. As soon as he begins to fall behind, take responsibility for doing the report yourself, if need be, to meet the deadline	3.53	2.93
8. Point out firmly, but politely, how he is holding up the report	5.34	5.37
9. Avoid putting any presuresure on him because it will just make him fall even more behind	2.75	2.97
10. Offer to buy him dinner at the end of the week if you both meet the deadline	5.50	4.20
11. Ignore his organizational problem so you don't give attention to maladaptive behaviour	2.03	1.63

chance, resolving to yourself to keep him better informed about your activities in the future' as a relatively good solution, while western expatriate managers suggest it is a relatively bad strategy.

Situation 6 asks managers to rate the quality of the following 11 strategies for meeting the goal on a 1 'extremely bad' to 7 'extremely good' point scale. Table 6.21 illustrates host Chinese managers' and western expatriate managers' mean rates for each strategy of situation 6 for comparison.

As shown in Table 6.21, overall host Chinese managers and western expatriate managers have the same tendency on the 'bad-good' dimension to all the 11 available strategies of situation 6 except the strategy 10. Overall Chinese managers think the strategy 'offer to buy him dinner at the end of the week if you both meet the deadline' to situation 6 is a quite good solution, while western expatriate managers regard it as a neither good nor bad strategy.

6.3.3 Accumulation of Managerial Tacit Knowledge Over Time

The present research also examines whether the longer the subjects exposure to managerial functions, the higher their levels of accumulated managerial tacit knowledge. The context of subjects' work environment was determined by investigating whether their working time had been spent predominantly performing managerial or non-managerial functions. These data were collected using self-developed items within the demographic section of the survey instrument where participants were asked to choose a length box referred to how long they have been in a managerial role. Briefing sessions were held with all respondents in the study to impressure on them that this part of the survey was concerned specifically with managerial functions involving the management of human as well as other resources such as finance and/or materials. Participants were encouraged to contact the researchers if there were any doubts about the item. In the present research, 18.8 % of participated host Chinese managers have been in a managerial role for less than 3 years; 24.1 % with 3–5 years; 31.6 % with 5–10 years; and 25.6 % over 10 years. As shown in the results of correlation analysis of all metric variables, the correlation between the accumulation of managerial tacit knowledge and the time in a managerial role is significant. However, there is no significant relationship between the overall time in western MNCs and the accumulation of managerial tacit knowledge. Tables 6.22 and 6.23 presents the correlation between time in the managerial role, the overall time in western MNCs and the nine managerial tacit knowledge variables.

As shown in Tables 6.22 and 6.23, there is significant negative relationship between the time in a managerial role and situation 4 ($p < 0.05$), managerial tacit knowledge related to managing self ($p < 0.05$), situation 2 ($p < 0.01$), situation 5 ($p < 0.01$), situation 6 ($p < 0.01$), managerial tacit knowledge related to managing others ($p < 0.01$), and total managerial tacit knowledge ($p < 0.01$). It should be noted that scores measured by TKIM (Tacit knowledge inventory for managers) are expected to decrease rather than increase with advancing levels of tacit knowledge because these scores represent respondents' deviations from the expert/successful group. There is no significant relationship between the overall time in western MNCs and the nine managerial tacit knowledge variables. The results suggest that

Table 6.22 The correlation between the time in managerial role, time in MNCs and managerial tacit knowledge

	S1	S2	S3	S4	S5	S6
Time in managerial role	−0.016	−0.304**	−0.108	−0.178*	−0.256**	−0.244**
Overall time in western MNCs	0.120	−0.021	−0.087	−0.004	0.077	−0.090

Note S referred to Situation
*$p < 0.05$; **$p < 0.01$ (two-tailed)

Table 6.23 The correlation between the time in managerial role, time in MNCs and managerial tacit knowledge

	Self	Other	Total
Time in managerial role	−0.218*	−0.354**	−0.387**
Overall time in western MNCs	0.102	−0.099	0.001

Note S referred to Situation
*$p < 0.05$; **$p < 0.01$ (two-tailed)

the longer host Chinese managers exposure to managerial functions, the relatively higher their levels of accumulated managerial tacit knowledge. Therefore, the present research further examines the enhancement of host Chinese managers' levels of accumulated managerial tacit knowledge along with them being in managerial roles over time. In this study, the sample of 133 host Chinese managers is divided into four groups based on how long they have been working in a predominantly managerial context. The first group has been in managerial role for 3 years or less; the second group for over 3–5 years; the third group for over 5–10 years; and the fourth group for over 10 years. Table 6.24, 6.25, and 6.26 illustrate the results of ANOVA of the nine managerial tacit knowledge variables by work length in managerial roles.

As shown in Tables 6.24, 6.25, and 6.26, there are significant differences in managerial tacit knowledge variables scores across groups on situation 2 (F = 4.590, $p < 0.01$), situation 5 (F = 3.583, $p < 0.05$), situation 6 (F = 3.104, $p < 0.05$), managerial tacit knowledge related to managing others (F = 6.398, $p < 0.01$), and total managerial tacit knowledge (F = 7.982, $p < 0.01$). Specifically, it shows an enhancement on levels of accumulated managerial tacit knowledge related to managing others and total managerial tacit knowledge as host Chinese managers being longer in a managerial role. It is reasonable to conclude that, based

Table 6.24 Results of ANOVA of the nine managerial tacit knowledge variables by length in managerial role

	S1		S2		S3	
	Mean	s. d.	Mean	s. d.	Mean	s. d.
First group	0.570013	0.1620630	0.667039	0.2584629	0.587553	0.2012614
Second group	0.592119	0.1418485	0.586618	0.1964675	0.573793	0.1432273
Third group	0.578589	0.1763636	0.562358	0.1249788	0.551623	0.1359398
Fourth group	0.569141	0.1651455	0.497034	0.1308052	0.545525	0.1118491
ALL	0.577817	0.1614336	0.571172	0.1832458	0.562152	0.1459843
df	3		3		3	
F	0.134		4.590**		0.534	

Note *$p < 0.05$; **$p < 0.01$ (two-tailed)

Table 6.25 Results of ANOVA of the nine managerial tacit knowledge variables by length in managerial role

	S4		S5		S6	
	Mean	s. d.	Mean	s. d.	Mean	s. d.
First group	0.591647	0.1383575	0.571799	0.1969833	0.616556	0.2200041
Second group	0.535983	0.1238939	0.512325	0.1367721	0.555182	0.1544839
Third group	0.528048	0.1387913	0.461869	0.1516969	0.517046	0.1083669
Fourth group	0.515852	0.1289670	0.462249	0.1129458	0.509822	0.1189117
ALL	0.538794	0.1339029	0.494770	0.1536242	0.543080	0.1521386
df	3		3		3	
F	1.756		3.583*		3.104*	

Note $*p < 0.05$; $**p < 0.01$ (two-tailed)

Table 6.26 Results of ANOVA of the nine managerial tacit knowledge variables by length in managerial role

	Self		Others		Total	
	Mean	s. d.	Mean	s. d.	Mean	s. d.
First group	0.577820	0.1246108	0.623716	0.1642903	1.201536	0.2195903
Second group	0.546809	0.0780927	0.571864	0.0921241	1.118673	0.1151497
Third group	0.522835	0.1044027	0.543675	0.0673200	1.066511	0.1289870
Fourth group	0.515747	0.0883279	0.517461	0.0559277	1.033208	0.0882740
ALL	0.537127	0.1005513	0.558801	0.1021897	1.095928	0.1500779
df	3		3		3	
F	2.327		6.398**		7.982**	

Note $*p < 0.05$; $**p < 0.01$ (two-tailed)

on analyses of the results of the correlation and the ANOVA tests, the longer host Chinese managers have been in a managerial role, the higher their levels of accumulated managerial tacit knowledge.

Appendix H: Correlation Matrix (Host Chinese Managers)

Means, standard deviations and inter-correlations for all research variables

	Mean	SD	1	2	3	4	5	6	7	8
1. Gender	1.51	0.502	_							
2. Age	2.17	0.510	0.091	_						
3. Time in MNCs	4.57	0.568	−0.101	0.512	_					
4. Time in managerial role	3.47	1.105	−0.153*	0.317*	0.445*	_				
5. Job position	2.41	0.565	−0.056	0.302*	0.417**	0.309*	_			
6. AC-CE	8.26	8.494	−0.218*	−0.011	0.215*	0.187	0.190	0.72		
7. AE-RO	4.09	12.602	−0.053	−0.104	−0.371**	0.216*	0.112	0.225**	0.73	
8. Managerial tacit knowledge	1.188	0.150	0.031	−0.107	−0.119	−0.270**	0.318**	0.118*	−0.017	0.80

n = 133; $*p < 0.05$; $**p < 0.01$
Coefficient alpha reliabilities are reported in parentheses in the correlation diagonals
Gender 1 male, *2* female

Chapter 7
Discussion and Conclusion

This chapter integrates the results of the previous chapters concerned with validating the expatriate learning model for adjustment and provides limitations of this research, and its implications. In this process, the researcher first summarizes and discusses the results of the examination of 9 hypotheses that correspond to 3 research questions. This section includes western expatriates' adjustment in China, western expatriates' learning style transitions, western expatriates' accumulation of managerial tacit knowledge, western expatriates' development of adaptive flexibility over time in China, and the relationships between these learning outcomes. Second, this chapter summarizes the differences between western expatriate managers and host Chinese managers working in the same MNCs in terms of learning styles and levels of accumulated managerial tacit knowledge. Third, limitations of this research are discussed. In the end, the researcher explores other important implications and future research avenues relevant to this study. These implications pertain to three disciplinary areas: Cross-cultural adjustment research, Global manager development studies, and expatriate management studies.

7.1 Summary of the Results of Research Questions

7.1.1 Expatriate Adjustment

In this study, the researcher extended the study of the expatriate experience by invoking an experiential learning view to investigate cross-cultural adaptation through expatriate learning and adapting a theory of knowledge acquisition to examine expatriate manager development. The research first presented its empirical support and extended studies to the international adjustment model of Black et al. (1991) and then explained its findings in relation to expatriate learning and development during their international assignments.

Y. Li, *Expatriate Manager's Adaption and Knowledge Acquisition*,
DOI 10.1007/978-981-10-0053-9_7

7.1.1.1 Expatriate Adjustment and Current Assignment Tenure

Research hypothesis 1 is associated with the relationships between the current assignment tenure and expatriate adjustment in China. Result of the test of Hypothesis 1 led to this hypothesis being refuted. Inability to 'adjust' to foreign environments has been cited as one of the failure (Takeuchi et al. 2005; Okpara and Kabongo 2011). Black et al. (1991) integrated perspectives from both domestic and international adjustment literatures and developed a comprehensive theoretical framework of international adjustment (discussed in Sect. 2.2). Bhaskar-Shrinivas et al. (2005) contend that Black et al.'s model is the most influential and often-cited theoretical treatment of expatriate experiences. Our research provided empirical support and extended studies to this model. Results of the study revealed that there is no direct significant relationship between the current length of assignment tenure and expatriate adjustment. The effects of current assignment tenure on expatriate adjustment depend on that of the mediators, such as individual characteristics. The results suggest that expatriate adjustment is independent of the general length of assignment tenure, but dependent on how expatriates learn and develop during their international assignments.

7.1.1.2 Expatriate Adjustment and Previous International Experience

With regard to anticipatory adjustment, the results demonstrated that managers' previous experiences of international assignments positively influenced their international work adjustment in the host culture. Black et al. (1991) contend that previous international adjustment experiences would provide more information from which uncertainties could be reduced and accurate expectations formed. Moreover, the results revealed that managers' previous overseas work experiences significantly facilitated their international adjustment via expatriate learning. Expatriate managers with previous international experience find it easier to learn using the host culturally dominant learning modes and become more matched with the host country. The results suggested that the group of 42 western expatriates with previous overseas work experience adapt significantly better than that of 79 non-experienced western expatriates. The exploratory examination indicated that the 79 non-experienced western expatriate managers adapt better if they learn by the concrete and reflective learning modes rather than the abstract and active learning modes. In addition, having family members coming from different countries, especially from Greater China, will enhance the adjustment of western expatriates. However, in light of 42 western expatriate managers with previous international assignment experience, the research results illustrated an insignificant relationship between the AC-CE learning dimension and expatriate adaptation in China. The association of the mediating variables with expatriate adaptation was also insignificant.

One possible explanation may lie in the small sample size. The sample of this group ($N = 42$) might be difficult to enable regression analysis to detect a significant relationship between them. Another explanation is that the western expatriate managers of this sub-group have already learned a way of living in different cultures from their previous international experiences. Several international assignment researchers identified the importance of previous overseas experiences for adaptation and success (Black 1988; Okpara and Kabongo 2011). Their previous international experiences may not require the western expatriate managers to learn using the concrete mode that is regarded as an undeveloped mode for non-experienced western expatriates.

7.1.1.3 Expatriate Adjustment and Learning Style

The results found support for the relationships between the two learning style variables: AC-CE and AE-RO, and expatriate adaptation in China. Results of the tests of Hypotheses 7a and 7b provided support. Furthermore, based on the results of regression analysis of three aspects of expatriate adaptation in detail, it shows that the AC-CE learning dimension significantly negatively affect the socialization adjustment and work adjustment, while the AE-RO learning dimension only significantly affect the socialization adjustment. The findings of the exploratory analysis also illustrated that having an international family member and a number of previous international assignment experience significantly affected expatriate adaptation. The results suggest that western expatriate managers who have an international family, especially when the family member comes from greater China, adapt better in cross-cultural context in China. Moreover, the findings revealed that western expatriate managers without experience in previous overseas assignment will adapt better in China if they learn by the concrete and reflective modes rather than the abstract and active modes.

(a) The Abstract-Concrete learning dimension and expatriate adjustment
    In answer to the first research question of 'How do Western expatriate managers adapt when working in China', this concerns the relationship between the AC-CE learning dimension and expatriate adaptation. Concrete western expatriates adapt better in China than abstract western expatriates. This result is congruent with that of Hypothesis 2a: the relationship between AC-CE and the length of international assignment tenure in China. Based on the results of exploratory analysis of three aspects of expatriate adaptation in detail, it shows that the AC-CE learning dimension significantly negatively affect the socialization adjustment and work adjustment, but not the general adjustment. The significant relationship between the AC-CE dimension and expatriate adaptation further stresses the general requirements of the concrete learning mode for cross-cultural adaptation. According to the findings from the previous literature, cross-cultural environments commonly call for expatriates to learn through concrete experience (Yamazaki and Kayes 2004, 2007). If western expatriates meet this requirement, they will become adapted to their cross-cultural environment more effectively. In contrast, abstract western

expatriates will not adapt well unless they meet this requirement that expatriates learn using the concrete experience mode.

(b) The Active-Reflective learning dimension and expatriate adjustment
In answer to the first research question of 'How do Western expatriate managers adapt when working in China', this concerns the relationship between the AE-RO learning dimension and expatriate adaptation. The research findings demonstrated that reflective western expatriates adapt significantly better in China than active western expatriates. This result is also congruent with that of the test of Hypothesis 2b: the relationship between AE-RO and the length of international assignment tenure in China. A combination of these findings from examination of Hypothesis 2b and 7b provides a logical pattern for cross-cultural adaptation of western expatriate managers in China. Western expatriate managers are shifted from the active to the reflective learning mode over time on account of the environmental influence of the reflective mode in China. In this respect, reflective western expatriates can be said to be more matched with the Chinese milieu than active western expatriates. Because of this match, therefore, reflective western expatriates adapt better than active western expatriates.

7.1.1.4 Expatriate Adjustment and Adaptive Flexibility

The first research question associated with 'How do Western expatriate managers adapt when working in China', is associated with the relationship between expatriates' levels of adaptive flexibility and expatriate adjustment in China. The results provided support for this relationship. Western expatriate managers with higher levels of adaptive flexibility adjust significantly better to their international assignment in China.

Whilst Black et al. (1991) cite evidence of individual characteristics of self-efficacy and relational skills as having positive relationships with expatriate adjustment, others (e.g. Maertz et al. 2009; Berry 1997; Alagic and Rammington 2009) have highlighted the importance of individual learning characteristics for developing and exhibiting culturally appropriate behaviours to fit with the host culture. The results provided empirical support that cross-cultural adaptation of expatriates entails the association of individual learning styles and adaptive flexibility. Summarizing the literature reviewed, the research started with the cross-cultural assumption that Westerners' learning orientations are generally more toward Active Experimentation (AE) than Reflective Observation (RO) and more toward Abstract Conceptualization (AC) than Concrete Experience (CE), while Chinese are generally oriented more toward RO than AE and more toward CE than AC. Results of the study revealed that the degree of adjustment were higher when expatriates' learning styles were matched with the host culture and lower among those whose learning styles were incongruent with the host culture. The results suggest that the concrete and reflective modes of learning need to be learned by western expatriates for adjustment to their international business contexts where these learning modes are culturally dominant. Unlike learning style, which refers to more generic adaptive competencies to the world (Kolb 1984), adaptive flexibility describes how an individual learns to adapt to changing circumstances and deal with environmental complexity. Yamazaki and Kayes (2004) proposed that adaptive flexibility is a key component of successful cross-cultural adjustment. The present research demonstrated that expatriate managers with greater levels of adaptive flexibility adjust significantly better to their international assignments in the host country. As a result, the researcher proposed that expatriate's learning styles and adaptive flexibility are important individual characteristics when considering international adjustment.

7.1.2 Expatriate Learning

A significant number of international HRM researchers have proposed that the successful adjustment of expatriates will hinge on how well they learn from experiences in these foreign operations (e.g. Ratiu 1983; Yamazaki and Kayes 2007; Ng et al. 2009; Armstrong et al. 2011). The present research further investigated a unique aspect of cross-cultural adjustment through expatriate learning. The results revealed that western expatriate managers developed adaptive flexibility according to the change of learning styles from AC to CE, from AE to RO learning mode for their international adjustment. Western expatriates' learning styles obviously shifted toward the concrete and reflective learning modes over time when they work in China. This phenomenon may be possibly interpreted not just as a change of learning orientation but as a developmental change in challenging learning situations for cross-cultural adjustment. Kolb's (1984) Experiential Learning Theory of development points out that a consequence of the developmental change of learning styles come out with a greater degree of adaptive flexibility when people face different learning situations. Furthermore, the research provided empirical support for Mainemelis et al.'s (2002) proposition that 'individuals with balanced learning styles demonstrate higher levels of adaptive flexibility' in cross-cultural contexts.

The present study started with the cross-cultural assumption that American and western European learning styles in business contexts tend to be dominantly distributed in the area of Converging learning style, while Chinese learning styles typically show Diverging learning styles. Results of the examination of western expatriate managers' learning styles allowed the researcher to analyze this cross-cultural assumption in light of Westerner's learning styles. The results of the Learning Style Inventory scores of 121 western expatriate managers illustrate that western expatriate managers exhibited their learning preferences for the abstract and the active modes, the combination of which makes the Converging learning style. Considering the business world, the Converging learning style of western expatriates can be regarded as one of their prominent learning characteristics. Therefore, this part of the results is consistent with the cross-cultural assumption in this research. However, the results of the Learning Style Inventory scores of 133 Chinese managers illustrate that host Chinese managers working in western MNCs exhibited their learning preferences for the abstract and reflective learning modes, the combination of which makes the Assimilating learning style. Even the first group of host Chinese managers, who had been working in western MNCs in China for 5 years or less, showed their preferences more toward the abstract conceptualization learning mode. This part of the results is inconsistent with the cross-cultural assumption in this research.

With regard to the second research question 'what do western expatriate managers learn from their international assignments in China', this concerns the relationship between the AC-CE learning dimension and length of international assignment tenure in China. This section summarizes all research results regarding the relationship between the AC-CE learning dimension and length of assignment tenure in China. Both the SEM result and the correlation analysis show that there is a significant, negative correlation between AC-CE and the length of assignment tenure. This transitional movement of the learning style of western expatriate mangers in the AC-CE learning dimension agreed with the prediction derived from ELT and the cross-cultural assumption in this research. The results showed that learning style distribution moved from Converging to Accommodating. The transition to the concrete learning mode was also affected by gender and the number of previous international assignment. The results suggest that western expatriate managers will become more concrete and less abstract if they have more previous international assignment experiences. Moreover, the results demonstrated that female expatriate managers show more learning preferences for concrete experience over abstract conceptualization when they work in China. In other words, female expatriate managers find it easier to develop concrete experience learning mode in cross-cultural context.

The assumption of the present research is that the learning characteristic of the business environment created by the majority of Chinese employees in China is toward the concrete learning mode. However, the learning preferences on the AC–CE dimension of 133 host Chinese managers, who work with the investigated western expatriate managers in the same MNCs, were contrary to this assumption. The learning preferences of participated host Chinese managers are toward the abstract learning mode rather than the concrete learning mode. This raises a future research question: if host Chinese managers prefer to learn from abstract conceptualization rather than concrete experience, should the business environment of western MNCs in China be predominated by the learning mode of abstract conceptualization or concrete experience? All in all, this opposite direction is meant to stress that the concrete mode rather than the abstract mode is important for western expatriates who are trying to adapt to their cross-cultural environment. Yamazaki and Kayes (2007) argue that the concrete learning mode is essential and very important for expatriates to learn for their cross-cultural adaptation. Ratiu (1983) contends that successful international managers tend to be concrete learners rather than abstract learners, suggesting that the development of the concrete learning mode is a pivotal key for successful adaptation. The concrete learning competencies such as: developing relationship with locals and colleagues, interpersonal respect, and great sensitivity to the needs of others make a difference to expatriates for cross-cultural adaptation. These interpersonal skills are associated with the concrete experience learning. It would be reasonable to conclude that the concrete learning mode is required by western expatriates to learn for effective performance and adaption to cross-cultural contexts. Such a requirement would tend to drive western expatriate managers to be shifted to the concrete learning mode.

With regard to the second research question 'what do western expatriate managers learn from their international assignments in China', this also concerns the relationship between the AE-RO learning dimension and length of international assignment tenure in China. Results of the SEM and the correlation analysis, along with the regression analysis, indicated that western expatriates' learning styles significantly changed toward reflective observation over time. This transitional movement of the learning style of western expatriate mangers in the AE-RO learning dimension agreed with the prediction derived from Experiential Learning Theory and the cross-cultural assumption in this research. This shift is interpreted as a requirement for western expatriate managers' adaptation to their cross-cultural circumstances. Mastering the reflective mode of learning would, therefore, facilitate western expatriate managers to perform effectively within the Chinese business world. In addition to this finding, the results of regression analysis showed that having an international family member and the number of previous overseas experiences negatively affect the shift of AE-RO. The results suggest that western expatriate managers that have an international family, especially the family member from Greater China, become more reflective and less active when they work in China. This is consistent with the discussions in the literature review that Chinese prefer to learn through reflective observation rather than active experimentation in comparison with other nationalities. Through western expatriates' intensive interactions with their Chinese family member, they would have many opportunities to learn about Chinese ways of life. In addition, the results suggest that western expatriate managers with more previous international assignment experience find it easier to develop a reflective learning mode in China compared to those with less previous overseas work experience.

In terms of the importance of the reflective learning mode for western expatriates in China, the results are consistent with the previous findings presented in cross-cultural research. Hall (1977) contends that westerners need to learn to make sense from Chinese high-context communication patterns. Li and Scullion (2010) suggest that western expatriates need to develop information gathering and analysis skills for their local competence to acquire tacit knowledge in Chinese business environment. These skills are clearly associated with reflective observation learning mode (Kolb 1984; Baumard 1999). Overall, the cross-cultural and expatriate studies are congruent with the empirical quantitative findings that western expatriates' learning styles are shifted toward the reflective learning mode over time for their cross-cultural adaptation in China.

Results of the study revealed that western expatriate managers with higher levels of managerial tacit knowledge related to managing-self adjust significantly better in their international work assignments. The results suggest that individuals' levels of accumulated managerial tacit knowledge are also able to predict success in work environments in cross-cultural context. An increasing amount of literature is now linking various forms of learning styles to tacit knowledge (e.g. Sternberg et al. 2000; Barkema et al. 1998; Armstrong and Mahmud 2008) and the present study showed evidence that participants' learning styles were associated with the accumulation of managerial tacit knowledge in cross-cultural context. Levels of accumulated managerial tacit knowledge were higher when expatriates' learning styles were matched with the host culture (e.g. Diverger) and lower among those whose learning styles were incongruent with the host culture. The results also revealed that expatriates' levels of accumulated managerial tacit knowledge related to managing others were positively related to the concrete learning mode. Experiential Learning Theory suggests that people with concrete experience learning preferences are more adept at establishing personal relationships and communicating effectively. This research provided empirical support that the learning characteristics of CE mode are closely associated with the nature of managerial tacit knowledge related to managing others. The present research also proposed that expatriates' learning preferences for reflective observation would positively influence their accumulation of managerial tacit knowledge related to managing self. However, this hypothesis was not supported in the study's findings. One possible explanation is that even through the learning characteristics of RO mode are closely associated with the nature of managerial tacit knowledge related to managing self, the content of managerial tacit knowledge emphasizes in action-oriented situations. Moreover, results of the study revealed a significant difference in levels of accumulated managerial tacit knowledge between successful and novice groups in cross-cultural context, which is consistent with previous research in the field in domestic context (Wagner and Sternberg 1986, 1987; Armstrong and Mahmud 2008) and, in part, confirms the validity of the present study. The study also revealed that the accumulation of managerial tacit knowledge is unrelated to the length of expatriate's assignment tenure. This finding lends support to the belief that it may be how people learn from experience rather than the length of experience that matters (Ng et al. 2009).

7.1.3 Expatriate Learning Model for Adaptation

This section integrates the discussions about the results of examination of 9 hypotheses and the cross-cultural assumption into the expatriate learning model for adaptation. The present research illustrated that the AC-CE learning dimension plays an important role in the cross-cultural adaptation of western expatriate managers to China. The AC-CE learning dimension is not only associated with the cross-cultural adaptation of specific cultural contexts, but also connected with a general requirement for cross-cultural adaptation. Research findings of the study showed: (1) a change of western expatriate managers' learning styles from the abstract mode to the concrete mode over time; (2) a significant relationship between the AC-CE learning dimension and the acquisition of managerial tacit knowledge related to managing others; and (3) a significant relationship between the AC-CE learning dimension and the development of adaptive flexibility. These findings are consistent with the need for concrete experience learning mode for adaptation (socialization adjustment and work adjustment). Particularly, the cross-cultural adaptation of western expatriate managers, especially those who have no previous international experience, is dependent on learning to make the transition from the abstract mode to the concrete mode. This finding strengthens the idea that the concrete learning mode is a general requirement for expatriates' adaptation. Li and Scullion (2010) suggested that interpersonal relationship skills are significantly related to the success of expatriate managers working in emerging markets. Yamazaki and Kayes (2004) contend that interpersonal skills are importantly required for expatriates' adaptation, no matter which countries expatriates go to or come from. Their study supports the notion that the concrete learning mode is demanded from cross-cultural environments and needs to be learned for adaptation. A shift of learning in the AC-CE learning dimension possibly tends to be directed toward the concrete learning mode when expatriates are transferred to a new assignment location. It would be reasonable to propose that concrete experience with its learning abilities is a general requirement of expatriates' adaptation in cross-cultural contexts.

In addition, the present research also examined the learning styles of host Chinese managers that work with the participated western expatriates in same MNCs in China. The overall learning preferences of host Chinese managers are toward the abstract learning mode rather than the concrete learning mode. Especially, the mean score of host Chinese managers on the AC-CE learning dimension learning dimension is significantly higher than that of western expatriates. Moreover, host Chinese managers' learning styles shifted from the concrete learning mode to the abstract learning mode over time when they work in western MNCs' subsidiaries in China. This finding further strengthens the assumption that the learning orientations of Western business culture are more toward abstract conceptualization than concrete experience and also, the concrete learning mode is a general requirement for expatriates' adaptation.

Empirical findings of this research consistently revealed that the AE–RO learning dimension is importantly involved with cross-cultural adaptation: a change of western expatriate managers' learning styles from the active learning mode to the reflective learning mode over time. The findings are consistent with the need of reflective observation for socialization adjustment in China. The results first suggest the AE-RO learning dimension illustrates cross-cultural differences in learning styles and thus, this learning dimension will enable us to illustrate cross-cultural learning styles as environmental characteristics. Second, the learning style difference in the AE–RO learning dimension between one culture and another is directly associated with cross-cultural adaptation. Therefore, such difference in the AE–RO learning dimension will make it possible to predict an adaptive direction of learning styles in cross-cultural contexts. In terms of expatriates' contexts, the AE–RO learning dimension can explain how the host country differs from the home country in learning styles as an environmental characteristic. For example, Chinese learning styles are more reflective and less active, American and Western Europe learning styles are more active and less reflective. The learning style difference in this dimension can then allow us to predict an adaptive direction in expatriates' learning styles in cross-cultural contexts. Based on the results of this research, western expatriates' learning styles tend to be changed from active experimentation to reflective observation if they work in China. As an opposite adaptive direction, it can be predicted that Chinese expatriates' learning styles are likely to be shifted from the reflective learning mode to the active learning mode if they work in American business contexts. This receives support from the present research. In this study, host Chinese managers shifted significantly from the reflective mode to the active mode when they continually worked in western MNCs' subsidiaries over time. One empirical comparative study about the relationship between learning styles and one of Hofstede's (1997) cultural dimensions also support the perspective that the AE–RO learning dimension is directly related to cross-cultural learning styles. Auyeung and Sands (1996) contend that the AE–RO learning dimension is related with the individualism-collectivism cultural dimension. In their research, accounting students in China and Hong Kong, a representative of collectivism, are more reflective; while accounting students in Australia, a representative of individualism, are more active.

Kolb (1984) refers to cross-cultural differences in the AE–RO learning dimension in Experiential Learning Theory (ELT). He contends that the active learning mode has come to dominate the reflection mode in western human society (1984). Exemplification of this domination refers to western technological society in contrast with eastern cultures that emphasize the reflective learning mode in traditional disciplines such as Confucian and yoga (Kolb 1984). The previous empirical evidence and theoretical views are consistent with the perspective that the AE–RO learning dimension illustrates cross-cultural differences in learning styles. Consequently, it would be reasonable to conclude that the AE–RO learning dimension makes it possible for us to differentiate one culture from the other. Since the AE–RO learning dimension is representative of a cross-cultural difference in learning, this dimension can be applied as dealing with the cultural transition of learning for adaptation. Because of a cultural difference in learning styles in this dimension, a shift from one learning mode to the other may occur for cross-cultural adaptation. That is, adaptation to one culture would particularly require learning an undeveloped mode that was not used in the other culture in this learning dimension. In this research, a learning style transition from the active mode to the reflective mode can be regarded as a cross-cultural adaptation of western expatriates.

7.2 Limitations

This section summarizes the limitations of this research. First, this research focused only on the examination of the change of Western learning styles in Chinese business contexts, empirical research of expatriates' adaptation in various cross-cultural contexts will be required. Second, the population of this study is all western expatriate managers in China, but the sample was composed of western expatriate managers who mostly engaged in IT, Manufacturing, Finance, and Logistics industries in Beijing and Shanghai. The sample provided a relative benefit for the elimination of demographic variations as potential errors, while it became biased against the population. Other industry areas and locations must be examined for generalization against the population. Third, the present research was designed to examine the change of learning styles and knowledge acquisition in a cross-sectional study under an assumption that all people have similar traits and common experiences over time. A longitudinal study should be conducted to examine how expatriates change according to their learning styles. The longitudinal design with quantitative and qualitative methods will provide rich information about the phenomena of expatriates' learning and adaptation to cross-cultural contexts. Fourth, expatriate performance on the international assignment should be examined for evaluating entire expatriate success. In particular, in order to reduce the potential for common source bias, future research could use a different source to assess managers' job performance. Managers' supervisors and their Human Resource Department could be asked to provide the details of the managers' job performance. Examination of expatriate performance would provide us with a better picture of entire expatriate success.

Moreover, demographic scales should be improved for evaluating mediating variables, particularly the adaptation scale of spouse and children. Future research should employ research instruments to grasp and evaluate the overall adaptation of expatriates' families. Finally, the cross-cultural assumption made for this study (i.e. Chinese learning styles are typical of Diverging learning style and American and western European learning styles are Converging learning style) was based on mostly theoretical findings and limited empirical findings. Examination of western managers' learning styles prior to their overseas assignments would provide us with a better picture of entire expatriate learning processes. Such studies will also shed a light on deeper understanding of western expatriates' international adaptation.

7.3 Suggestions for Future Research

This section outlines potentially interesting future research directions. This research proposes that concrete experience learning mode with its learning abilities is a general requirement of expatriates' adaptation in cross-cultural contexts. To test this proposition, future studies could be empirically conducted in four patterns of cross-cultural contexts by combination of the home and host culture in the AC–CE learning dimension. The first pattern is the combination of the abstract (home) and the concrete (host). The present research is related to the first pattern. The second is the combination of the concrete (home) and the abstract (host). This pattern is the opposite of the first one. This research question is representative of the following one: are Chinese expatriates' learning styles further changed toward the concrete learning mode over time if they work in an American business context? The third is the combination of the concrete (home) and the concrete (host). The following is presented as a specific research question: are Chinese expatriates' learning styles further changed toward the concrete learning mode over time if they work in Japan or south Korea? The fourth is the combination of the abstract (home) and the abstract (host). This research question is representative of the following one: are American expatriates' learning styles changed from the abstract learning mode to the concrete learning mode over time if they work in the UK? If all of the four patterns result in the direction to the concrete learning mode, then the proposition that the concrete learning mode is generally required for expatriates' adaptation would be supported sufficiently.

The present study also supported one adaptive direction from the active to the reflective learning mode. In this research, western expatriate managers learning style 'shifted' from the active mode to the reflective mode for their cross-cultural adjustment in china. To strengthen the generalization of this cultural learning mode, a future study could focus on the other adaptive direction from the reflective mode to the active mode. For this purpose, researchers need to pay attention to cross-cultural contexts in which expatriates with the reflective learning mode culturally developed are assigned to a country that emphasizes the active learning environment. An example of this cross-cultural context is Chinese expatriates who work in America or the UK. The following is posed as a specific research question: are Chinese expatriates' learning styles changed from the reflective mode to the active mode over time if they work in America? The examination of this research question will further deepen our understanding of expatriates' adaptation in cross-cultural contexts. Moreover, future research in examination of western managers' learning styles prior to their overseas assignments would provide us with a better picture of entire expatriate learning processes.

This research demonstrated that managers' levels of accumulated managerial tacit knowledge are able to predict success in work environments in cross-cultural context and learning style may be a significant factor accounting for differences in levels of managerial tacit knowledge. Future research is needed to identify other variables that mediate the acquisition of tacit knowledge in cross-cultural contexts. Empirical research of the interaction between tacit and explicit knowledge and the mechanisms by which they are intertwined would also lead to further advancements in the area of developing managers. Future research could also examine the difference of levels of accumulated managerial tacit knowledge between expert and novice groups in a variety of other national and cross-cultural contexts. This would be helpful in determining whether the present findings and implications can be accepted with confidence and generalized to other groups of managers.

7.4 Conclusions and Implications

There is a dearth of studies that have researched learning in the context of cross-cultural adaptation or knowledge acquisition during the course of expatriate managers' international work assignments. Furthermore, there is only very limited understanding of how expatriates develop and become successful global managers during their international assignments. The results of this study have provided empirical evidence that expatriates' learning style, adaptive flexibility, and previous international experience influence their cross-cultural adjustment. Results also suggest that the development of adaptive flexibility and the accumulation of tacit knowledge through experiential learning may be impacted by individuals' learning styles. Most previous empirical research associated with expatriate success has focused on expatriates' performance and adaptation (Bhaskar-Shrinivas et al. 2005) and few have considered the importance of assessing the effectiveness of international assignments in the context of expatriate learning. This study has demonstrated that expatriate learning greatly influenced expatriates' cross-cultural adjustment and the knowledge acquisition by expatriates is an important strategic outcome from their international assignments. Outcomes of the study have a range of implications for theory, experiential learning, global manager development, expatriate management, and future research in these areas as follows.

According to Kolb (1984), interplay between people and the world shapes learning style at five levels: psychological types, educational specialization, professional career, current job, and adaptive competencies. Several cross-cultural Experiential Learning studies indicated that learning styles differ from one culture to another, suggesting that the culture of a country around people may be the sixth level of interplay between people and the world. The present research lent support to this view from a pseudo longitudinal study of how western expatriate managers adapt, learn, and develop in MNCs in China. It provided the empirical findings that people' learning styles are changed over time in a cross-cultural environment where the home and host cultures differ in learning styles. These findings are meant to emphasize that the learning characteristics of culture, especially the reflective and active learning modes, must necessarily be considered as a crucial factor upon learning styles so that we can understand individual learning styles with integration. However, because this research focused only on the examination of the change of Western learning styles in Chinese business contexts, empirical research of expatriates' adaptation in various cross-cultural contexts will be required to understand people' learning styles holistically in light of relationships between the people and the cultural environment.

MNCs believe in international assignment mechanisms to enhance their global management effectiveness (Caligiuri 2006; Collings et al. 2007). The present research has provided empirical support that international assignment intervention is beneficial to global manager development. To the extent that a cross-cultural environment facilitates managers to learn using the undeveloped learning modes and develop adaptive flexibility for their adjustment, this research demonstrated that expatriate learning and adaptation entails the development of the manager. In other words, international assignment intervention is an effective experiential approach for manager development. The processes of cross-cultural adaptation can be seen as an analogy with the individual development conceptualized in the Experiential Learning Theory. Kolb (1984) suggest the potential longer term value of intentionally mismatching to increase adaptability, help learners overcome weaknesses in their learning style, and develop a more integrated approach to learning. Reasonably, international assignments, especially to the host country with high cultural differences, can be interpreted as an experiential learning mechanism that MNCs expose their managers to a mismatched learning environment in order to help them develop a wider repertoire of coping behaviors and learning strategies. Expatriate managers that can learn to use a variety of problem-solving and learning strategies, and apply them in situations that do not match with their natural learning style, 'may be more able to perform effectively across a wider range of situations than managers with limited stylistic versatility' (Hayes and Allinson 1988), or we could say 'think globally'.

This study also demonstrated that managers' levels of accumulated managerial tacit knowledge are able to predict success in work environments in cross-cultural context and learning style may be a significant factor accounting for differences in levels of managerial tacit knowledge. The field of research exploring tacit knowledge in expert/novice groups in a variety of professions has been all confined to domestic context. One significant contribution of the present study is that the previously reported phenomenon that expert-novice groups within the same professional context differ in their levels of accumulated tacit knowledge has been extended to cross-cultural context. Evidence suggests that most learning to manage occurs through practices (Sternberg et al. 2000) and expatriates need a certain period of time to adapt to their international assignment (Black et al. 1991; Shaffer et al. 1999; Yamazaki and Kayes 2007). Therefore, how can anticipatory cross-cultural training provide effective support for expatriate adaptation? One way is to blend formal approaches, like an introduction of host culture, with informal learning that takes place in work-based problem scenarios. From this, the real cross-cultural problems and real cross-cultural needs are dealt with in the context of learning. On the basis that the present research confirmed the context-dependent nature of tacit knowledge, cross-cultural training may beneficial from more deliberate attempts to closely match training content with situations that are consonant with the specific cross-cultural context being considered.

Tung (1987) reported that the average assignment term of European expatriates is 4.67 years, while that of American expatriates is 2 years or less. The sample of this research showed the mean score of 3 years (36.5 months). There is no guideline and rule for the assignment posting periods. Such periods may depend on the overseas strategies of MNCs in each country. However, if MNCs are concerned about the effectiveness of expatriates' performance, findings of this research should be considered one of the important components to determine how long expatriates take to effectively adapted to cross-cultural settings. This research suggests that western expatriate managers seem become quite effective in concrete experience learning mode after 3 years and become effective in reflective observation learning mode after 5 years. International assignment literature points out that the American MNCs see greater values in rotating expatriates between a series of overseas assignments rather than keeping them in a single post (Hocking et al. 2007; Osland et al. 2006). Tahvanainen (2005) argues that a longer period of overseas assignment makes expatriates go native and identify strongly with local norms. As a negative side, however, American expatriates may not have sufficient time to learn from overseas experiences and then may perform ineffectively (Hocking et al. 2007). With less learning and adaptation, shorter posting periods of American expatriates would make them feel more pressure and stress under higher expectations of the fulfilment of their overseas duties. Therefore, the examination of learning style transition in cross-cultural environments should be done in order to understand optimum posting periods as a strategic and practical issue to MNCs and as a psychological and mental issue for expatriates and their families.

As discussed in Chap. 2, several cross-cultural and international assignment researchers demonstrate the importance of cultural matches between the person and the environment for effective adaptation (Black and Mendenhall 1989, 1990; Dickmann and Doherty 2008; Dowling et al. 1999). The lowest failure rates of expatriates' assignments depend upon expatriate selection according to various contextual circumstances (Farh et al. 2010; Furuya et al. 2009; Shin et al. 2007). An effective adaptation strategy for expatriates success in their international assignments might entail a selection process through which to screen for the identification of expatriates' characteristics that are properly fit to the host country. Although there are thought to be several factors to determine who should be selected as overseas assignees such as technical skills and knowledge, foreign language capabilities, or previous overseas experience, MNCs should examine the learning styles of candidates for overseas assignees. This research suggests that concrete experience is a general requirement for expatriates' adaptation. If candidates are very abstract, it can be expected that they will need to exert much more effort to become adapted to cross-cultural environments. In contrast, concrete candidates will find it easier to adapt themselves to the new world than their abstract counterparts, although the concrete candidates may experience greater cultural shock on account of their inherent sensitivities to outside environments. In addition, MNCs should investigate the learning characteristics of their overseas subsidiaries in order to identify the degree of the learning style difference between candidates and the host country. The present research suggests that the active-reflective learning dimension is related to the cross-cultural adaptation to specific contexts. If there is a big difference between candidates and the host country is this learning dimension, they will need a large amount of time for adaptation. In this respect, the smaller difference between them will produce more effective adaptation than the bigger difference.

Women are still underrepresented in expatriate assignments (Altman and Shortland 2008; Halsberger 2007; Lazarova 2006). GMAC's (2010) relocation trends survey mentions a historical average of 20 % women in expatriate assignments. In this research, only 13.2 % of the research sample were female expatriates.

The reason for their under-representation often stems from prejudice against women by the decision makers within MNC headquarters exerted through informal selection methods (Harris 2002; Hocking et al. 2004). There is a growing body of research investigating the differences in patterns of adjustment to their cross-cultural environment between female and male expatriates and the different variables influencing their adaptation outcomes (Altman and Shortland 2008; Caligiuri 2000; Yamazaki 2010). Many studies showed that women can be successful abroad (Altman and Shortland 2008) and some researchers content that female expatriates tend to be better adapted than male expatriates overall (Varma et al. 2006; Haslberger 2007; Reiche et al. 2011). This research contributes to the growing evidence from a learning perspective by demonstrating that female expatriate managers found it easier to develop a concrete learning mode in cross-cultural context and as a result, had better international adjustment. Results of the study also demonstrated that female expatriates adapted better in the building and maintaining of relationships with host nationals. Therefore, this study proposes that MNCs need to assess carefully the conditions for success and the different support mechanisms women and men may require in order to be successful when working abroad. It would be an injustice and a waste of talent to continue to exclude women from expatriate ranks, especially given the findings relating to gender differences in this research.

References

Alagic, M., & Rimmington, G. M. (2009). Improving intercultural communication competence: Fostering bodymindful cage painting. *Journal of Intercultural Communication, 12*, 39–55.

Altman, Y., & Shortland, S. (2008). Women and international assignments: Taking stock—A 25 year review. *Human Resource Management, 47*, 199–216.

Armstrong, S. J., & Mahmud, A. (2008). Experiential learning and the acquisition of managerial tacit knowledge. *Academy of Management Learning and Education, 7*(2), 189–208.

Armstrong S. J., van der Heijen B. I. J. M., & Sadler-Smith, E. (2011). Intellectual styles, management of careers, and improved work performance. In L. Zhang, R Sternberg, & S.G. Rayner's (Eds.) Handbook of intellectual styles: Preferences in cognition, learning and thinking. New York, NY: Springer.

Auyeung, P., & Sands, J. (1996). A cross-cultural study of the learning style of accounting students. *Accounting and Finance, 36*, 261–274.

Baumard, Paul. (1999). *Tacit knowledge in the organization*. London: Sage.

Barkema, Hariy G., & Vermeulen, F. (1998). International expansion through start-up or acquisition: A learning perspective. *Academy of Management Journal, 41*(1), 7–26.

Berry, J. W. (1997). Immigration, acculturation, and adaptation. *International Journal of Applied Psychology, 46*, 5–34.

Bhaskar-Shrinivas, P., Harrison, D. A., Shaffer, M. A., & Luk, D. M. (2005). Input-based and time-based models of international adjustment: Meta-analytic evidence and theoretical extensions. *Academy of Management Journal, 482*, 25–281.

Black, J. S. (1988). Work role transitions: A study of American expatriate managers in Japan. *Journal of International Business Studies, 19*, 277–294.

Black, J. S., & Mendenhall, M. (1989). A practical but theory-based framework for selecting cross-cultural training methods. *Human Resource Management, 28*(4), 511–539.

Black, J. S., & Mendenhall, M. (1990). Cross-cultural training effectiveness: A review and a theoretical framework for future research. *Academy of Management Review, 15*(1), 113–136.

Black, J. S., Mendenhall, M., & Oddou, G. (1991). Toward a comprehensive model of international adjustment: An integration of multiple theoretical perspectives. *Academy of Management Review, 16*, 291–317.

Caligiuri, P. M. (2000). Selecting expatriates for personality characteristics: A mediating effect of personality on the relationship between host national contact and cross-cultural adjustment. *Management International Review, 40*, 61–80.

Caligiuri, P. M. (2006). Developing global leaders. *Human Resource Management Review, 18*, 219–228.

Collings, D. G., Scullion, H., & Morley, M. J. (2007). Changing patterns of global staffing in the multinational enterprise: Challenges to the conventional expatriate assignment and emerging alternatives. *Journal of World Business, 42*, 198–213.

Dickmann, M., & Doherty, N. (2008). Exploring the career capital impact of international assignments within distinct organizational contexts. *British Journal of Management, 19*, 145–161.

Dowling, P. J., Welch, D. E., & Schuler, R. S. (1999). *International human resource management: Managing people in a multinational context* (3rd ed.). Cincinnati: South-Western College Publishing.

Farh, C. I. C., Bartol, K. M., Shapiro, D. L., & Shin, J. (2010). Networking abroad: a process model of how expatriates form support ties to facilitate adjustment. *Academy of Management Review, 35*(3), 434–454.

Furuya, N., Stevens, M. J., Bird, A., Oddou, G., & Mendenhall, M. E. (2009). Managing the learning and transfer of global management competence: Antecedents and outcomes of Japanese repatriation effectiveness. *Journal of International Business Studies, 40*(2), 200–215.

GMAC. (2010). *Global relocation trends: 2010 survey report*. Oak Brook, IL: GMAC Global Relocation Services.

Hall, E. T. (1977). *Beyond culture*. Garden City, NY: Anchor Presures/Doubleday.

Hayes, J., & Allinson, C. W. (1988). Cultural differences in the learning styles of managers. *Management International Review, 28*, 75–80.

Halsberger, A. (2007). *Gender differences in expatriate adjustment*. Paper presented at the Academy of Management annual conference, Philadelphia.

Harris, H. (2002). Think international manager, think male: Why are women not selected for international management assignments? *Thunderbird International Business Review, 44*(2), 175–203.

Hocking, J. B., Brown, M., & Harzing, A.-W. (2004). A knowledge transfer perspective of strategic assignment purposes and their path-dependent outcomes. *International Journal of Human Resource Management, 15*, 565–586.

Hocking, J. B., Brown, M., & Harzing, A.-W. (2007). Balancing global and local strategic contexts: Expatriate knowledge transfer, applications, and learning with a transnational organization. *Human Resource Management, 46*(4), 513–533.

Hofstede, G. H. (1997). *Culture and Organization: Software of Mind*. New York: McGraw Hill.

Kolb, D. A. (1984). *Experiential learning: Experience as the source of learning and development*. Englewood Cliffs, NJ: Prentice-Hall.

Lazarova, M. B. (2006). International human resource management in global perspective. In M. J. Morley, N. Heraty, & D. G. Collings (Eds.), *International HRM and international assignments*. Basingstoke, UK: Palgrave MacMillan.

Li, S., & Scullion, H. (2010). Developing the local competence of expatriate managers for emerging markets: A knowledge-based approach. *Journal of World Business, 45*, 190–196.

Maertz, C. P, Jr, Hassan, A., & Magnusson, P. (2009). When learning is not enough: A process model of expatriate adjustment as cultural cognitive dissonance reduction. *Organizational Behaviour and Human Decision Processes, 108*, 66–78.

Mainemelis, C., Boyatzis, R. E., & Kolb, D. A. (2002). Learning styles and adaptive flexibility: Testing experiential learning theory. *Management Learning, 33*(1), 5–33.

Ng, K. Y., Dyne, L. V., & Ang, S. (2009). From experience to experiential learning: Cultural intelligence as a learning capability for global leader development. *Academy of Management Learning and Education, 8*(4), 511–526.

Okpara, O., & Kabongo, D. (2011). Cross-cultural training and expatriate adjustment: A study of western expatriates in Nigeria. *Journal of World Business, 46*, 22–30.

Osland, J. S., Bird, A., Mendenhall, M. E., & Osland, A. (2006). Developing global leadership capabilities and global mindset: A review. In G. K. Stahl & I. Bjorkman (Eds.), *Handbook of research in international human resource management* (pp. 197–222). Cheltenham, UK: Edward Elgar Publishing.

Ratiu, I. (1983). Thinking internationally: A comparison of how international executives learn. *International Studies of Management and Organization, 13*(1–2), 139–150.

Reiche, B. S., Kraimer, M. L., & Harzing, A. W. (2011). Why do international assignees stay? An organizational embeddedness perspective. *Journal of International Business Studies, 42*(4), 521–544.

Shaffer, M. A., Harrison, D. A., & Gilley, K. M. (1999). Dimensions, determinants, and differences in the expatriate adjustment process. *Journal of International Business Studies, 30*, 557–582.

Shin, S. J., Morgeson, F. P., & Campion, M. A. (2007). What you do depends on where you are: Understanding how domestic and expatriate work requirements depend upon the cultural context. *Journal of International Business Studies, 38*(1), 64–83.

Sternberg, R. J., Forsythe, G. B., Hedlund, J., Horvath, J. A., Wagner, R. K., Williams, W. M., et al. (2000). *Practical Intelligence in Everyday Life*. New York: Cambridge University Presures.

Takeuchi, R., Tesluk, P. E., Yun, S., & Lepak, D. P. (2005). An integrative view of international experience. *Academy of Management Journal, 48*(1), 85–101.

Tahvanainen, M., Welch, D., & Worm, V. (2005). Implications of short-term international assignments. *European Management Journal, 23*, 663–673.

Tung, R. L. (1987). Selection and training procedures of U.S., European and Japanese multinationals. *California Management Review, 25*, 57–71.

Varma, A., Toh, S. M., & Budhwar, P. S. (2006). A new perspective on the female expatriate experience: The role of host country national categorization. *Journal of World Business, 41*, 112–120.

Wagner, R. K., & Sternberg, R. J. (1986). Tacit knowledge and intelligence in the everyday world. In R. Sternberg & R. Wagner (Eds.), *Practical intelligence: Nature and origins of competence in the everyday world*. New York: Cambridge University Presures.

Wagner, R. K., & Sternberg, R. J. (1987). Tacit knowledge in managerial success. *Journal of Business and Psychology, 1*(4), 301–312.

Yamazaki, Y. (2010). Expatriate adaptation: A fit between skills and demands among Japanese expatriates in USA. *Management International Review, 50*, 81–108.

Yamazaki, Y., & Kayes, D. C. (2004). An experiential approach to cross-cultural learning: A review of competencies for successful expatriate adaptation. *Academy of Management Learning and Education, 3*(4), 362–379.

Yamazaki, Y., & Kayes, D. C. (2007). Expatriate learning: exploring how Japanese managers adapt in the United States. *International Journal of Human Resource Management, 18*(8), 1373–1395.

MIX
Papier aus verantwortungsvollen Quellen
Paper from responsible sources
FSC® C105338

If you have any concerns about our products,
you can contact us on
ProductSafety@springernature.com

In case Publisher is established outside the EU,
the EU authorized representative is:
Springer Nature Customer Service Center GmbH
Europaplatz 3, 69115 Heidelberg, Germany

Printed by Libri Plureos GmbH
in Hamburg, Germany